The Holocaust
in American Film

The Holocaust in

Judith E. Doneson

THE JEWISH PUBLICATION SOCIETY
Philadelphia · New York · Jerusalem   5747 · 1987

American Film

Copyright © 1987 by Judith E. Doneson
First edition   All rights reserved
Manufactured in the United States of America
Library of Congress Cataloging in Publication Data

Doneson, Judith E.
   The Holocaust in American film.

   Bibliography: p. 233
   Filmography: p. 247
   Includes index.
   1. Holocaust, Jewish (1939–1945), in motion pictures.
2. Antisemitism in motion pictures.   3. Moving-pictures—
United States.   I. Title.
PN1995.9.H53D66   1987   791.43'09'09358   87-2634
ISBN 0–8276–0281–2
      0–8276–0298–7 (pbk.)

The still photographs in Chapters 1–3 are courtesy of
The Museum of Modern Art/Film Stills Archive, New York City.

The still photographs in Chapter 4 are used with the
permission of Worldvision Enterprises Inc., New York City.

Photo research by Linda R. Turner

Designed by Adrianne Onderdonk Dudden

*To my mother, Florence, my brother, Michael,
and in memory of my father, George J. Doneson.*

Acknowledgments

It is my great pleasure to be able to thank those who helped me along the route to completion of this work.

I am grateful to the staffs of the following offices: The American Film Institute; the Jewish Film Archive of the Hebrew University and the World Zionist Organization; the Margaret Herrick Library of the Academy of Motion Picture Arts and Sciences; the ULCA Film Collection; the UCLA Department of Special Collections, where I was assisted with the Stanley Kramer Collection; the ULCA Theater Arts Library; the University of Southern California Archive of Performing Arts; and the Wisconsin Center for Film and Theater Research at the State Historical Society of Wisconsin.

In particular, I am grateful to Lia van Leer, founder and director of the Israel Film Archive; Sheba Skirball, librarian at the Israel Film Archive; Murray Wood, who allowed me to view the files of the Jewish Film Advisory Committee at the Community Relations Council of the Los Angeles Jewish Federation; Herbert Brodkin, who gave me permission to view production files of *Holocaust* at Titus Productions, Inc.; Thomas De Wolfe of Titus Productions, Inc., for his assistance; Geoffrey Wigoder and Phil Gerard, for their help; and my friend, Yitzchak Mais, Director, Yad Vashem Museum.

Grants from the Memorial Foundation for Jewish Culture, the Hebrew University of Jerusalem, and the Institute of Contemporary Jewry of the Hebrew University were important in helping me to carry out this work.

I am deeply appreciative to those with whom I have worked at The Jewish Publication Society—to the Editor-in-Chief,

Sheila F. Segal, the Managing Editor, Barbara Spector, and to Linda Turner, who researched the stills.

I was fortunate to be guided throughout this study by two people whom I greatly admire—Professor Yehuda Bauer and Professor George L. Mosse.

Professor Irene Eber of the Hebrew University gave freely of her knowledge and friendship. Judy Goldberg typed so very fast. Phyllis, Jonathan, and Michael Leef and Lottie Loew never complained, no matter how long they waited for me.

My brother Michael Doneson was always there—professionally and personally—with advice, criticism, and whatever I needed.

My mother, Florence Doneson, is always there—for everything.

J.E.D.
St. Louis-Jerusalem, 1987

Contents

The Holocaust
in American Film

Introduction

As the Jews of Warsaw were being destroyed around him, Warsaw ghetto diarist Emmanuel Ringelblum painfully wondered: "Does the world know about our suffering? And if it knows, why is it silent?"[1] For the past forty years (and, one suspects, for eternity), artists, academics, and theologians have searched, perhaps in vain, for an answer to Ringelblum's beseeching query, which spoke also for the rest of European Jewry. It is imperative to question how the same humanity, of which we are all a part, abandoned the Jews; to try and understand the process of destruction that resulted in the loss of two-thirds of European Jewry—six million Jews. Yet how does one comprehend an event that defies comprehension? "I who was there do not understand," writes Elie Wiesel.[2] One searches endlessly for the proper language to describe the Holocaust, but nothing is ever adequate. It challenges normal responses to explain how a modern, cultured Germany, ruled by the National Socialist government, marshaled its scientific knowledge, its arts, its political system for the purpose of committing genocide. As Hannah Arendt succinctly states:

> Twentieth century political developments have driven the Jewish people into the storm center of events; the Jewish question and anti-semitism, relatively unimportant phenomena in terms of world politics, became the catalytic agent first for the rise of the Nazi movement and the establishment of the organizational structure of the Third Reich ... then for a world war of unparalleled ferocity, and finally for the emergence of the unprecedented crime of genocide in the midst of Occidental civilization.[3]

The Holocaust, the destruction of European Jewry, has undeniably left its imprint on contemporary history. It has become a metaphor as well as a paradigm for modern tragedy. Its language evokes perceptions of fear and despair, persecution and suffering. This is especially true in America where in recent years it has been common to hear the Watts ghetto in Los Angeles compared with the Jewish ghettos of Europe, the massacres in Vietnam compared with Auschwitz, and the plight of the Boat People with that of European Jewish refugees. Americans derive much of their contemporary language of catastrophe from the Nazi destruction of the Jews. Further, the Holocaust has established its official place in American society, institutionalized in the form of a federally backed national museum and educational center to be built in the capital near the Washington Monument. And a major television network invested millions of dollars in a four-part series entitled, simply, *Holocaust.*

Yet, paradoxically, the Holocaust played little if any role in the lives of most Americans, Jew or gentile. In order to understand its impact we can begin with the question posed by Paul Lazarsfeld in his introduction to *The Apathetic Majority*, a study based on responses to the Eichmann trial: "By what process is an event turned into an influence?"[4] Or, in terms of this work: How and why has the Holocaust entered into the popular imagination of the American people to such a degree that it seems to have become almost a part of the American experience?

Certainly cinema offers one route into the collective mind. Film helps to shape popular attitudes and simultaneously reflects popular attitudes—social, political, and cultural. Indeed, historian Arthur Schlesinger, Jr., believes: "The fact that film has been the most potent vehicle of the American imagination suggests all the more strongly that movies have something to tell us not just about the surfaces but about the mysteries of American life."[5] Therefore, by examining how the American cinema and, more recently, films made for television deal with the rise of National Socialism and the Holocaust, how they signify meaning of the event for Americans, we can understand one important influence that has given an image and shape to the Holocaust. In what context does the Holocaust become relevant for a people who have no tangible understanding of its dimensions because they have not experienced it? The Holocaust enters America as a "refugee" event. Following the traditional path of refugees, the event had to be shaped and molded in order to make it comprehensible to an American public.

The immediate impact of the Final Solution came largely

through the media. Camera teams filmed the horrors that remained of the concentration camps after the liberation—piles of bodies, crematoria, stacks of personal possessions—and the skeletal survivors. It was the shock of seeing these pictures and reading accounts in the press of what was discovered in the camps that brought the reality of the Holocaust to the attention of the public.[6] This realization of the horrors of the Final Solution turned the Holocaust, both for Jews and gentiles, into a watershed event, clearly influencing America's attitudes toward its Jews. Whereas anti-Semitism had peaked during the war, only "a few short years later, America appeared to emerge from the war against Hitler as a nation in which anti-Semitism was miraculously dead."[7] However, the initial shock passed as America entered into the postwar recovery and the event was no longer "news."

Educators should have been the ones to ensure that the Holocaust was taught to new generations. But this simply did not happen. Various studies indicate that in all educational areas—religion, social studies, history—in secondary schools as well as universities, most texts either minimally treated the Holocaust or virtually ignored it altogether.[8]

Instead, films for commercial release and for television have been instrumental in helping to assimilate the Holocaust into the popular consciousness. And no wonder, as it is a powerful, seductive medium. Author and critic Alfred Kazin says of movies that they "are really insidious, they please us so easily. They are one of the great drugs of our time, as irresistible as sex and liquor. I am an addict. . . ."[9] Leo Rosten, in his study on Hollywood, recounts the story of a mob of frenzied fans swarming through Penn Station in New York City to greet actor Edward G. Robinson, while they did not recognize his fellow passenger, Herbert Hoover. Even prior to America's entry into the war, Rosten points out, "American movies became pawns in the gigantic game of power and conquest. Hollywood's product was outlawed in Germany, Italy, Soviet Russia, and in the nations which fell under the heel of conquest."[10] It is perhaps an act of justice that American films, as we shall see, eventually return to Europe and frequently serve as a catalyst in Europe's confrontation with its immediate past. For as television critic Michael Arlen so succinctly puts it: "Now it is the camera that provides our points of reference, our focus."[11]

Film can create and revive memory, especially in its capacity as a popular entertainment. So when it approaches a subject like the Holocaust, it brings an enormous potential to educate. This sometimes poses a problem for those more concerned with the aesthetics of film; "art" is often ignored for the sake of mass appeal.[12] Although the question of artistic merit can influence the reception of a film, nonetheless, films valued for their aesthetics will find their place in the history of the cinema as art: This work focuses on film in its historical context and must necessarily bypass film as art. More frequently than not, it is the least successful films in the eyes of the serious critics that exert the strongest influence on the public. Some of the films we discuss may disappear into oblivion, much like paintings and painters famous in their time but today unknown. With film, however, due to its availability through television and video recorders, many will survive longer. With this in mind, let us analyze the efforts of film and television to create and preserve the memory of the Holocaust.

At this juncture, it is important to define Holocaust film. Let us say, simply, that this includes any films that reflect what historian Raul Hilberg describes as a step-by-step historical process,[13] beginning with the laws of April 1933, which removed Jews from the civil services in Germany, and ending in 1945, when the last concentration camps were liberated and the war ended. This includes the gradual evolution to destruction, as well as the destruction itself, which culminated in the death of six million Jews. A film that captures elements of the earliest persecutions of the Jews in Germany can be called a Holocaust film. Likewise, a film that refers to the period when Nazi anti-Semitism grew increasingly worse is a Holocaust film. And in the broadest interpretation, a film influenced by the Holocaust is also termed a Holocaust film.

Even in allowing for so broad a definition, it remains for us to understand why an event foreign to the American experience has succeeded in penetrating the American imagination. Why the Holocaust in American cinema? French films about World War II and the Holocaust, for example, touch on their own history, as do Polish, Czech, and Italian films on the subject. One recalls the explosive reaction in France when *The Sorrow and the Pity* (1970) appeared to challenge the myth of the French nation backing the resistance.[14] The matter most closely connecting America to the Holocaust was its refusal to allow Jewish refugees entry into the United States—in retrospect, a tragic decision for the Jews, one that also countered a myth of America as a land of refuge. Indeed, this theme would eventually appear in the American cinema in the film *Voyage of the Damned* (1976). On the whole, however, the Holocaust plays a minor part in the scheme of American history. Nonetheless, American films on the Holocaust have been the most influential in bringing the event to the attention of an international audience. There seem to be no European films on the Holocaust that can compete with the popular success of *Judgment at Nuremberg* (1961) or *Holocaust* (1978). Ironically, the most successful films utilize American symbols and language to convey an American perception of the (European) Holocaust. In effect, we are talking about the Americanization of the Holocaust.

The move toward Americanization must be in a direction meaningful to Americans, for whom the Final Solution was a foreign event. Therefore, the Holocaust functions as a model, a paradigm, or a framework for understanding history. It is a metaphor that teaches a lesson. In film, it tends to reflect general societal trends. It may serve, for example, as a guide for contemporary action, perhaps in connection to civil rights or antiwar protest. The absorption of the Holocaust into the American psyche has been a cumulative process. As is pointed out in *The Apathetic Majority*:

> By concentrating on highly salient issues and by ignoring long-run effects research has overlooked a possible powerful cumulative mass media effect on issues which remain of low salience for extended periods of time. On such issues, the majority do not take the trouble to become even minimally informed so that they can arrive at an independent judgment. Rather, when it becomes appropriate for them to have an opinion, they search for clues as to what proper opinion is. A natural source is the impressions they have been absorbing almost subliminally from habitual, if superficial, attention to mass media. This would appear to be the process through which the apathetic majority formed their generally favorable opinion about the [Eichmann] trial. They were primed to form this opinion not only by what they discerned to be the proper attitude from their limited exposure to the trial via the mass media, but by prior exposure to what may be described as a long-term propensity on the part of the mass media to present stories about Jews in a sympathetic light.[15]

The cumulative effect of a series of films on the Holocaust has been to create a lasting image of the event in the mass mind. Since these films tend to reflect contemporary trends, they help make the Holocaust meaningful to an audience for whom the Final Solution is a foreign event. At the same time, they strive to place the Holocaust in its proper historical context—as the attempted genocide of European Jewry by the Nazis.

As a product of the society that produces it, film serves as a primary source of evidence for the historian.[16] Therefore, like a more conventional document, a film must be "read" and analyzed for what it can tell us about the period in which it was created. In this regard, American films that deal with the Holocaust serve a dual function. Yes, they focus on themes portraying National Socialism and the persecution of the Jews; but they also explore contemporary issues that were and are germane to American society at the time of their appearance. Consequently, the analysis must proceed on both levels: on the salient level, the one that depicts the Holocaust itself; and on the latent level, the one that explains a particular film's contemporary meaning. The two are connected, of course. On the salient level, the Holocaust operates as a metaphor for the discourse taking place on the latent level. Thus the event—the Holocaust—is a function of its current environment as well as a reflection of its own history.

This study begins with films made before, during, and soon after the war. They all focus on anti-Semitism, as they are influenced by Nazi persecution of the Jews. These films, which appeared between 1934 and 1947, lay the foundation for the films that follow in that they establish the image of the Jew that evolves from a foreign stereotype to an Americanized figure. Once the Jew is at home in America in the popular imagination, then the Holocaust can be absorbed as an "immigrant" event, ultimately to be brought into the American consciousness.

The study considers certain key phenomena signifying trends that either influence or are influenced by the films in question: demystification, democratization, universalization, trivialization, politicization, commercialization, and popularization. These phenomena, reflected in the films, are related to similarly shifting directions and patterns occurring at the same time in American society. For example, the earliest film under discussion, *The House of Rothschild* (1934), seems to be the first American film made in response to the implementation of the initial Nazi anti-

Jewish laws in Germany as well as the first American film to focus on anti-Semitism. Although the tone of the film is ambiguous, its major thrust is to demystify the Jew, that is, to explain the seemingly mysterious and obscure characteristics of the European image. This coincides with a period when immigrants were no longer arriving by droves on America's shores; the Jew in the United States was becoming a recognizable American; the European Jew, by contrast, was still strange. Shortly after the war, *Gentleman's Agreement* (1947) appeared, its denunciation of anti-Semitism clearly a response to the Holocaust. But it too reflects the Americanization and democratization of the Jew, a shift in America toward the social acceptance of minority groups as full-fledged Americans.

Universalization of the Holocaust becomes a major postwar theme: In *The Diary of Anne Frank* (1959), the Holocaust becomes a symbol for the suffering of all people; in *Judgment at Nuremberg* (1961), it is shared history; in *The Pawnbroker* (1965), it is compared history. Not until *Holocaust* (1978) does the event take on its specific Jewishness, at which time it also becomes a universal message for mankind. Moreover, when *Holocaust* was broadcast, the issue of trivialization erupted, as critics accused the show's creators of trivializing the actual event. The issue of trivialization of the Final Solution is an especially sensitive one. In the example of *Holocaust*, its detractors perhaps confused trivialization with commercialization and popularization, both of which are endemic to American television.

In an analysis of these films, several aspects of the historical discourse must be considered. For example, *The Diary of Anne Frank* is adapted from an actual document of the war. The manner in which the film (and play) treat the *Diary* raises the question of historicity: How closely must the writers adhere to the original in order not to lose the authentic mood of the *Diary* as a historical document? *Judgment at Nuremberg* introduces documentary footage into a fictional context. *Holocaust* stirs up a polemic over its form as a docu-drama—the blending of fact with fiction. The portrayal of the Holocaust through this form of art challenges us to consider the (perhaps mistaken) notion of the importance of historical accuracy as opposed to the accuracy of the mood of history.

We also examine the changing image of the Jew. In the films made in the early period, from 1934 until 1947, we witness an evolution from a highly stereotyped figure, to that of the Jew as a symbol for mankind—finishing, finally, with the Americanized Jew. After the war, there is less concern with specific traits and more attention paid to Jewish behavior in the face of destruction. This involves the image of the Jew as a weak figure and the related argument over whether the Jews' passivity helped contribute to their deaths. Historian George L. Mosse points out how crucial the images in nineteenth-century German popular literature were in influencing the mass mind by creating a stereotype "that in the end came to haunt Jews and Gentiles alike."[17] The portrayals in these films form a picture that establishes an image of Jewish behavior during the Final Solution as well as a portrait of the contemporary Jew. The effect of these images remains to be seen.

In summary, then, American films on the Holocaust have helped to integrate the Holocaust into the American tradition. This study examines the myths that surround the Holocaust and considers how the Holocaust, used as a metaphor for some aspects of contemporary history, alters or distorts the actual event. It analyzes, too, the various images of the Jew projected in these films. In attempting to understand these elements that together form a picture of the Holocaust in American film, perhaps we can better understand the role of the Holocaust as an influence on the American consciousness. There is a scene that speaks to this issue in the 1943 film *Watch On the Rhine* (based on Lillian Hellman's play). The hero, Kurt, a member of the European resistance, visits America with his American-born wife. Kurt tells two of her relatives that they cannot understand his world, and if they are fortunate, they never will. The truth of this statement is obvious. Still, film offers the possibility that some of this world can be explained, in the hope that no one will be forced to understand—experience—such conditions again.

One

Reflections of Anti-Semitism in Film and the Nazi Persecution of the Jews: 1934–1947

A

uthor and sociologist Leo Rosten, in his extremely enlightening study on the Hollywood colony, observes:

> The very success of Hollywood lies in the skill with which it reflects the assumptions, the fallacies, and the aspirations of an entire culture. The movie producers, the movie directors, the movie writers, and the movie actors work with stereotypes which are current in our society—for they, too, are children of that society; they, too, have inherited and absorbed the values of our world. But Hollywood, through the movies, reinforces our typologies on an enormous scale and with overpowering repetitiveness.[1]

Between 1934 and 1947, American society moved from the depths of the Depression, through the New Deal and its era of political liberalism, on to prewar anxieties, the horror of World War II, and postwar recuperation. Hollywood was there to capture it all, reflecting "the assumptions, the fallacies, and the aspirations of an entire culture." In the 1930s, the film industry created a world of fantasy and prospered, as it attempted to pull its audience out of the social and political doldrums. It was the era of the Hollywood musical. At the same time Hollywood began to confront issues of importance, tackling, for example, themes of social conscience in films like *Mr. Smith Goes to Washington* (1939), *Juarez* (1939), and *The Grapes of Wrath* (1940). And as the war became more of a threat, Hollywood produced films with Nazi themes, such as *Confessions of a Nazi Spy* (1939) and *The Mortal Storm* (1940). For, while Americans struggled to move out of the Depression, Hitler, having been elected Chancellor of Germany in 1933, embarked on his "plan" to control Europe and free it of a major menace—the Jews. Thus these two factors—the Depression, with its internal consequences, and

Hitler, an international threat—became overriding influences in American life at that time.

For world Jewry, the rise of the Nazis signaled a turning point in their history. From the time the Nazis came to power until their defeat, they focused their attention on the solution of the "Jewish problem." Already in 1933, Jews living in Germany who anticipated serious trouble or who were used to wandering or who were just scared began requesting visas to immigrate to America. These visas, however, were not readily obtained, as they had once been, because of the quota system established in the United States as a result of the Immigration Act of 1924. Some in America immediately perceived the threat posed by Hitler. American Supreme Court Justice Louis Brandeis remarked already in 1933: "The Jews must leave Germany."[2] The Jews were in danger; no one yet knew to what extent. But a process was set in motion that would end in 1945 with two-thirds of Europe's Jews destroyed.

Knowing the limitations of hindsight, it is with caution that we address the question: To what extent did Hollywood, known as a "Jewish" industry, feel the Nazi threat to the Jews to be a major concern? The American cinema has offered various portrayals of Jews and Jewish life since its inception,[3] some dealing with anti-Semitism. But during that dark period only three films stand out for having confronted the European danger and focused on anti-Semitism. Two of them we might call warning films: *The House of Rothschild* (1934) and *The Great Dictator* (1940). The third, *Gentleman's Agreement* (1947), came in the wake of the revelations of the destruction of European Jewry.* Why, one asks, did the persecution of the Jewish people in Europe play so minor a role in "Jewish" Hollywood at a time when movie production and movie attendance were at a peak? Was anti-Semitism aimed at industry executives (anti-Semitism was increasing at a rapid rate with the general public) a factor contributing to the dearth of such films at that most urgent time? Or, one asks, how important was the European threat to the Jews in the minds of the film makers?

*It is interesting to note that in an industry in which Jews played so dominant a role, these three films were produced by non-Jews: *The House of Rothschild* and *Gentleman's Agreement* by Darryl F. Zanuck, a Nebraska-born Methodist, and *The Great Dictator* by Charlie Chaplin, who was often mistakenly taken for a Jew.

Studying the three aforementioned films may perhaps yield some insights regarding this relationship between the American film industry and the Jewish problem in Europe. That is, by viewing the feature film as a historical document, we can find in it testimony of the times. Pierre Sorlin points out:

> If we were studying an historical text written at the same time, we would not compare it with the film version to see if it was true. We would instead try to understand the political logic of the account given in the book, asking why it emphasized this question, that event, rather than others. We should keep this same preoccupation in mind when analysing films.[4]

Sorlin points the way for this analysis of *The House of Rothschild, The Great Dictator,* and *Gentleman's Agreement,* three films that, despite their obvious differences, share a great deal in common. *The House of Rothschild* is a historical film confronting the present; the other two are living history, explicitly dealing with realities at the time of their appearance. The event under discussion in this study, that is, the process leading to and culminating in the Final Solution, is itself evolving over the course of this period. In 1934 everything is unknown; by 1947 the Holocaust is part of history. Nevertheless, each of the films, in its own way, is influenced by Nazi anti-Semitism and, more fundamentally, by the idea that the Jewish question must be solved everywhere—even in America. It is anti-Semitism, and, in a broader sense, hatred of "differentness," that is at the heart of these films. Jewish suffering, and the evolving horror of it, offers a lesson for all men on the evils of racism and bigotry.

This analysis of the function and meaning of the three films places them within their historical context. Society was in flux, and problems confronting the Jews then would, after the war, become less central as Jews grew more comfortable in America. In fact, it is the Final Solution itself that renders these problems unimportant. We examine anti-Semitism as an ideology, tracing the movement from European political anti-Semitism in *The House of Rothschild* to the American social anti-Semitism in *Gentleman's Agreement.* This suggests an interesting paradox. As the cinematic image of the Jew improves, anti-Semitism in the United States continues to grow, until it peaks in 1944. We might say that film, in opposition to the social realities, is establishing standards of correct behavior and attitudes for Americans.

In looking at how the three films present the various facets of anti-Semitism, we find portrayals derived from the notion of the international Jewish conspiracy that is expounded in *The Protocols of the Elders of Zion*. We also find stereotypes commonly associated with Jews in America. These three films, as we demonstrate, reflect popular attitudes toward the persecution of Europe's Jews and attempt to deal with these attitudes in a didactic manner that stresses the importance of tolerance and equality. We hope, through our analysis, to arrive at a better understanding of the reluctance on the part of Hollywood film makers to confront the Jewish issue on film. At the same time a picture emerges that offers some insight into the Jewish condition in America from 1934 until 1947.

The House of Rothschild seems to be the first American feature film to deal directly with the problem of anti-Semitism. Yet the timing of this historical film on the rise of the Rothschild financial empire is somewhat questionable. It was the middle of the Great Depression (an event that helped bring the Nazis to power in Germany); unemployment in both Europe and the United States was at a peak; several European countries, conforming to tradition, blamed the Jews for their economic woes. In fact, by way of contrast, anti-Semitism seemed to play a minor role in America's response to the Depression. Instead, President Hoover and the banks bore the blame. Even political fringe groups led by Father Coughlin and Huey Long did not resort to anti-Semitism, at least not until almost the end of the Depression, toward the end of the 1930s.[5] Nonetheless, as historian John Higham brings out:

> Perhaps the most important symbiotic link between Jewish and American values ... lies in the very economic sphere that modern anti-Semitism has tried to exploit. As an ethnic group, Jews have traditionally emphasized the materialistic, competitive values of business life that are so deeply ingrained in American culture. The prestige America confers on the businessman—the man of thrift, enterprise and rational calculation—has ordinarily encompassed the Jew. Nowhere does this deference appear more vividly than in the immense respect Americans felt for the House of Rothschild during a great part of the nineteenth century.[6]

In other words, an ambivalence tied to admiration, on the one hand, and distrust based on notions of power, on the other hand, connected Jews and money in the minds of Americans. This ambivalence pervades the film *The House of Rothschild*, especially given its appearance in the middle of the Depression.

Pierre Sorlin observes that "historical films are concerned with the problems of the present. . . . On the surface, they deal with historical events . . . but from the vast range of possible choices, film-makers have singled out those characters, circumstances and dates that have a direct bearing on contemporary circumstances."[7] What, then, is the intent in *The House of Rothschild*? To prevent the Jews from becoming scapegoats during a period of economic crisis? A subconscious desire to display symbols of Jewish wealth and thereby offer an explanation for America's woes? The film begins in the ghetto and ends with the Rothschilds (Jews) controlling the outcome of Europe's wars. Might we conclude that the Jews should have remained in the ghetto, where their influence was restrained? Above all, we see members of the Rothschild family in every major European capital; their interests lie not in their respective countries, but in the advancement of their own family and in a united Europe. Does this not hint that Jews are foreigners wherever they are, loyal to no country, only to themselves? Could this have influenced attitudes toward immigrant Jews in the United States? In seeking to clarify these and other questions that are suggested by the film, we find that its vision is indeed both ambivalent and ambiguous.

Recalling *The House of Rothschild* as Hollywood's first film to focus on anti-Semitism, the film's scriptwriter Nunnally Johnson was overwhelmed at producer Darryl Zanuck's willingness to approach such a theme at the time. From Johnson's point of view, as Leonard Mosley writes in his biography of Zanuck:

> It was 1933 and Adolf Hitler and the Nazis had just come to power in Germany. Not only were the newspapers and newsreels full of pictures of the Brownshirts on the rampage in Berlin and Munich, but the smell of anti-Semitism reeked strongly enough to drift across the United States. From a purely commercial point of view, it was a controversial movie to be making at the time. . . . Zanuck . . . was stimulated by the prevailing conditions, and felt that here was a Page One film if ever there was one, its story brought up to date by the happenings in Nazi Germany.[8]

Johnson recounts an incident of a Jewish film executive telling Zanuck that people would cheer the film's anti-Semitic speeches;

yet he also recalled that there was some concern that the film was too pro-Jewish in a saccharine manner and that many Jews would be made uncomfortable by it.[9] The film's vision is indeed ambiguous with its negative Jewish stereotypes and simultaneous sympathy for the eternal suffering of the Jews. One can add that despite the foreignness of the Rothschilds, their story is at the heart of the American dream—the rise from poverty to success. And yet, on another level, they embody attributes that Americans found distasteful in Jews at that time. A mixed message indeed!

The film is divided into two sections. The first introduces us to the Rothschilds in the ghetto, from which the family influence spreads to the great banking houses in the major capitals of Europe. The equivocal portrait of the family incorporates both the negative traits attributed to the Rothschilds and the apologetics offered to explain these traits. The second section depicts the Rothschilds, now a dynasty controlled by Nathan in London, helping Europe to defeat Napoleon—and thus proving their (and the rest of the Jews') value to the societies in which they live. Both segments of the film combine, paradoxically, antipathy with concern for the contemporary Jew, along with a warning about the serious threat facing European Jewry.

The film opens on Jew Street in Frankfurt (in Prussia) in 1780. The camera moves through a dark crowded ghetto to the home of Mayer Amschel Rothschild—money changer, dealer in coins—founder of the dynasty. These early scenes reveal the Jew: a lover of money, a conniver. This unromantic figure tricks the gentile and he seeks to control society. His physical image reinforces the accepted American stereotype of the Jew.

Money is the central theme of the film and the central topic of discussion at the Rothschilds. Indeed, the Jew as Shylock—mercenary and dishonest—is a persistent image. Mayer, waiting eagerly for some money to arrive, rubs his hands together like the old lecher dreaming of the young beauty. He calls his wife "Mama"—a sign that Jews do not conform to the traditional Western ideal of romantic love but that money is their love—their passion. Mayer complains to his wife in one scene about an agent who tries to take advantage of him: " . . . planning to rob this poor old Jew and here I was so innocent. . . . Always make them think they're clever." In other words, outwit the gentile by deceiving him.

The following illustrates the scheming ways of the Rothschilds. The tax collector approaches. Mama hides their valuables in a secret cellar. The family changes to old, tattered clothing. The children are told to "look hungry." Mayer gives the tax collector false books to check. The latter, wise to this ploy, asks for the real books and demands a large sum in taxes. Even as Mayer whines that he cannot possibly raise the sum, the tax collector trips on the rug hiding the cellar door. It may be, Mayer decides, that he can raise some money after all.[10]

The film attempts to offset this scheming image by offering an explanation for the Rothschilds' actions. As Mayer says:

> I have to cheat the tax collector before my own children. . . . I want to be honest with them. But they won't let us. We are Jews—taxed to death, forbidden to learn a trade, to own land. . . . They send men here to rob us. So work and strive for money. Money is power. Money is the only weapon a Jew has to defend himself with.

In this way he tells the audience why Jews are greedy and deceptive; and at the same time, he passes on this legacy of "money equals power" to his children.

The concept of the international Jewish conspiracy figures as another prominent theme in the film. It is evoked when a dying Mayer offers his parting wisdom to his children, advising them to open banking houses in the major European capitals but to remain loyal, above all, to each other as one family. Now, *The Protocols of the Elders of Zion*, which voices the conspiracy theory, was known in America, a complete version having been published there in 1920. Also in 1920, Henry Ford published a series of articles on the "international Jew" in his *Dearborn Independent*. (The influence of these themes of conspiracy and control was felt mainly among the rural population, who feared city life and industrialization.[11] In any event, more likely than not, they were not a large part of the audience for a film like *The House of Rothschild*, which enjoyed high critical acclaim as well as success at the box office.) It is strange to find echoes of such blatant anti-Semitic themes in a film that ostensibly wishes to convey a positive image of the Jew—especially during the Depression. There are other problematic sections as well. The film hints at negative popular notions connected to the legend of the wandering Jew. Thirty-two years after Mayer's death, we learn, the Rothschild empire is established throughout Europe. On screen, a map indicates in graphic fashion the extent of the family's domain. We see the heads of Europe at the mercy of the Rothschilds, whom they need in order to finance the war against Napoleon.

At this point, however, the ambiguous portrayal begins to take on more positive overtones, as the film evinces its concern for the contemporary plight of German Jewry threatened by the Nazis. One reviewer at the time realized that *The House of Rothschild* is about Hitler, Göring, and Goebbels more than it is about Prussia on the eve of Waterloo,[12] a most perceptive and accurate observation, as we see from a closer look at the characters in the film. The major European leaders are based on historical figures: Prince Metternich in Vienna, Talleyrand in France, Wellington in England, and of course Napoleon. Only Count Ledrantz of Prussia is fictional; and he is the one who gives voice to unfounded, irrational hatred for the Rothschilds and, indeed, for all Jews. Although it is historically correct that the Jews suffered persecutions during the period of the rise of the Rothschilds, since Ledrantz is himself a fictional character he may be taken to symbolize both a contemporary figure or, in this case, state—Germany—and a contemporary message—that a grave threat looms over German Jewry in 1934. The following scenes reinforce this notion.

Ledrantz uses his influence to prevent the Rothschild banks from participating in an important loan to France. Nathan then "manipulates" the bond market in order to compel the ruling European powers to include the House of Rothschild in the loan. They acquiesce, but Ledrantz warns Rothschild that his victory may be bought too dearly, a prophecy that proves all too true. For, Nathan returns to the ghetto in Frankfurt where his aged mother still lives only to find mobs stoning the buildings. Later, Captain Fitzroy, an aide to Wellington in love with Nathan's daughter Julie, arrives at the ghetto home to make sure that she is safe. Nathan then tells Fitzroy that the relationship with Julie must be ended, for he is not of their race. Says Nathan: "Go into the Jewish quarter of any town in Prussia today and you'll see men lying dead: Jewish people killed by your people for but one crime—that they're Jews." And finally, in a later scene, Ledrantz receives the following note: "Dresden—entire ghetto reduced by fire. It is estimated that five thousand Jewish refugees crossed the border into the Netherlands"; indeed, the very direction of the flow of Jewish refugees during the early years of National Socialist rule.

The viewer is left with the impression that the Jews can purchase their safety with money, as when Ledrantz is pressured into halting anti-Jewish violence in order to persuade the Rothschilds to agree to finance Europe in its second war against Napoleon (after his escape from Elba). This belief that Jewish wealth can buy anything perhaps mirrored a commonly accepted stereotype. Possibly there was even some truth in this presumption during the early stages of the Nazi regime. After the war began, however, at a time when no amount of money could have saved Jewish lives, it is possible that the persistence of the stereotype hindered people from coming to the aid of European Jewry.

Again, we confront the paradox that runs throughout the film: that of the cunning, powerful Jew who is also an oppressed victim. This uncertainty may have been a reflection of the uncertainty of the American view of the Jew. Surveys taken in the thirties found the following traits to be considered to typify Jews: shrewdness, persistence, industriousness, aggressiveness, love of money (and unscrupulous and successful in getting it), clannishness, lack of refinement, and foreign religious customs. Simultaneously, positive qualities attributed to Jews included: success in making money, ambitiousness, aggressiveness, and loyalty to family and to fellow Jews.[13] The overlap is telling. And the attitude of Americans toward the Rothschilds epitomizes this dual vision: They were admired for their achievements, yet despised for the way they had accomplished them.

There is, however, no ambiguity or ambivalence with regard to the physical image of the Jew. Incidentally, this is not the first time George Arliss, who plays both Mayer and Nathan, had acted the role of a Jew. He was famous for his screen portrayal of Disraeli as well as his theatrical interpretation of Shylock. As a non-Jew playing Jewish roles, he had ample opportunity to study prevailing stereotypes—which he incorporates into the roles of Rothschild father and son. Might the film makers have decided to have one actor play both characters in order to convey a "sameness" that highlights the stereotypical aspects of the roles? Mayer Amschel, dressed in black, wears a thick skullcap on his long, sidelocked hair; he has a prominent hooked nose on his bearded face, banal even in the stereotype. His figure is bent,

conditioned by generations of Talmud study and praying; he ges-
ticulates when he talks; in sum, the archetype of the ghetto Jew.
Nathan looks exactly like his father, only without the beard and
with a top hat in place of a skullcap. He must always be reminded
to remove his hat when he is in company—an atavism of his
religious inheritance that is, of course, bad manners in English
society. Father and son in combination yield a complete stereotype. Past and present share the same face, the same blood, and
the same personality—a visual metaphor for Jewishness in the
public imagination, immediately recognizable and comprehensible to an American audience. This reinforces a popular perception of the Jew as a race in which the over-all image is bio-
logically fixed.[14]

This image of the Jew did not, in fact, originate in the United
States but in the Anglo-European cultural milieu. John J. Appel,
in his article "Jews in American Caricature," writes: "Conniving,
swindling, rich, wicked and yet comic Jews in the Elizabethan
Shylock tradition predominated among the Jews depicted in
American plays performed during the first three-quarters of the
nineteenth century." And during the latter part of the nineteenth
century cartoons in illustrated weeklies created in the American
popular imagination a picture of the unscrupulous and dishonest
Jew. With the decline of the illustrated weeklies early in this
century, the stereotypes were appropriated by vaudeville, bur-
lesque, and movies.[15] However, these images are not altogether
negative, for just as we observe contradictory images in *The
House of Rothschild*, Appel finds the same phenomenon in the
cartoons of the illustrated weeklies:

> How puzzling and contradictory the contents of *Puck* and other il-
> lustrated weeklies appear today! . . . drawings of Jewish merchants
> with immense beaks and grotesque gestures enticing customers into
> stores, are intermingled with tributes to Jewish sobriety and indus-
> try. . . . Cartoons and editorials defending Jews against their detrac-
> tors, cartoons welcoming Russian Jewish immigrants as more desir-
> able than the Irish, alternated with illustrations and jokes reducing
> the Jewish condition to all-pervasive concerns with money and gain
> achieved through commercial acumen combined with fraud and
> stealth.[16]

The paradoxical vision of the Jew persists in films like *The House
of Rothschild*, as a review in the *Motion Picture Herald* states

The House of Rothschild (1934). Mayer Amschel Rothschild (George Arliss, far right) is a bent, side-locked, bearded, hook-nosed figure who wears a skullcap and represents "the archetype of the ghetto Jew."

The House of Rothschild (1934). Nathan (George Arliss) looks exactly like his father, only he has no beard, wears a top hat in place of a skullcap, and now controls a banking dynasty centered in London.

about Arliss's performance: "Where else can you find an actor who can so beautifully unite the demoniac and the human."[17]

That the film appears in the middle of the Depression is not without significance. In *Crowds and Power*, Elias Canetti discusses inflation as a crowd phenomenon; money, like crowds, comes in large numerical units. During times of inflation, money increases numerically but decreases in value; it loses its continuity; it becomes worthless. Men, at its mercy, depreciate along with the unit on which they rely and with which they equate themselves. They, in turn, seek out something worth less, something to treat as valueless. Hitler found the Jews, as Canetti explains:

> They [the Jews] seemed made for it: their long standing connection with money, their traditional understanding of its movements and fluctuations, their skill in speculation . . . all this, in a time of doubt, instability and hostility to money. . . . The individual Jew seemed "bad" because he was on good terms with money when others did not know how to manage it.[18]

The potential to incite the crowd with visible symbols of Jewish money and power existed in America, too, which shared the same stereotypes. We have already mentioned the American fascination with the Rothschilds. Oscar Handlin adds: "The conception of Jewish interest in money deepened into the conviction that Jews controlled the great fortunes of the world. . . . Every American had heard of the Rothschilds."[19] Rudolf Glanz captures the power of the Rothschild myth over the minds of Americans when he calls it "a need to express the essence of capitalism in one great human example, that was, moreover, no individual fortune doomed to extinction, but a family undertaking, continuing from generation to generation."[20] That is to say, the rich Jew embodied aspects of the American dream—stability, continuity, hope, and possibility. Instead of blaming the Jew for inflation, Americans saw that, with his keen knowledge of money, he might help cure the nation's economic woes. Perhaps the film makers sought to exploit America's admiration for capitalism in offering a sympathetic portrayal of the wealthy Jew that would supersede the negative side of the stereotype. Indeed, the film Rothschilds are not frivolous squanderers. Rather, they place great importance on the duties of the rich and powerful to safeguard society and the nation; they are the very paradigm of noblesse oblige.

The fact that anti-Semitism was neither institutionalized nor widespread in political rhetoric was reason enough for the film makers not to fear the consequences of connecting Jews to money. Their goal, perhaps, was to reinterpret an accepted historical image in order to demystify the Jew of the present. True, he was still the "imagined" Jew, an anomaly in American life. Yet he had won acceptance within the larger society. He was not an enemy. Perhaps their goal was to alter popular anti-Semitic notions fed by large-scale Jewish immigration earlier in the century. For as John Higham indicates: "The problem of anti-Semitism in America ultimately needs to be viewed in relation to mass immigration," that is, to the fear of being overrun.[21] In what should be a positive ending to the film, Nathan is knighted by the king of England in appreciation of his and his people's contributions to their "adopted" land. But here too a positive element is negated—in this instance by a slip of one word. That word, "adopted," separates the Jews from the rest of the English—or American—citizenry. The film makers themselves may well have been influenced on the subconscious level by the identical stereotypes that they eschewed on the conscious level. This would account for the persistently ambiguous portrait of the Rothschilds as symbol of the Jews. We must therefore emphasize again that even the most overtly positive aspects of the film are fraught with contradictions. For example, Mayer's apologetics after the visit of the tax collector offer strange logic as to why the Jews are "forced" to cheat; or the suggestion that assimilation is a viable solution to the "Jewish problem" (via the intended marriage of Nathan's daughter Julie to a gentile) is certainly a threat to Jewish continuity. And although the film challenges the validity of political anti-Semitism by emphasizing the contributions of the various Rothschilds to their respective societies, it depicts the success of the Rothschilds only in terms of financial manipulation.

The salient historical concepts in *The House of Rothschild* were surely strange to Americans: closed ghettos, the court Jew, emancipation. More likely, the themes of money, power, and control would linger in the minds of its audience, especially coming on the heels of the 1929 stock market crash, as we see Nathan controlling London's financial markets. It is obvious that the continuity of deep-seated stereotypes was not so easily broken, even by those who consciously set out to do just that. Although Amer-

The House of Rothschild (1934). Jew Street, in Frankfurt's Jewish ghetto of 1780, provides the backdrop for this lovers' tryst between Captain Fitzroy (Robert Young) and Nathan's daughter, Julie (Loretta Young).

icans did not scapegoat the Jews for their economic troubles, anti-Semitism did begin to increase during the 1930s. For the Jews, hope centered on the desire expressed by Mayer Amschel to his children as he lay dying: "And remember this before all: that neither business nor power nor all the gold in Europe will bring you happiness till we, our people, have equality, respect and dignity."

This hope notwithstanding, in the Europe of the 1930s Mayer's dream for his people was a rapidly disintegrating illusion. The warning in *The House of Rothschild* of the threat against the Jews was becoming reality. One year after the film appeared the Nuremberg Laws were enacted in Germany. The process by which conditions continued to deteriorate culminated in 1938 with *Kristallnacht*. The Evian Conference to solve the "refugee" problem also took place in 1938, but without much success. Furthermore, the Jews' problems in Europe did not elicit much sympathy from the American public. A majority of those questioned in a 1938 poll were "apparently seduced into condoning the persecution of European Jewry by the idea that it was at least in part the victims' own fault." Without doubt most respondents, who probably knew little about those in Europe, were expressing their feelings about Jews in America.[22] Their vision was blinded by the circumference of their understanding of American Jewry.

In spite of political realities in Europe, from 1934 until 1939 Hollywood shied away from films dealing with anti-Semitism— or even fascism, a decision undoubtedly influenced by the strong isolationist sentiments prevailing in the United States. Hollywood probably feared being accused of using film to propagandize on behalf of "Jewish brethren" overseas. In addition, perhaps box office sense ruled the day: an American public apathetic about Jewish conditions in Europe would not buy tickets to see films dealing with the subject. Interestingly, anti-fascist activities in Hollywood antedated the swing in American public opinion and diplomacy. Even so personal politics and activism did not intrude into the films of the day: "Anyone who attends the movies regularly must be impressed by the fact that Hollywood's output is to an overwhelming degree distinguished by utter political innocuousness."[23]

Then, in 1939, Hollywood also began to respond to the Nazi threat through motion pictures. Warner Brothers produced *Confessions of a Nazi Spy*, a quasi documentary based on the true story of a Nazi fifth column in the United States. The film does not concern itself at all with the Jewish problem. On the contrary, it might even have harmed European Jewish efforts to gain American visas, for the film suggests that refugees might pose a threat to America's security. As we have already noted, American anti-Semitism cannot be understood without reference to mass immigration. This film reinforces what was already a problematic situation for those wishing to immigrate, although at that time, refugees were not yearning for the "golden land"—they were hoping just to survive. The failure of the Evian Conference coupled with the State Department's unbending adherence to immigration quotas established America's position on refugees. Hollywood's entry into the political arena was of no help to the Jews.

Even as more feature films began to deal with war themes, their success with the public was minimal. The fact is, not many filmgoers were interested in political films. According to one report in 1941:

> The relative apathy of movie-goers for such films as *Confessions of a Nazi Spy, Escape, Mortal Storm*—each an honest courageous effort and an excellent movie—is reflected in their moderate or disappointing reception at the box-office. In 194 separate surveys made by Dr. George Gallup, it was found that only New York audiences seem to want pictures with political content involving Hitler and the Nazis.[24]

New York may have welcomed such political films because it was the largest urban Jewish center in America as well as the home of most immigrants with something at stake in Europe. The feelings of New Yorkers, apparently, were not those of the rest of the country.

One film maker chose to resist the prevailing mood and make his picture "for the Jews of the world," as he was once quoted as saying. Charlie Chaplin's *The Great Dictator* (1940) stands out during that bleak period as a document reflecting deep concern for the oppressed Jews in Europe. The film was not an easy task to undertake. The truth is, as Chaplin prepared *The Great Dictator* he received warnings from several quarters not to proceed. Isolationists objected. So did crypto-Nazis. Indeed, Chaplin's own studio, fearing financial losses, did not want to see the picture made. The most revealing complaint, made to the Motion Picture Association, came from a high Nazi official who said that

Confessions of a Nazi Spy (1939). A Nazi meeting, held somewhere in New Jersey, where Bund members met regularly.

Chaplin's playing Hitler will "naturally lead to serious troubles and complications."[25] Chaplin, however, was not a politician. He saw himself as a humanitarian, and in his film he captured the danger facing the Jews as no other film maker would during the war.

The Great Dictator begins during World War I, set in a mythical country called Tomania. Its plot goes as follows: A Jewish barber saves the life of a fellow Tomanian soldier named Schultz but is himself injured and hospitalized with amnesia. The war ends. A new and insane political movement ruled by Hynkel the dictator rises in Tomania. One day the barber wanders out of the hospital and returns to the ghetto. Innocent of political events, he becomes a target for the storm troopers because he fights back when they mistreat him. He is unharmed thanks to Schultz, now a Tomanian VIP. In the meantime, the barber falls in love with a Jewish orphan, Hannah. Schultz opposes Hynkel's anti-Jewish policy and flees to the ghetto. Both he and the barber are arrested there and sent to a concentration camp. They escape. Hynkel's men mistake the barber for the dictator and bring him to speak to the cheering crowds in newly conquered Osterlich. It is then that the barber/Hynkel delivers his famous speech—a plea for mankind to save itself.

The Great Dictator lends itself to revealing comparisons with *The House of Rothschild.* The two films share many of the same structural elements, both in setting and theme, yet they differ markedly in the manner in which they employ those elements. Both, for example, use the ghetto locale, but in *The House of Rothschild* it is dark and somber, whereas in *The Great Dictator,* it is spacious and light. George Arliss and Charlie Chaplin play dual roles in their respective films. The Arliss role of Rothschild father and son intimates a "sameness" of all Jews, a genetically determined type that remains unchanged and unchangeable from generation to generation, an idea almost racist by definition. Chaplin, on the other hand, plays two distinctly opposing roles—the Jewish barber and the dictator, who, in turn, illustrate an inner struggle between good and evil, with the Jew representative of the good in man. Chaplin thus avoids defining the Jew by any particular traits and makes of him a universal symbol. There is no general stereotype in *The Great Dictator.*

As mentioned earlier, *The House of Rothschild* hints at a negative but popular interpretation of the legend of the wandering

The Mortal Storm (1940). "Remember your duty" says a Storm
Troop officer (Robert Stevenson), when Margaret Sullavan
pleads to Robert Young for help in finding her arrested father.
This is the story of a German family split by the Nazis' rise to
power.

Jew: the Jew as an international businessman. Now, Chaplin's barber can be associated with the legend as well, for, generally, the famous tramp is known in all his films as a wanderer. But it is doubtful that Chaplin means his barber to symbolize the Jew as a victim in a theological sense, that is, as one punished for the death of Christ. Instead, the barber is a symbol of man's struggle; he assumes the burdens of the world; he functions as an omen; and he is representative of all humanity—all of which are possibilities in the context of the legend.[26] In *The Great Dictator*, the barber, a victim of amnesia, operates outside the realm of any specific historical time, tied not to any particular event in history but to all events. From the hospital he simply wanders into the ghetto, only to witness the beginning of its destruction. The Jew here is no longer a wanderer for the sake of world domination, as might be seen in *The House of Rothschild*, but rather a wanderer for the cause of humanity, indicating, on the level of myth, a softening of the Jewish image.

Both films, though, are clearly concerned with the threat to Europe's Jews. When *The House of Rothschild* appeared, the danger was incipient. By the time *The Great Dictator* premiered, events had progressed far along the road to destruction, although many preferred to disregard Chaplin's warning. He uses newspaper headlines, some of actual events, others relating to the persecution of the Jews in the ghetto, in order to transmit a sense of the urgency and reality of events in the film, especially as they pertained to the Jews. In fact, the film, a story of the battle between the Tomanians [Germans] and the Jews, is a warning. Hynkel lashes out against the Jews to the Tomanian masses. References are made to poison gas and to "getting rid of the Jews," the scapegoat for Tomania's problems. Storm troopers mistreat the Jews in the ghetto. But the Jews are courageous in the face of persecution. The barber fights back. Hannah fights back.

In *The House of Rothschild*, the figure of Ledrantz is fictionalized, thereby removing him from a historical context in order to stress his character as symbolic of Nazi Germany. Chaplin, too, turns to fictional characters, but with a difference. In *The Great Dictator*, all of the fictional figures are assigned symbolic names which are easily recognizable, in a contemporary historical setting. Only the Jews retain their identity, qua Jews, as a

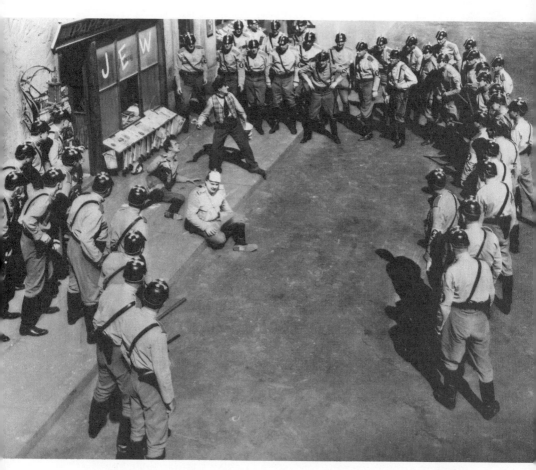

The Great Dictator (1940). A Jewish barber (Charlie Chaplin) becomes the target for Tomanian storm troopers when he fights back.

means of emphasizing the severe danger and persecution confronting them.

In contrast to the earlier film the money theme plays a minor role in Chaplin's work. His Jews are working people—barbers, laundresses, grocers—reflecting the film's more socialist, New Deal vision, indeed, a mood very unlike that of Rothschild-style capitalism! But even Chaplin errs on one crucial point: Hynkel, in need of money to finance the invasion of Osterlich, softens his stand against the Jews, hoping to convince the rich Jew Epstein to provide the funds. This notion of the wealthy court Jew— Chaplin's one lapse into stereotype—leaves the unfortunate impression that Jews could, at that late date, buy their way out of danger. In this regard, Chaplin too misunderstands the reality of Hitler's anti-Jewish policy.

Religion figures in both films as well. One film is distinctly Jewish; the other, universalistic, incorporating a secular theology. The Rothschilds, at least in the ghetto, wear skullcaps and kiss mezuzahs on doorposts; their ways are foreign. Chaplin's Jews do not observe the Jewish religion. Instead they function as a symbol for a society founded on the Judeo-Christian ethic. Assimilation becomes a goal for the Rothschilds, whereas the barber espouses a liberal, humanist tradition—perhaps a form of assimilation.

Chaplin's secular theology has Christian associations. For example, the Jews flee Tomania to nearby Osterlich, in the historical context, obviously a reference to Austria. (Similarly, Garbitsch is Goebbels, Herring is Göring, Tomania is poison, or Nazi Germany.) Yet Chaplin also intends his choice of names for people and places to evoke additional connotations and levels of meaning. In this light, we might allow for Osterlich as a theological symbol. *Oster* means Easter in German; *lich* or *licht* means light. The Jews have fled to "Easter Light" where they seek security and salvation—a secular resurrection. And when the barber, having been mistaken for Hynkel, speaks to the newly conquered citizens of Osterlich, his words bear a resemblance to the central theme of Christ's Sermon on the Mount: "I want to help everyone—Jews, gentiles—all. . . . We have lost our way. . . . We need kindness and humanity, universal brotherhood." In other words, "love thy neighbor."

The House of Rothschild accentuates the "differentness" of the Jews, suggesting that, nevertheless, they can be important to

The Great Dictator (1940). The barber falls in love with Hannah (Paulette Goddard), a Jewish orphan, and together they fight back when the Jews become Hynkel's scapegoat—proving that Jews are courageous in the face of persecution, thus becoming "the weathervane of society" and "the symbol of humanity."

their "adopted" lands. *The Great Dictator* perceives the Jew as the bellwether of society: When the Jew is in danger, so is mankind. That is to say, *The House of Rothschild* is an apologia for the Jew and allows him, as a marginal, stereotyped figure, to approach the center; *The Great Dictator*, on the other hand, has a grand vision with the Jew at its center as the archetypical man.

The image of the Jew in *The Great Dictator* is more a function of Chaplin's humanitarian vision than a reflection of popular consensus, for, if anything, anti-Semitic sentiments were increasing in America. In *The Great Dictator*, the anti-Semite is unequivocally the "bad guy," making the Jew a more sympathetic figure, whereas to some extent the stereotype in *The House of Rothschild* justifies gentile attitudes toward the Jew. In other words, in films that portray "anti" themes, either the victim or the oppressor must bear the guilt; as the image of the Jew evolves from *The House of Rothschild* to *The Great Dictator*, the guilt is transferred from the victim to the oppressor. The victim is no longer responsible for the opprobrium heaped upon him. Chaplin's film, then, is a cinematic turning point. The Jew reaches the peak of humanity, indeed, he is the very symbol of humanity itself. He bears no resemblance to any previously established stereotype—such that, there may not be another American film whose vision of the Jew is so eloquent.

At the time of its release, one aspect of *The Great Dictator* aroused considerable controversy and criticism: the use of humor in the film. The review in the *Hollywood Citizen* more or less captures the essence of the critique: "It's hard to be funny about war when war is ravaging humanity."[27] Does Chaplin, through his use of comedy, especially his mocking of Hitler, trivialize the horrifying urgency of the events of the day?

When the comical aspects of *The Great Dictator* are considered, it must be remembered that political comedy is anathema to totalitarian regimes. To laugh at a dictator, to mock a person who envisions himself the earthly equivalent of God, is tantamount to committing the crime of blasphemy. In fact, author Richard Grunberger points out that in Germany "the penalty for anti-Hitler jokes was death," so that anti-Nazi humor became a means of expressing resistance.[28] As an interesting aside, a portfolio of more than sixty Saul Steinberg drawings was discovered recently among the declassified documents at the National Archives. Steinberg, known for his drawings in *The New Yorker*, had been recruited during the war by the Office of Strategic Services to work for the Office of Morale in Washington. His cartoons ridiculing Hitler were dropped behind enemy lines in hopes of inspiring resistance.[29] The Jews, themselves, believed that by telling jokes against Hitler, they too were offering resistance. The idea was: "If you do not possess the physical force to overthrow him, there is no more effective way to fight a dictator than to make a laughingstock of him."[30] What better method is there to attack people who live in fear of humor than to mock them? Clearly, Chaplin hoped through *The Great Dictator* to use his own superb talent to expose Hynkel/Hitler before it was too late.

Perhaps a more relevant question might be: Is *The Great Dictator* funny? Certain scenes contain elements of humor, most glaringly the slapstick sequences between Hynkel and his rival, Napaloni. However, at no time does Chaplin make fun of the Jews. There are scenes that are sweetly humorous in their pathos, as, for example, when the Jews are to select the one who will blow up a government building based on whoever finds a coin placed in his pudding. Hannah places coins in all of the desserts to point up the absurdity of the Jews taking on the Tomanians' fight when they had yet to figure out how to save themselves. In effect, *The Great Dictator* is not funny. Its laughter originates in despair. As Bosley Crowther writes in his *New York Times* review of the film: "If 'The Great Dictator' seems less funny than anything Chaplin has done before it is because the evil which he is exposing seems more immediate and threatening."[31]

Chaplin wrote in his autobiography that had he known of the horrors of the concentration camps, he might not have made *The Great Dictator*.[32] Nonetheless, one cannot fault him for making the effort while there still seemed to be time to do something about the Nazi evil. Through his depiction of the Jew as the symbol of good, he demonstrates that goodness and justice are unconquerable. As was once said of Chaplin: "All his life Charlie has lived on the edge of things . . . but he has behaved with decorum . . . and when the last moment arrives he has no regrets because he has a clear conscience."[33] One can say, in addition, that rather than trivializing events of the day, Chaplin, in *The Great Dictator*, focuses attention in a most serious and urgent manner on what was to be one of the great tragedies of civilization—the Nazi genocide against the Jews. He does this

The Great Dictator (1940). Slapstick sequences between Hynkel (Chaplin) and his rival dictator, Napaloni (Jack Oakie) provide some comic relief in *The Great Dictator*. Chaplin hoped to expose Hynkel, or Hitler, by mocking the absurdity of dictators and making a laughingstock of Hynkel.

throughout the film and, again, in his final speech, which many critics found to be incongruous with the rest of the film. At the time, the film was not as popular as Chaplin had anticipated—"because," according to Hannah Arendt, "his underlying humanity had lost its meaning. Man had stopped seeking release in laughter; the little man had decided to be a big one." And, further,

Today, it is not Chaplin, but Superman. When, in *The Great Dictator*, the comedian tried, by the ingenious device of doubling his role to point up the contrast between the "little man" and the "big shot," and to show the almost brutal character of the Superman ideal, he was barely understood. And when, at the end of the film, he stepped out of character, and sought, in his own name, to reaffirm and vindicate the simple wisdom and philosophy of the "little man," his moving and impassioned plea fell, for the most part, upon unresponsive audiences.[34]

There is no doubt, especially in light of his final speech, that Chaplin wants his audience to respond in some active way to his plea.

Unfortunately, those who seemed to be most "influenced" by *The Great Dictator* were a group of senators who supported isolationist policies in America. In September 1941, Senator Bennett Clark of Missouri and Senator Gerald Nye of North Dakota introduced a Senate resolution calling for an investigation of what they perceived to be prowar propaganda in Hollywood films. The initial argument for the resolution was made by Nye in a speech in St. Louis, Missouri, at a meeting of the America First Committee. It was then that Nye attacked such movies as *The Great Dictator* because he felt they were propaganda aimed at bringing America into the war. He cited the names of those he believed controlled the eight major film companies in Hollywood, all "Jewish sounding" names, including Darryl Zanuck, who Nye probably thought was Jewish.[35]

In Nye's opening testimony at the hearings, he found it necessary to deny charges of anti-Semitism aimed at him after his St. Louis speech. He claimed that those Jews who criticized him for so-called Jew-baiting took their cues from the heads of the film industry. He insinuated that the actions of some Jews who desired America's entry into the war would cause other Jews to suffer. He concluded his opening remarks with the "hope" that "our Jewish people will so conduct themselves as to invite more of such spirit as ours. Unfortunately, certain of them are not doing so."[36] In effect, Nye accused the Jews of not being sufficiently "American" and of not acting in America's interests. Rather, as recent immigrants themselves, their concern was for other Jews in Europe—an accusation to which Jews were most sensitive. Later in his testimony, Senator Nye added: "Indeed, in Hollywood it is understandable when one speaks not of the foreign policy of the United States, but the foreign policy of Hollywood. . . . I would myself call it the most potent and dangerous fifth column in our country."[37] When Nye was questioned in the Senate about films he found objectionable, he admitted that the only picture he had seen was *The Great Dictator*, the one film that focused on the threat to the Jews.

Nye's intentions were perceived clearly in a letter to Ed Raftery, United Artists' legal adviser (United Artists was also Chaplin's studio):

I take it your industry is more or less sensitive to popular notions and I am sorry that little crucifixion business is starting up. . . . Doubtless the intention of . . . Mr. Nye is to advertise the enthusiasm of American Jews for the war, and thereby make American participation unprofitable.[38]

Darryl Zanuck's testimony bore witness to the tone of the investigation:

At the outset, it seems necessary to state my personal background. . . . My mother and father were both born in the United States of America. My grandparents, on both my mother's and father's side, were born in the United States of America. My parents and grandparents were regular attendants and life long members of the Methodist Church.[39]

Zanuck sounded as if he were out to prove that he had no Jewish blood to the German Ministry of Interior rather than offering testimony at a hearing of the United States Senate. But whether it was motivated by anti-Semitic, anti-Hollywood, or truly intense isolationist feelings, the mood of the investigation only reinforced the hesitancy with which Hollywood executives approached the anti-Nazi theme in films.

In any case, the events of 7 December 1941 put a quick end

to the investigation. Hollywood began in earnest making war films aimed at involving Americans in what was now their war, too. But none focused on the persecution of Europe's Jews, whose attempted genocide had by then already begun.[40] Perhaps, this was because those who headed the film industry feared corroborating Nye's accusations of the supposed Jewish self-interest in wanting to aid European Jews. America at war had to present a united front in fighting fascism, and ethnic interests might have been considered un-American.

Hollywood was ready to join in, using film to aid the American defense effort. The leaders of the motion picture industry had established the War Activities Committee (WAC) of the Motion Picture Industry. After Pearl Harbor, on 18 December 1941, Roosevelt appointed his personal assistant and Director of the Office of Government Reports, Lowell Mellett, as Coordinator of Government Films. Certain rules provided guidelines for film makers; decision-making was left to their discretion on the basis of "voluntary self-discipline." In June 1942, the *Government Information Manual for the Motion Picture Industry* was issued,[41] its purpose being to advise film makers on what was considered important to include in films helping the war program. The manual suggests, for example:

> There are still groups in this country who are thinking only in terms of their particular group. Some citizens have not been made aware of the fact that this is a people's war, not a group war.

And, in addition: "We must emphasize that this country is a melting pot." Clearly, the government would consider any emphasis on individual or specific group needs as un-American. With the memory of the recent Senate investigations still fresh, it is obvious why Hollywood might have hesitated to emphasize the persecution of the Jews in Europe. As the manual explains: "We must emphasize that this (is) a people's war."

Hollywood, nonetheless, was confronted on the issue in 1943, when the American Jewish Congress made direct pleas to the leaders of the film industry for a picture dealing with the genocide in Europe.[42] Rebuffed by their contacts, it seems, the Congress then wrote to Lowell Mellett, at that time chief of the Bureau of Motion Pictures of the Office of War Information, asking him to intervene with industry leaders regarding the urgency of such a film. Mellett's Bureau spoke to various studio heads, and in February 1943 he communicated their reaction to the AJC:

> ... it might be unwise from the standpoint of the Jews themselves to have a picture dealing solely with Hitler's treatment of their people, but interest has been indicated in the possibility of a picture covering various groups that have been subject to the Nazi treatment. This of course would take in the Jews.

This is exactly the route that Hollywood took. Anti-Nazi films, like *To Be Or Not To Be* (1942) or *The Seventh Cross* (1944), included Jews among the victims of Nazi persecution, never singling them out.

The preceding example hints at a phenomenon that was already apparent at the Evian Conference in 1938. Although the major concern of the conference was how to save the Jews, reference was always to "refugees." The group most in danger was not to be singled out, but was to be rescued as refugees, not as Jews. In this way the persecution of the Jews was officially universalized. By 1943, Hollywood had picked up on this notion. Americanization, the theme of the *Government Information Manual for the Motion Picture Industry*, precluded focusing on particular interests; it rejected the notion that the treatment of the Jews was "unique in its horror," as the American Jewish Congress wrote to Mellett. The Jews were simply victims among other victims, who would not receive special treatment—at least, not in America. In fact, Mellett went so far as to attempt to dissuade studios from making films dealing with anti-Semitism in America because they might suggest distasteful parallels with Nazi Germany.

The irony of such incidents is that, studies showed, "far from evoking sympathy, the Nazi persecution apparently sparked a rise in anti-Semitism in this country."[43] A letter written by Herman Shumlin, director of *Watch On the Rhine*, to Albert Hackett and Frances Goodrich, the husband-wife team who wrote the script for the 1944 film *The Hitler Gang*, intimates a necessity to avoid too much emphasis on the suffering of the Jews:

> I received your "Hitler" script and have read it. . . . There are a couple of places in it which make me a little anxious. As to the point about the references to the Jews, I think you have handled them

To Be or Not To Be (1942). Maria Tura (Carole Lombard), the star of a troop of Polish actors who, through their various guises both on stage and off, manage to foil the Nazis.

very well. But I do get a feeling that when Hitler begins pounding away on the Jews, it would be better if he did not pound at this point alone. There is a frightening positiveness about a repetition of a simple statement. It begins almost to take on the quality of truth. Did Hitler in these early days not also attack other groups?[44]

Shumlin's point, of course, is that the more an issue is stressed, the more convincing it becomes. Emphasis on the Jew as victim, in an atmosphere that is already negative, might lead a viewer to wonder why the Jew is always the "chosen" victim—and, ultimately, to believe that the Jew might in fact be deserving of punishment. The Jew then bears the guilt for being the victim. According to one survey taken during the war, 10 percent of Americans approved of Hitler's treatment of the Jews,[45] perhaps not a large percentage in absolute terms, but in the light of Hitler's Jewish policy, it becomes overwhelming.

Yet again, in 1943, Hollywood was given reason to avoid the Jewish problem in Europe in the form of accusations from members of Harry S. Truman's Senate Committee, which was hearing testimony regarding the war effort. Despite the glowing testimony of Colonel K. B. Lawton, Chief of the Army Pictorial Division of the United States Signal Corps, about Hollywood's participation in the war effort, the committee questioned, among other things, whether the movie industry was profiting from military training films and how some major executives managed to get officers' commissions. One committee member, Senator Ralph O. Brewster, felt that "recent citizens were not appropriate film makers for the war effort, that the War Department should hang out a sign saying only 'seasoned citizens' may apply." His words seemed to echo the sentiments expressed by Senator Gerald P. Nye in 1941, "that the moviemakers were insufficiently American in origin, intellect and character."[46] So the continuing accusations aimed at industry leaders, insinuating that they were aliens—along with the government's emphasis on fighting the war together as Americans and the increasing anti-Semitism in the United States—go a long way toward explaining Hollywood's decision to avoid the subject of the persecution of the Jews.

Another factor in this equation may have been the American Jewish community's lack of political power and ability to influence the American policy at that time (a situation that would change in the postwar period). America's Jews supported Roosevelt overwhelmingly, and there was little chance they

The Seventh Cross (1944). George Heisler (Spencer Tracy), the only one of seven fugitives from a German concentration camp to elude the Gestapo.

would change this allegiance. Thus the Jewish vote was assured. In addition, the Jewish community itself was slow and chaotic in its response to the persecutions in Europe. Indeed, their often ineffectual attempts at helping European Jewry came, in part, as a result of their external weakness.

Difficult as it is to believe, as we have noted, general resentment against the Jews increased during most of the war and reached a climax in 1944.[47] Opinion polls in 1945, after the mass killings in Europe were common knowledge, showed that 75 percent of the respondents had not changed their attitudes toward American Jews.[48] Paradoxically, during the war no one wanted to see films dealing with the persecution of the Jews in Europe; but after the war, according to a 1945 poll, 39 percent wished to see films of the horrors that took place in the concentration camps, 60 percent thought such films should be shown in cinemas throughout the United States, and 89 percent thought they should be shown to all Germans.[49] Apparently, Americans believed there was a lesson to be learned from the genocide against the Jews, only they were not yet convinced that it was their lesson.

For, even after the knowledge of the camps had been graphically unfolded, a refugee problem persisted. Lacking the urgency of the thirties and forties, it was, instead, a matter of the survivors living in crowded displaced persons camps in the occupied zones of Europe. Many wanted to come to the United States. However, popular opinion still seemed to favor the anti-Semites. The Citizens Committee on Displaced Persons, founded in 1946, made it a point in their propaganda to stress that of the 400,000 DPs they hoped would gain entry into the United States, only 20 percent were Jewish.[50] This was done, apparently, to appease the American public who, according to the opinion polls, were not anxious to receive refugees, perhaps the majority of whom they felt were Jews.

With the world no longer innocent of the knowledge of the death camps and the DP problem, Hollywood returned to the subject of anti-Semitism. The results of the war, combined with the heightening of anti-Semitic feelings in the United States, had instilled the sense that "it can happen here." In the shadow of the European experience, film makers took it on themselves to explain to Americans the danger of anti-Semitism. This time the focus in the films would be on full-fledged American Jews, not immigrants or refugees.

Several war films featured Jewish characters, generally soldiers who had proven their bravery and loyalty to America on the battlefield. This was actually a continuation of the policy of the Office of War Information to encourage film makers to include Jews along with other minorities as soldiers fighting for the American cause.[51] But this image was a problematic one, as film critic Pauline Kael observes:

> By a quota system, war films admitted carefully selected minority representatives, clean-cut Jewish and Negro soldiers whose participation in the national defense apparently gave them a special claim to equality over and above mere membership in the human species. Can it be that even in liberal thinking there is a stigma which can be rubbed off only if minority characters behave heroically.[52]

The idea, clearly, was to convince American audiences, especially the anti-Semites among them, that the minority soldier, in this case the Jew, was a "true" American who fought side by side with "established" Americans. This self-conscious desire on the part of film makers to avoid negative stereotyping had as its adjunct the fear of making their Jews too real, that is, too easily identifiable, of attributing to them characteristics that might be misconstrued and, in turn, foster anti-Semitism. The result was an exaggerated portrayal of the qualities of goodness and wisdom, making of the Jew a one-dimensional figure.

The Jew in *Crossfire* (1947), the first postwar film to focus on and attack anti-Semitism, is a decorated war hero. However, he plays a relatively minor role, as the film concentrates on the gentile characters: the soldier who murders the Jew and the detective who solves the case (and while doing so preaches the evils of anti-Semitism). Pauline Kael poses a relevant question with regard to the characterization of the Jew in *Crossfire*. "Suppose the murdered man was a draft dodger, or a conscientious objector, would the fanatic [also an American soldier] have been justified in killing him?"[53] In other words, where prewar films rely on commonly accepted Jewish stereotypes, postwar—post-Holocaust—films substitute a new stereotype, the "Americanized" Jew, who, betraying no Jewish content or nuance of character, is a person just like any other American, what Miss Kael calls a "liberal" stereotype.

Gentleman's Agreement (1947), the next major film to center on the Jews and anti-Semitism after *The House of Rothschild* and *The Great Dictator*, captures in its characters the essence of the liberal stereotype while also sharing many motifs in common with its two predecessors. The knowledge of the Holocaust looms large in the film's warning to the American public about the dangers that can result in a society where anti-Semitism thrives. It was also a factor for those who created the film's publicity, as the Twentieth-Century Fox Release Synopsis shows: "Phil finds prejudice cropping up fast—flicks here and flicks there of insult that tap constantly on the nerves. No yellow armbands, no marked park benches, no Gestapo, no torture chambers—just a flick here and a flick there."[54]

Gentleman's Agreement, then, is the only one of the three films to take place on American soil in a particularly American milieu. The story is about journalist Phil Green, who comes to New York with his mother and young son Tommy to write a story on anti-Semitism for *Smith's Weekly*. He decides to pose as a Jew for several weeks in order to "feel" anti-Semitism firsthand. In his guise as Jew, he meets Jewish self-haters and apathetic liberals. He experiences various forms of discrimination, not life threatening, merely inconvenient. The Jews in *Gentleman's Agreement* do not suffer persecution as they do in *The House of Rothschild* and *The Great Dictator*.

The Jewish ghetto, which figures in *The House of Rothschild* and *The Great Dictator*, interestingly, also has a place in *Gentleman's Agreement*. Phil brings his family to New York, a type of ghetto in that it has the largest urban concentration of Jews in the world. Moreover, New York, with its cosmopolitanism, might be considered by the average citizen as the outskirts of America, much as the Jew often finds himself on the margins of society. New York, then, becomes a logical starting point for the elimination of anti-Jewish prejudice in the United States.

As in *The House of Rothschild* and *The Great Dictator*, one actor plays dual roles, in this case, the gentile who poses as the Jew and, in the process, negates the belief that physical appearance defines the Jew. Yet, the old stereotype is invoked at least once. When he decides to pass as a Jew, Phil looks at himself in the mirror. The idea will work. After all, he says to himself, he has dark hair and dark eyes like his friend Dave Goldman. He has no accent, no Jewish mannerisms. Neither does Dave. Then

Phil gestures toward his chin, somewhat like Nathan Rothschild, as if wondering what he will do about a beard. In essence, he applies many of the attributes of the stereotype to himself with the result: the gentile, posing as a Jew, is still a gentile. In trying to negate the stereotype he actually reaffirms it, which adds another dimension to his character, that of an alter ego to his (Jewish) best friend. Phil is the gentile equivalent of Dave Goldman. The two men clearly resemble one another, only everything about Dave is more "Jewish": He has curlier hair, he has a slight bend in his nose, he is a little swarthier, he is shorter. So, in spite of "liberal" efforts to cancel it, a stereotype prevails, albeit a more subtle one.[55]

Beyond the question of stereotypes, the Jews in each of the three films symbolize particular qualities that are relevant to the particular thrust of the film in question. In *The House of Rothschild*, the Jews represent money, power, and manipulation, despite the apologetics for these traits. In *The Great Dictator*, the Jew stands for universalism, hope, and a humanitarian world. In *Gentleman's Agreement* the fact that Phil can play both Jew and gentile signifies that there is a common denominator among men: Americanism. Even in the choice of family name, Green is neutral; he can be either Jew or gentile. And Phil himself is "green"—naïve, innocent. He reflects the popular ideals of American society—liberty and equality for all regardless of race or creed—ideals that needed to be reaffirmed. His way of life is "American." He comes from a close nuclear family in which we see deep intergenerational respect. Even the furnishings in his home are colonial style, indicating his rootedness in all that is American. Kathy, his girl friend, symbolizes the flaw in this otherwise perfect picture. She, in her own way, undermines the American ideal, not because she is vicious or nasty but because by her failure to do battle with anti-Semitism she participates in perpetuating it. Anti-Semitism, after all, is un-American; and, indeed, the notion of "un-American" was to set the tone in society following the end of the war and into the fifties. Discrimination, ethnic identity, and belief in foreign ideologies would be considered un-American, while equality, sameness, and belief in the "American way" would define the true American.

This film, like the other two, also incorporates elements of the wanderer motif. Phil is widowed and comes from California to New York. When he and Kathy (who initially suggests the article to her uncle, the editor of *Smith's Weekly*) quarrel over his passing as a Jew, he decides to return to California. He is on the move, looking for a place to settle.

Now, whereas the theme of the three films is anti-Semitism, each deals differently with it as well as with the Jews themselves. The Jews in *The House of Rothschild* are visibly Jewish, both in manner and dress. Religious customs are important in their lives, at least in the first segment of the film. However, assimilation is a viable and seemingly desirable option. The Jews bear the blame for their personality traits but are vindicated by the apologetics offered on their behalf. *The Great Dictator* leaves no room for ambiguous interpretations. The Jews are blameless victims. Yet Chaplin's Jews have no Jewish identification other than that they live together in the ghetto. *Gentleman's Agreement*, on the other hand, defines the Jew by his religious label. Early in the film, Phil's son Tommy asks what a Jew is. Phil answers by saying that some people go to churches, and some, like Jews, go to churches called synagogues and temples, that is, that only religious affiliation distinguishes one person from the next. But what does this mean? Does he refer to traditions, celebrations, or prayer? In the context of the film, religion is a label with no underlying substance. Church or synagogue affiliation is simply part of being an American. And therefore Jewish identification is a function of anti-Semitism, as we see from Phil's decision to pose as a Jew. He can "experience" what it means to be Jewish through anti-Semitism. This, indeed, is the problem of the gentile, as Jean-Paul Sartre writes in *Anti-Semite and Jew*. And Phil makes it his problem. The film assumes that a Jew is not Jewish by virtue of a shared culture and history (which Phil, of course, does not experience); it is the gentile who makes the Jew "Jewish" by being an anti-Semite.

None of the Jewish characters in the film has any visible connection to Jewish culture or tradition. Irving Weissman, the industrialist, thinks anti-Semitism is best kept under cover—Why call attention to the Jews?—an attitude held by many American Jews at the time. Phil's secretary Elaine Wilofsky changes her name to Elaine Wales in order to be accepted and does not want other Jewish "types" to ruin things for her. Incidentally, as the only Jew who is given a negative character (and an unimportant job), she is also the only one given a distinctly Polish-sounding name, perhaps reflecting an attitude that the Eastern European

Jew is inferior to the more cultured and westernized Central and Western European Jews. Professor Lieberman, the Einstein figure, is a Jew to spite the gentile, although he is a nonbeliever. Dave Goldman, the returning soldier (thus the script is able to introduce the "Jew as soldier") happens to be Phil's best friend (and the Jewish equivalent of Phil). It is Dave who tells Phil, after Tommy is beaten up because he is "Jewish," " . . . now you know what it's all about." To be Jewish is to be a victim. By focusing solely on discrimination, being a Jew is like having an illness. As Kathy says when praising the virtues of being a gentile, "it's like being happy you're well and not sick."[56] The only way to cure the affliction is for Jews to be like everyone else, that is, American. It would seem that the more American the Jew becomes, the sooner he will be "well." Therefore, the film does not identify any overtly identifiable Jewish traits.

Gentleman's Agreement does not picture the stereotypes that had shaped the American image of the Jew; rather, it attempts to explain the inherent danger and prejudice that result from such stereotypes. Phil's dual role is meant to emphasize that religion is the only distinguishing factor between Jew and gentile. The film is really about a post-Holocaust American dilemma: that American practice fails to conform to the American creed, a notion that Gunnar Myrdal applied to his study of black-white relations in America.[57] In effect, *Gentleman's Agreement* becomes the first film to focus on Jews whose underlying theme is guilt. Although the Holocaust is not mentioned once in the film, its unspoken influence is present to guide the American away from anti-Semitic prejudice.

We conclude this section by reiterating that, influenced by the rise and fall of the National Socialist regime, only three American films, truly a tiny number in light of the reality of Nazi anti-Jewish policy, focused on anti-Semitism with the intent of striking a blow against it. All three films enjoyed critical acclaim; they were each nominated in several categories for Academy Awards. *Gentleman's Agreement* went on to win three Academy Awards, including best picture.

Indeed, these films reflect a trend in the easing of stereotypes, which made life far more comfortable for the American Jew. In the earliest of these films, *The House of Rothschild*, we find the European stereotype, distinctly Jewish, and a warning about the dangers inherent in political anti-Semitism. Yet the traits attrib-

Gentleman's Agreement (1947). Phil Green (Gregory Peck) is a journalist "posing" as a Jew in order to "feel" anti-Semitism and to write a story for *Smith's Weekly*. Dave Goldman (John Garfield), the returning soldier, is Phil's best friend and his Jewish equivalent. Kathy (Dorothy McGuire), Phil's girlfriend, is against his posing as a Jew. She praises the virtues of being a gentile: "It's like being happy you're well and not sick."

uted to the Rothschilds were at that time accepted by Americans as accurate. *The Great Dictator*, the sole film made during the war to focus on the threat to the Jews, veers away from European-influenced anti-Semitic stereotypes and portrays the Jew as a symbol of a kindly universe in its vision of a better future—even while its warning about the persecution of the Jews becomes reality. Hollywood's immediate response to the Holocaust comes in *Gentleman's Agreement*, a film that, in attempting to fight social anti-Semitism, presents the Americanized Jew, albeit a one-dimensional figure that Pauline Kael, in her discussion of the characterization of minority groups in film, would call "a democratic disease."[58] It is this "disease" that becomes a portent of the next fifteen years, for Americanization, as reflected in *Gentleman's Agreement*, would come to mean "sameness"—conformity; there would be no room for differentness, either social or political, in the United States. No doubt, this improved image, reflected in other films as well, could only help to lessen the acceptance of negative stereotypes, thus providing a better atmosphere in which to live.

Paradoxically, however, this evolution from the European to the American Jew could also cloud the very issues that inspired these films in the first place. By Americanizing the Jew, films also begin to Americanize, to democratize Jewish history. And, as the Jews come to symbolize more universal ideas in films, the Holocaust too becomes a symbol, thereby diminishing its centrality as an event in the history of the Jewish people.

Two

The Diary of Anne Frank in the Context of Post-War America and the 1950s

In 1947 a journalist visiting displaced persons camps could not help but compare the continuing presence and influence of the war and destruction in Europe to the atmosphere in the United States: "America has already come out of the war, has almost forgotten it. Even the post-World War II mood is in back of us."[1] Indeed, distance kept the physical reality of the war out of the lives of Americans. For them the postwar period was a time of unparalleled prosperity for all. The Depression and the war were already history, although, inevitably, new problems and concerns appeared to supplant the old.

A major postwar theme was the fight against Communism, one totalitarian ideology having replaced another as the target of American political passions. But whereas fascism was regarded as a right-wing movement, Communism was identified with the left wing, resulting in a more conservative mood in America to replace the New Deal liberalism of the war years.[2] The House Committee on Un-American Activities (HUAC) hearings, beginning with the "Hollywood Communists" in 1947, soon dominated the political scene, creating an environment of fear, suppression, and mistrust—the age of McCarthyism—that would haunt the "liberal" American image.

But this is not the only perception of the period. Robin M. Williams, Jr. offers a description of postwar America that points to a more liberal social attitude.

> Since the end of the Second World War, events in the domestic political and administrative arena have served mainly to extend and reinforce . . . institutionalized universalism. . . . The task of elaborating and extending ethical universalism undoubtedly was made easier by the end of large-scale immigration and by the increasing cultural similarity of "majority" and "minority" Americans.[3]

So, despite the atmosphere of suppression and fear generated by McCarthyism, the Supreme Court decided that segregating black school children from the white school system was unlawful. And anti-Semitism, which had escalated during the war and peaked in 1944, began to decline, making life for the Jews more comfortable than they had perhaps thought possible.

"Un-American" seemed to be an underlying motif for all factions, both liberals and conservatives, in an odd combination of suppression and liberalism. Yes, it was un-American to be associated with the Communist Party (and those who were found themselves blacklisted, their lives often destroyed). But it was also un-American to be anti-Semitic or to prevent blacks from participating in the American dream. The opposition, in both instances, to "un-American" would come through the "democratic," "American," "universal" approach.* Politically, this meant one dared not be too different. And socially, the trend was to accept the principle of equality for minority Americans.

It is in this environment that *The Diary of Anne Frank* makes its appearance and, in fact, becomes representative of the postwar period and the 1950s. The vicissitudes of the *Diary* very much parallel the prevailing tendencies of the period. Anne's diary, first published in Holland in 1947, made its appearance in America in the early fifties. It was dramatized and later turned into a film, which appeared in 1959. Over the course of those years *The Diary of Anne Frank* evolved from a particularly European work written by a young Jew hiding from the Nazis in Holland to a more Americanized, universal symbol.

As we recall, major films focusing on anti-Semitism and influenced by the persecutions in Europe see the Jew evolve from a European type to a definite American personality. (The Holocaust influenced as well—though not always explicitly—the trend in film to democratize all minority characters.) *The Diary of Anne Frank* is an exemplum of this tendency and becomes one of the first popular symbols of the Holocaust. With it comes, however, not only the democratization of Jewish characters, but the democratization of Jewish history. This was what the times demanded.

Of the few American films made in the late forties and the

*These terms often become interchangeable when referring to the process of "equalization" or "sameness" beginning in America.

fifties dealing with the Holocaust, only *The Diary of Anne Frank* would leave its mark over time. The *Diary*, as a play and film, is rooted in American traditions of the fifties, even though it deals with earlier events foreign to Americans, gentiles as well as Jews. The Holocaust, although it had little meaning for Americans, nevertheless had an impact on America's attitudes toward its Jews[4]; and Anne's diary becomes a symbol of the Holocaust for Americans. In this inquiry into the history of the *Diary*, we consider three general issues related to it: the universalization of the Holocaust, the cinematic image of the Jew, and questions of historical accuracy.

The *Diary* contributes importantly to the universalization of the Holocaust, that is, adapting and adjusting images of the Holocaust in order to allow a broad consensus of the population to identify with the event—this, inevitably, at the cost of its Jewish particularity. The Holocaust as a universal symbol of suffering allows Americans to find significance in an event that they did not experience. As a result, the theatrical and cinematic representations of the *Diary*, while not avoiding the Holocaust, veil its uniqueness.

In tracing the *Diary's* history as it evolved into a play and then a film, we can better understand how this process of universalization unfolded. Included here are a discussion of author Meyer Levin's war against Anne's father, Otto Frank, because Levin believed, among other things, that Anne's message had been bastardized. At the time, this battle focused a good deal of attention on the *Diary*. Does the Americanization, and ultimate universalization, of the Holocaust through the *Diary* mirror America's attitude toward its Jews and other minorities—the growing phenomenon of "sameness"? Or does it signify a blatant desire to alter the Jewish meaning of the Holocaust? Meyer Levin argues in this last regard, that there was a Communist/Stalinist influence, through Lillian Hellman's input, that purposefully robbed the *Diary* of its Jewish specificity.

In addition to the predominant theme of universalization, we examine the cinematic image of the Jew. Are the Jews portrayed as weak figures? If so, what are the implications? How does Israel influence this image? And finally, we deal with questions of historicity. How important is historical accuracy? What role does it play in universalizing the *Diary's* message? And what is the significance of the film's content in relation to broader issues concerning America? In answering these and other questions, we see just how the Americanizing/democratizing/universalizing of the Holocaust through one of its first popular symbols, *The Diary of Anne Frank*, mutes the particular message of Jewish suffering while, at the same time, it also serves to imprint the Holocaust on the American popular imagination.[5]

A brief look at some events that shaped the environment of the late forties and the decade of the fifties helps to explain the direction the *Diary* took in its adopted home. In 1947, the Hollywood Motion Picture Project, later to be known as the Jewish Film Advisory Committee, was formed in Los Angeles; retired film producer John Stone was its first director. The Project's founders were worried about anti-Semitism and concerned about the portrayal of Jews in the media (although the Project was created at a time when anti-Semitism was waning in the United States). Funding was provided by the National Jewish Community Relations Advisory Council, the American Jewish Committee, and the Anti-Defamation League. The Project sought, not always successfully, to work closely with Hollywood film makers, not as censors but as advisers, in order to avoid negative portrayals of Jews in film and television and, further, to improve the image of the Jew in the minds of Americans.[6]

The same year also saw the House Committee on Un-American Activities (HUAC) swing into action, and Hollywood once again came under investigation. It seems that the belief in and fear of the influence of film constantly brought Hollywood under public political scrutiny. This time Communism was the culprit. The defendants, who came to be known as the "Hollywood 10," were the first of many to be brought before the Committee and subsequently blacklisted by the film industry. The industry's initial reaction, according to the Association of Motion Picture Producers, was one of anger: "Hollywood is weary of being the national whipping boy for Congressional Committees."[7] Yet in the end they submitted. At a meeting at the Waldorf-Astoria Hotel in New York City, the studio executives publicly pledged not to employ Communists knowingly or others who might advocate the overthrow of the United States government "by any illegal or unconstitutional methods."[8] Their pledge was to be binding throughout the fifties, and it destroyed many careers along the way. Although the initial hearings had some anti-Semitic overtones, attributed mainly to Congressman John Rankin of Mississippi, anti-Semitism was not at the core of McCarthyism and played a minor role, if any, at future hearings.

During the first hearings, "Holocaust terminology," today commonplace, was used as a referent to explain the atmosphere of suppression created by the hearings. For example, Dalton Trumbo, one of the original "10," testified before the Committee, stating: "For those who remember German history in the autumn of 1932 there is the smell of smoke in this very room."[9] And at one point he shouted at Chairman J. Parnell Thomas: "This is the beginning of an American concentration camp."[10] One could say that the Holocaust, along with its symbols, had already come to be considered a watershed event, the standard to which future disasters and persecutions, minor or major, would be compared. The Holocaust, in other words, was becoming part of the vernacular of tragedy.

In any case, the prevailing theme in America was the fear of the Communist threat and the Cold War. In 1948 the Russians took Czechoslovakia, and most of Eastern Europe became a Soviet satellite; in 1949 the revolution in China established Communist dominion there. Espionage trials in the United States became commonplace. Whittaker Chambers testified that Alger Hiss had been passing state secrets to the Russians and that there were Communist cells among government personnel. Julius and Ethel Rosenberg were tried and later executed on charges of espionage. And the senator whose name would become synonymous with the period made his appearance.

During the time Senator Joseph McCarthy headed the hearings, "the thrust was to establish anti-Communism as the religion of America, with Communism as the antireligion. It cut across sectarian lines and blended with the secularized faith of America."[11] McCarthy was not interested in investigating people of minority ethnic groups. Contrary to what was feared, there was no anti-Semitic slant to his charges; indeed, several of his main advisers were Jewish. And surveys from the period show that those who supported McCarthy were no more anti-Semitic than those who opposed him.[12] In fact, major Jewish organizations, while opposing McCarthyism, did not denounce either HUAC or McCarthy by name. The American Jewish Committee even had a staff member whose job it was to discover areas of Communist infiltration into Jewish communal life.[13] The goal of the HUAC hearings was to "stigmatize" and thereby destroy the reputation of anyone who was or had been associated with the Communist Party, for most of the "subversives" were already known to intelligence agencies. This objective was to be achieved by compelling "friendly" witnesses to "name names," that is, by creating a system of informers. An atmosphere of fear and mistrust prevailed.[14] Most witnesses informed in order to keep their jobs, others, out of fervent anti-Communist beliefs. Some, like Lillian Hellman, refused to cooperate. Although she was able to avoid imprisonment, many other defendants were given prison sentences for refusing to inform.

Hollywood was completely intimidated by the hearings. There were those, as for example Edward Dmytryk, director of *Hitler's Children* and *Crossfire*, who tried to resist but in the end broke down and submitted. Films were cleansed of any obvious "subversive" messages. This was as close as the American film industry ever came to being politically controlled. Film makers were simply too frightened to address subjects in film that might be politically questionable. Adrian Scott, producer of *Crossfire* and one of the original "Hollywood 10," wrote: ". . . the blacklisting of other men was in reality the blacklisting of the liberals' own ideas."[15]

Given the tense atmosphere created by the HUAC hearings, not only in Hollywood but throughout the country, many leaders in the Jewish community feared the possible connection of being Jewish with being a Communist traitor in the popular mind.[16] However, polls taken at the time reveal that the image of the "Jewish Communist" did not increase during the period.[17] Nonetheless, there were other channels that might have stimulated anti-Semitic activity, for example, the establishment of the State of Israel. Yet this had little impact on American attitudes toward Jews,[18] and actually the majority of Americans came out in support of Israel. Anti-Semites might also have been aroused by the close ties between Jews and emerging black political activists. During the decade of the Supreme Court ruling against segregation—beginning the struggle of blacks for equality—Jews were especially committed to integration. Yet, surprisingly, they were not particularly associated in the public mind with the black struggle.[19]

Contrary to expectations, then, the trend in the United States was toward a decline in anti-Semitism as well as a decline in the acceptance of traditional anti-Semitic images. Added to this was Congressional legislation against social discrimination. Jews began to mingle more with non-Jews and to assimilate into the mainstream of American society,[20] in keeping with the universalist tendencies that defined the mood of the fifties. "Americanization" was a goal for minorities: equality and freedom as well as conformity and assimilation were ideas to be found on both the left and the right. The liberals, in calling for equality, sought "sameness" for minority groups, whereas the anti-Communist conservatives' notion of freedom was to protect the "American way," in this case, freedom from enemy influence. As Will Herberg has suggested, America "really has a common religion in the 'American way of life.'"[21]

And the Jews conformed to the principles of the day. They tried not to "stand out." In the arts, this expressed itself in what Henry Popkin called "de-Semitization": out of misguided benevolence, "Jewish characters, Jewish names, the word 'Jew'" itself are expunged. According to Popkin, the attitude (perhaps unconscious) went as follows: "If we pretend that the Jew does not exist, the reasoning goes, then he will not be noticed; the anti-Semite, unable to find his victim, will simply forget about him." Those involved in the arts attempted to reflect the "American" experience rather than a specifically Jewish one. Arthur Miller, for example, in his plays *All My Sons* (1947) and *Death of a Salesman* (1949), situates his characters in a vaguely Anglo-Saxon Protestant environment—although, in fact, he involves them in familiar Jewish scenes in his treatment of business life and family.[22]

In keeping with their avoidance of overtly visible Jewish characters in the arts, politically the Jews associated themselves with liberal, universalistic causes; many who were involved in the civil rights movement would never have dreamed of being involved with Jewish causes. Jewish organizations themselves extended their activities to include other minorities. A report from the Jewish Film Advisory Committee (JFAC) explains their particular philosophy:

> But the offices' interest is not limited to the Jewish community itself. It is aware that a hurt inflicted on one minority group is a hurt inflicted on all minority groups—and in turn, on all humanity. And

it has, therefore, fought for freedom for all people—for their liberty and their right to pursue happiness wherever they are.[23]

Within this context of the quest for universal meaning in American society *The Diary of Anne Frank* becomes a universal symbol. The American history of the *Diary*, from its inception as a play until it appeared as a film, illustrates how the universalizing process began to take shape—what influenced this process, why it happened, and why it was necessary.

The *Diary* itself, though a chronicle of Anne's experiences during the war years, is actually not an account of the war. Anne was cut off from external events and received her information about the world outside her attic either from the radio or from the Christian protectors who visited daily. For this reason, her diary lacks the tragic details of the unfolding of the process of genocide found in other diaries from the period. Emmanuel Ringelblum and Chaim Kaplan, for example, kept daily records of the Nazi destruction against the Jews in the Warsaw ghetto and of the Jewish reaction to their persecution. Anne wrote mainly about her own inner turmoil and about the others with whom she was confined. For a young girl, her writing has unusual depth and insight; and the fact that she was a child lends a particular poignancy to her diary. But one may ask whether the diary would have been so important had she survived. Survivor accounts generally inform us of uprooting and deportation, of life in the ghetto, of life in a concentration camp, or of life as a partisan hiding in the forest. Anne's diary is more a personalized literary piece, influenced by the Holocaust, whose tragic implications are fostered by our knowledge of her fate—both in hiding and, finally, in Bergen Belsen—rather than specifically by what she writes. The war simply provides the backdrop. Otto Frank, Anne's father, expressed a similar view in a letter to Meyer Levin:

> As to the Jewish side you are right that I do not feel the same way you do. I always said, that Anne's book is not a warbook. War is the background. It is not a Jewish book either, though Jewish sphere, sentiment and surrounding is the background. . . . It is read and understood more by gentiles than in Jewish circles. So do not make a Jewish play of it.[24]

Precisely because he was closest to the material, Otto Frank understood the personal nature of his daughter's writing. And,

The Diary of Anne Frank (1959). Anne Frank (Millie Perkins) continues her studies under the guidance of her father, Otto (Joseph Schildkraut).

in addition to this, he wanted to memorialize her, which meant emphasizing the diary's universal aspects over its specific Jewish content in order to provide the general public with symbols with which it could identify.

The Levin-Frank connection began when Meyer Levin came across a copy of the *Diary* that had been published in Paris. He contacted Otto Frank, and they agreed that Levin would look for an American publisher.[25] Otto Frank also consented to allow Levin to attempt a dramatization of the work. The play was never produced because, Levin was told, it was not a good dramatic piece—a rejection that he felt was unjustified and that caused him great anguish until his death in 1981. Levin accused Lillian Hellman and other "intellectual pro-Stalinists" of ostracizing him and rejecting his play because both were too Jewish. He claimed throughout the years that the play that was produced—the one that became the legitimized version of the *Diary*—only served to destroy Anne's message by universalizing its Jewish aspects.[26]

As it happened, producer Kermit Bloomgarden, who had purchased the rights to the *Diary*, contacted Lillian Hellman (several of whose plays he had produced) and asked her to suggest a playwright. Miss Hellman proposed Albert and Frances (Goodrich) Hackett, a husband-wife writing team who worked in Hollywood. On her recommendation, they were hired.

Frances Goodrich kept her own diary while she and her husband worked on the play.[27] The sincerity with which they approached the material seems beyond question[28]; they read books on Dutch history, Jewish history, and Judaism. (The Hacketts are not Jewish—another point that angered Levin.) In one entry, Frances writes in her diary: "This is not like any other job we have done. Terrible emotional impact. I cry all the time." In a later entry: "We are brazen about asking people for help. But feel this play tremendous responsibility. It can mean so very much . . ." Upon completing their fourth version of the play, the Hacketts flew from Los Angeles to New York to present it to Kermit Bloomgarden and Lillian Hellman, both of whom felt it was too loyal to the *Diary* at the expense of dramatic structure. According to Frances's diary, everyone hated it, including Otto Frank.

Painful as it was for him to do, he wrote to the Hacketts to tell them what was wrong with the script:

... having read thousands of reviews and hundreds of personal letters about Anne's book from different countries in the world, I know
what creates the impression of it [sic] on people and their impres-
sions ought to be conveyed by the play to the public. Young people
identify themselves very frequently with Anne in their struggle during puberty and the problems of the relations mother-daughter are
existing all over the world. These and the love affair with Peter
attract young people, whereas parents, teachers and psychologists
learn about the inner feelings of the young generation. When I
talked to Mrs. Roosevelt about the book, she urged me to give permission for play and film as only then we could reach the masses
and influence them by the mission of the book which she saw in
Anne's wish to work for mankind, to achieve something valuable
still after her death, her horror against war and discrimination.[29]

Clearly, for Otto Frank the universal aspects of Anne's diary were
the most important. To interpret the *Diary* only as a Jewish tragedy might, in Mr. Frank's eyes, have reduced his daughter's
chances of "living" even after she died—a wish she expressed in
her diary.

So the Hacketts began to rewrite. They mailed the completed
fifth version of the play to Kermit Bloomgarden and Lillian Hellman for comments. According to Frances's diary entry of 5 September 1954: "Lilly ... was amazing. Brilliant advice on con-
struction." Again, they reworked the play, until finally, having
completed their sixth version, it was accepted by Kermit Bloomgarden.

Now, Meyer Levin's major complaint about the play throughout the years had been that it ignored the Jewish content of
Anne's book, a very apparent Jewishness, as in this passage:

Who has inflicted this upon us? Who has made us Jews different
from all other people? Who has allowed us to suffer so terribly up
till now? It is God that has made us as we are, but it will be God,
too, who will raise us up again. If we bear all this suffering and if
there are still Jews left, when it is over, then Jews, instead of being
doomed, will be held up as an example. Who knows, it might even
be our religion from which the world and all people learn good, and
for that reason only do we have to suffer now.[30]

Levin quite rightly viewed this as a central idea of the *Diary*. And
his anger was justified when in the final version of the play,
Anne's words had been changed to read: "We're not the only
people that've had to suffer. There've always been people that've

had to . . . Sometimes one race . . . Sometimes another . . . and yet . . ."[31] Levin attributed this change to Lillian Hellman's influence.[32] However, based on Frances Goodrich's diary, which clearly delineates Miss Hellman's input, it seems as if she had stopped contributing ideas after the fifth version or perhaps the sixth, the one accepted by Kermit Bloomgarden. Up until then, the lines in question still retained their Jewish focus: "We're not the only Jews that've had to suffer. Right down through the ages there have been Jews and they've had to suffer."[33] It was not until the seventh version that these lines were changed, most likely as a means of securing better audience identification with the subject and the characters. It does cast suspicion on Meyer Levin's insistence that Lillian Hellman was responsible for his losing the play because his version was too Jewish (although, in keeping with her beliefs, she might conceivably have supported introducing universal concepts into the play).

Levin charged that her pro-Stalinist politics influenced her attitude toward him. He was perhaps overly zealous in his accusation, for she herself was a victim of the McCarthy witch-hunt; it does not seem logical that she would support anything that even hinted at blacklisting another writer solely for his political beliefs. In fact, the move toward universalizing the *Diary* was part of the spirit of the times; conformity, or universalizing, was a motif adopted by liberals and conservatives. However, one concept in the play went too far in its universalizing mood and betrayed a misunderstanding, not of Anne's diary but of Nazi anti-Semitic ideology and the goals of the Final Solution.

We see this in the Hanukkah scene, which the writers considered to be at the heart of the dramatic structure of the play. Neither the play's director, Garson Kanin, nor the Hacketts wanted the Hanukkah song to be sung in the original Hebrew. The Hacketts explained their reasons to Otto Frank in the following letter:

> It would set the characters in the play apart from the people watching them . . . for the majority of our audience is not Jewish. And the thing that we have striven for, toiled for, fought for throughout the whole play is to make the audience understand and identify themselves . . . to make them one with them . . . to make them feel "that, but for the grace of God, might have been I."[34]

But, one might respond to the Hacketts, it was not by chance that Anne was hiding but by Nazi design—and, specifically, because she was Jewish. Under any circumstances, it would be nearly impossible for an American audience to identify with characters who had been victims of Nazi racial hatred and persecution. Therefore, in the name of historical honesty, the Hacketts should have made it absolutely clear that the Nazis had planned a genocide against the Jewish people; audience identification could come only from the realization that they, like the Franks, are part of the same humanity. The question the audience must confront becomes: How was it possible for the destruction of European Jewry to have occurred in the heart of Christian Europe? The insistence that *fate* chose the Franks is the supreme universalization, one which clouds rather than clarifies the Nazi reality. Otto Frank, however, supported the Hacketts in their interpretation, writing that it "was my point of view to try to bring Anne's message to as many people as possible even if there are some who think it is a sacrilege and does not bring the greatest part of the public to understand . . ."[35]

But the entire frame of reference of the *Diary* was foreign to Americans, in a way that was not for Europeans. The Hacketts were writing for people who had not experienced the Nazi occupation. This distinction is glaring in the correspondence between Margaret Scaltiel, French agent for the play, and Leah Salisbury, the Hacketts' agent, who presented their opinion in a controversy that arose over the French production. Miss Scaltiel wrote:

> I do not know where you were during the war, my dear Leah. But you were certainly not doing what nearly all connected with this play were doing. I personally am not brave, and I know I could not stand up against torture as so many did. And I never would have been taken alive. But everytime I went to Lyon to establish false papers and went around with them, I knew real terror. It is therefore quite unnecessary for you to explain the meaning of the play to us . . .[36]

In other words, the French nation, if not victims of the Final Solution, knew the horrors of the war and the occupation. Whatever devices the playwrights used to arouse audience identification would be unnecessary among people who could read the terror of the war in every scene. The naïve attempts at total universalization could only have been aimed at an American audience ignorant of what it meant to live in the midst of war.

Even as the play, which opened on Broadway in October 1955, was enjoying enormous success in America (including winning a Pulitzer Prize in 1956) and was being performed all over Europe, negotiations began for the rights to the film. In the end, it was Twentieth-Century Fox, the producers of *The House of Rothschild* and *Gentleman's Agreement*, who, in the fall of 1956, secured the rights. Meyer Levin was still pursuing Otto Frank in the hope that he might at least be given the chance to write the screenplay. Otto Frank, however, wanted the Hacketts to do the film, too, although the final choice lay with the studio.

Realizing that he had no hope of participating in any adaptation of *The Diary of Anne Frank*, Meyer Levin commenced legal proceedings against Otto Frank and Kermit Bloomgarden. In his complaint, he accused them of having shown his version of the play to the Hacketts, who then plagiarized its entire structure. Twentieth-Century Fox, concerned about the outcome of the suit, considered holding up production until the case was settled; Levin, it appears, had traveled to the West Coast in an attempt to influence studio executives.[37] He charged that the Hacketts had not only plagiarized his play but also had destroyed the diary's ideology with their notions of universalization.[38]

Eventually, studio executives overcame their hesitation and proceeded with plans to make the film. At the time, in 1957, a copy of the script was sent to John Stone, director of the Jewish Film Advisory Committee, whose job, we might recall, was to ensure a positive image of the Jew in the media. Mr. Stone wrote the following assessment of the script to director George Stevens:

> . . . this screenplay is even better than the stage play. You have given the story a more "universal" meaning and appeal. It could very easily have been an outdated Jewish tragedy by less creative or more emotional handling—even a Jewish "Wailing Wall," and hence regarded as mere propaganda.[39]

Stone wrote almost as if the Holocaust were an embarrassment to the Jews. He made it clear that, as a middleman between the film industry and the Jewish community, he was not interested in emphasizing the Jewish particularity of the *Diary*. (Jewish particularism was not popular in the fifties and was certainly at odds with the assimilationist tendencies that were becoming so prevalent.)

The president of Twentieth-Century Fox, Spyros Skouras, also saw the *Diary* as a universal film, but his vision was more likely related to profit motives and not ideology. A San Francisco newspaper quoted him as saying that he did not want to hold a benefit for any particular (meaning Jewish) organization because "this isn't a Jewish picture, this is a picture for the world."[40] A Jewish picture, he feared, might hurt box office returns. The Hacketts verified this when they wrote to Otto Frank that "they (the management) are so very anxious to make this picture have a universal appeal. And I think that is the right approach, don't you?"[41]

Following the success of the play, and realizing the even larger audience potential for the film, the Hacketts pursued their course of universalizing the *Diary's* contents. This did not mean totally disguising the particular Jewishness of the Holocaust. It did necessitate minimizing the horrors involved, which, with Anne's *Diary*, was not difficult. In this way, the likeness of all suffering is maintained for the purpose of audience identification: Whoever has faced adversity will surely identify with what happened to the Franks and Europe's Jews. Even so, the thrust remains ambiguous in that though the film does indeed universalize the Holocaust, it still succeeds in relating the specificity of the event for European Jewry.

The fundamental question is: In what ways does the film reinforce the specific Jewish aspects of Anne's diary, and in what ways does it alter or distort Anne's intent in order to broaden the appeal of the film? The tone of the script, in keeping with the diary, is extremely optimistic. It is clear in both that Anne and the others are in hiding because they are Jewish. In the beginning of the film, Anne explains the anti-Jewish laws using the term 'we'—we had to wear yellow stars—instead of 'Jews had to wear yellow stars,' as is written in the diary. Does this change the meaning of Anne's statement? Certainly not, for who else but Jews would be wearing the yellow star? When the dentist, Dr. Dussel, arrives at the secret annex, as Anne calls it, he is barraged with questions. So through him, in both the diary and the film, existing circumstances are revealed: conditions for the Jews are deteriorating; they are being arrested and deported daily. The emphasis is on the persecution of the Jews. Also in both diary and film, the fact that Dutch Christians visit and provide for the

Jews in hiding signifies an essential difference between the Jew and the Christian. The Christian can survive the occupation. He tempts trouble, however, when he helps the Jew.

A major attempt at universalization surfaces when the writers seek to achieve audience identification with the Jewish characters in hiding. This comes in one of the film's key scenes—the Hanukkah celebration. In the diary, Anne writes that they do not make a big fuss about the holiday. Yet it is the Hanukkah celebration that serves as a dramatic climax in the film. The Hacketts pick up on a minor event in the diary and use it to foster audience identification with those in hiding. That is, Hanukkah can be like Christmas—just a little different—an idea very much at home in the 1950s. Religion, the only barrier separating one American from another, is, as we remember, stressed in the film *Gentleman's Agreement*. But religious ritual, generally absent in films whose goal is to Americanize—to dissolve ethnic differences—should at least not be "strange." To make a "foreign" religious rite comprehensible, then, the Hacketts Americanize it by having it spoken in English, not Hebrew, a language that does not fit into the American landscape.

In this regard, a discussion similar to the one we focused on earlier within the context of the play came up. Should the Hanukkah prayers be recited in Hebrew in the film? Rabbi Max Nussbaum of Los Angeles, himself a survivor of the Holocaust, advised the Hacketts on this scene. He had felt at first that the service could take place in English but changed his mind because he believed in real life the prayers could only be spoken in Hebrew. The Hacketts disagreed and explained their opinions to him in the following manner:

> What we all of us hoped, and prayed for, and what we are devoutly thankful to have achieved, is an identification of the audience with the people in hiding. They see them, not as some strange people, but persons like themselves, thrown into this horrible situation. With them they suffer the deprivations, the terrors, the moments of tenderness, of exaltation and courage beyond belief.[42]

This desire for the audience to identify with an event that is beyond their comprehension once again emphasized the writers' seeming inability to understand the Holocaust and National Socialist ideology. To some extent this may have been because Holocaust historiography was only in its infancy. But it was also a

The Diary of Anne Frank (1959). The Hanukkah celebration serves as a dramatic climax in the film and represents the writers' attempts to achieve audience identification with the Jewish characters in hiding.

reflection of the general atmosphere in America, which encouraged the leveling of specific differences among its people.

There are sections in her diary in which Anne speaks explicitly about Jewish persecutions, sections that could easily have been incorporated into the film were the film makers interested in doing so. For instance, Anne describes what she knows of deportations to the Dutch concentration camp of Westerbork and the life there. Elsewhere she writes: "I get frightened when I think of close friends who have now been delivered into the hands of the cruelest brutes that walk the earth. And all because they are Jews" (p. 48).* Or, she speaks of newly aroused anti-Semitism in Dutch circles where it never existed before. None of this is mentioned in the film. Was it feared that by stressing anti-Semitism too much, a reverse process would take place whereby viewers might find truth in it? The film makers opt to strive for a feeling of audience identification with the Jewish victims for the purpose of creating a universal antipathy toward all persecution. The Jews and the Holocaust, in other words, can be the symbol for the suffering of mankind.

In building on its newly found American traditions, the film resorts to a truly American phenomenon—the optimistic ending (which, in truth, is also in keeping with the optimistic tone of Anne's diary).[43] In a sneak preview in San Francisco, another ending was tried "which showed the girl in a concentration camp uniform swaying in a numb, miasmic fog . . . " Apparently, this was too tough for the audience and went against Twentieth-Century Fox's desire to have the film considered "hopeful despite all."[44] So instead, the film closes with Anne saying, "In spite of all, I still believe men are good." European audiences, by contrast, would have had little difficulty understanding the reality which took place (which is not to say that the concentration camp scene would have been a better ending). In fact, for the European viewer, the hopeful conclusion might have lessened any feelings of shame about what had happened to the Jews. Mainly, however, the ending indicates the need to fulfill American expectations of an optimistic finish, and in so doing, encourage the audience to identify with the film's characters. The film accomplishes this successfully, culminating a course that con-

*The edition of the *Diary* that is quoted in this chapter was published by Pocket Books, Inc. (Cardinal Edition) in 1959.

cludes with the *Diary*'s becoming one of the first universal symbols of the Holocaust.

Bruno Bettelheim, in working out his particular theories on Jewish behavior during the war, has offered an interesting interpretation of the universalization of the *Diary:* "The universal success of *The Diary of Anne Frank* suggests how much the tendency to deny the reality of the camps is still with us."[45] Bettelheim contends (based solely on the book, the play, and the film) that the Franks, having gone into hiding as a family unit and seeking to live a normal daily life, actually contributed to their own destruction because it helped them to deny the reality of the Holocaust. He views the *Diary* as a primary source that fosters and establishes an image of the Jews that persists until the present— that of a people contributing to their destruction by not resisting and by denying the reality of events.

Bettelheim has chosen to condemn the wrong party. It is unjust to blame the Franks for falling prey to the civilization that victimized them in the first place. The issue is more theological than psychological. Essentially the Jew is at the mercy of the Christian and Christian civilization. Permeating the film is a mood that forces the viewer to assume "that the Nazi terror was predicated on the failure of Christianity."[46]

The universal Christian tenet "love thy neighbor" forms the basis of the relationship between the Christian and the Jew; it assumes that the majority Christian will act in good conscience on behalf of the minority Jew when the latter is in trouble. At the same time, it is this dependency on the gentile that unavoidably makes of the Jew a passive, weak individual. Limited by the available alternatives, the Franks choose to hide and rely on good Christians to protect them. Yet they also fear that Christians, at some point, will turn them in. This is the film's thrust—the tenuous relationship between the Christian protector and the Jew who relies on him.

It is in this context that Anne's optimism is so important— and so troubling. It removes the guilt from those who were truly passive—the bystanders. Anne, the saintlike figure, bears the suffering for the viewer; she alleviates the viewer's guilt in saying that she still believes, in spite of everything, that men are really good. Bettelheim understands this ending as a negation of the reality of Auschwitz; that is, if man is good, then Auschwitz could not exist. (Anne, of course, wrote these lines before she had seen

The Diary of Anne Frank (1959). Anne, her family, the Van Daans, and Dr. Dussel wait in silence as they feel the end nearing.

a concentration camp.) We would propose, instead, that this ending really serves to reestablish the credibility of Christianity. It does not deny Auschwitz; rather, it forgives a lapse of Christian goodness. Anne as symbol of the Holocaust becomes as well the affirmation of post-Holocaust civilization because only she (and other victims) can forgive and hence allow man to live without guilt. Viewed in this way, the film is about universal forgiveness for the failure of a fundamental Christian belief.

Let us now return to Bettelheim. His theory of denial and passivity, which helped to establish and to perpetuate the myth of the sheeplike Jew, takes on new meaning when seen in the light of the glaring contrast to the new image of the Jew—the Israeli, the fighter. It is perhaps in this context that Bettelheim's theories become more important, especially in the popular imagination. Most films on the Holocaust to this day focus on the Jew as a passive victim rather than attempting to deal with, perhaps, Jewish resistance or Jewish partisans. By the time *The Diary of Anne Frank* appeared as a film, Israel had fought and won two major wars; the old idea of the Jew as introspective, feeble, unsoldierly was giving way to the vision of a warrior (an image highly touted in Israel at the time).[47]

In seeing that the Jews can fight back, therefore, the world can blame the Jews for their own inaction during the Holocaust. Perhaps, then, this Israeli image has been detrimental to the image of the diaspora Jew. Measured against these new criteria for Jewish behavior, the victim is judged guilty.

Thus, the film leaves us with an ambiguous vision. On the one hand, it seeks to alleviate, via Anne's forgiveness and hope, the guilt of the gentile world. On the other hand, looking to Israel as an alternative model, the viewer can blame the victim for his own impotence in the face of the Nazi destruction.

Apart from the preceding general themes and image projected in *The Diary of Anne Frank*, specific Jewish stereotypes play only a minor role in the film, although one particular scene, one that does not appear in the *Diary*, proves problematic. Mr. Van Daan steals food; Mrs. Frank, furious, wants to throw him out of their annex.[48] Mr. Frank responds to the selfish, petty action and to the ensuing fight as follows: "We don't need the Nazis to destroy us. We're destroying ourselves"—in essence, minimizing the Nazi persecutions by placing them on the level of petty squabbles. This scene serves to reinforce one of Bruno

Bettelheim's points: the failure of the victims to accept the reality of the gas chambers.[49]

This leads us to consider another important element in the film—its historicity. Speaking of film in general, Pierre Sorlin is correct to point out that to worry about mistakes in a historical film is to worry about a meaningless question.[50] It is not historical mistakes that concern us but rather the problems entailed in dramatizing a document that is itself history. The dramatic structure of the film states categorically that the *Diary* is authentic history; therefore deviations from its own statement may deceive the viewer. This occurs in several instances, with results that are even harmful to the memory of those who perished.

We can begin with the very obvious, the title, which indicates to the viewer that he will see a film based on a diary, although he may not be sure whether it is authentic or not. Since it is in fact real, there is an obligation to be true to its themes and ideas, to Anne's memory. Whereas she need not be quoted verbatim, it is essential not to distort her meaning.

The film's structure forces this issue of authenticity. Using a voice-over of Anne reading from her diary and then a fade into the dramatic sequences, the film gives the impression that these scenes are based on Anne's writing. The viewer believes that he is "reading" her diary throughout the film. If any elements are falsified, for whatever reason, then Anne's history becomes distorted. This is not to say that all films based on the Holocaust must be accurate in every historical detail. However, it is imperative that the film transmit honestly and authentically the precise images and beliefs of the document. How, then, is Anne's history reflected in the adaptations of her diary?

Already while the play was still in preparation, the importance of authenticity was conveyed to the Hacketts by producer Kermit Bloomgarden. He told them that "complete knowledge of the situation is vital to the dynamics of later events" and then added: "What is important is what she has not said in the diary. It is this that makes her tragedy so vital and meaningful to us, and why its impact is so shattering."[51] Yet Otto Frank apparently could not convince Bloomgarden to refer specifically to the authenticity of the *Diary* in the theater program. Frank told of the experience of a Dutch Jewish woman he knew who sat next to an American Jewish woman at a performance of the play in New York. The American woman told the Dutch woman that she had seen the play three times. When the latter mentioned that she had known Anne before the war, the American expressed amazement that the characters and events in the play were real.[52] In another incident, after Otto Frank had seen the film, he wrote to the Hacketts:

> . . . there are a great number of the younger generation who just do not understand what it is all about and that it is a true story. I spoke to youngsters who told me their classmates laughed right at the beginning when the truck came and there were people on it in "pyjamas." It seems that some sort of explanation should be given at the beginning—before the film starts.[53]

In such occurrences, where the historical mood is unclear, uninterpreted history fades even into comedy. Anne becomes a symbol. The reality and uniqueness of Anne and her diary are veiled.

In one particular scene the memory of one man is altered for the sake of dramatic development. Dr. Dussel, the dentist who shared a room with Anne, perished during the war. But his wife, Mrs. Charlotte Pfeffer, wrote to the Hacketts concerning the veracity of the script. She explained that the Hanukkah scene, which portrays her husband as an unbeliever who had not the faintest idea what Hanukkah is, distorts the facts. He had been a master of the Hebrew language and "his religion meant everything to him." She added that her husband, survived by a son and brothers, "was neither an inveterate bachelor nor a man without relations." Nor did she want him shown as a psychopath. "I think it enough that this had been done already in the play."[54] Anne's diary supports Mrs. Pfeffer's contentions.

The Hacketts replied that a play cannot mirror reality. In order to inform the non-Jewish audience about the Hanukkah service and its significance, they needed one character (Dr. Dussel) unfamiliar with it so that another character could explain it to him—and, hence, to the audience. To Mrs. Pfeffer's request for a copy of the film script, the Hacketts responded that they were not allowed to send it; and, in any case, they did not have the final say on the film.[55] The Dussel character remained as the Hacketts had styled him, a pernicious, even if unintended, assault on the memory of the individual as well as a cruel blow to his survivors. It clearly indicates a lack of imagination on the part of the Hacketts, who could find no other means to inform their audience about Hanukkah. For a man's biography is also history.

Not only does fidelity to individual history suffer. A similar lack of concern is evident when it comes to broader issues, as when the Hacketts change Anne's dialogue and, in so doing, distort her meaning. Once again, we return to the scene that so upset Meyer Levin, the one in which the writers substitute "all races" for "Jews" when Anne speaks of suffering through the ages. Levin complained about the removal of the specific Jewish content of this speech. But on the level of history, the change has even broader implications. Viewers who are aware of the diary's authenticity would reasonably assume that the play and the film are faithful to the document on which they are based. Not so. When André Maurois, in praising the play, "quotes" Anne: "Nous ne sommes pas les seuls à souffrir, . . . Il y en a d'autres. Et pas seulement les juifs . . . ,"[56] he is, in fact, unknowingly *misquoting* her. Anne's intent is replaced by that of her interpreters; the authentic becomes inauthentic; fiction merges with history to distort even the mood of history. As Levin saw it, this tampering with a document was a blatant attempt to universalize the Jewishness of the original. A successful attempt, for the universal images and ideas entered the popular mind. Louis de Jong, director of the Netherlands State Institute for War Documentation and historical adviser for the film, wrote to the film's director, George Stevens, in 6 April 1959 as follows:

> Of course, I as a historian have discovered here and there some slight touches and details which did not correspond with reality, but these will not hinder the general public and I realize that sometimes certain dramatic effects are necessary in a work of art, even if they did not occur in reality.[57]

He correctly assesses the role of historical detail in film. However, the purposeful alteration of the words of a document here indicates an intent to alter its meaning, which the film does for one reason—to reflect the events and the spirit of the fifties in America.

The Diary of Anne Frank becomes a symbol and a metaphor for that era. We are not the only ones to suffer, says Anne; sometimes one race, sometimes another. Her suffering stands for all suffering. The persecution of the Jews shows what can happen when racism prevails. In this way, the film serves as a warning to the American public, at the time very conscious of its discrimination against blacks. Clearly, the film is also a metaphor for another prevailing theme of the fifties—the HUAC hearings with its system of informers. For the end comes for Anne and the others in the secret annex because someone informs on them. The lesson is obvious; one connects Anne with those who found themselves blacklisted. The fear of being discovered that pervades the film reflects the fear in America that one's innocent past—perhaps a momentary flirtation with Communism—might destroy his future. *The Diary of Anne Frank* shows to what extent the informer can inflict damage.

In the sense that *The Diary of Anne Frank* can be seen as a comment on racial discrimination against blacks and on the danger posed by the informer, its message is a liberal one. At the same time, the universalization and Americanization of its content fit into the prevailing mood—one that was simultaneously repressive and liberal—a time when being "different" suggested either the wrong political attitude or the wrong social attitude. This European document, which deals with events foreign to Americans, becomes, through the play and the film, one of the first international popularizations of the Holocaust. That is, it is the American imagination that decides how the Holocaust is to be remembered, making it, ironically enough, an American memory. Through Anne Frank's diary, America becomes Europe's teacher on the moral implications of the Holocaust. For, as Pierre Sorlin observes: "Historiography, far from being universal, is subordinated to national traditions. In studying historical films, we must allow for the cultural backdrop against which history is defined."[58] It is against the historical backdrop of America in the 1950s, that *The Diary of Anne Frank* evolves from a European to an American work, into a universal symbol of the Holocaust. It is, as well, a factor contributing to what was to become the universalization of the Holocaust.

Three
Chaos and Social Upheaval: The 1960s and 1970s

Eichmann and *Nuremberg:*
Nazis on Trial in the 1960s

Professor Morris Dickstein has argued that during the 1950s, the Jew was on his way to becoming the American Everyman (to be supplanted by the black in the 1960s): "In the wake of the Holocaust the fate of the Jew, to many, had become a parable of the human condition—a drama of pointless, horrendous suffering which revealed the modern dimensions of terror and evil."[1] As the United States moved out of the decade of the fifties, with its preference for conformity and the distorted justice of the McCarthy era, the crisis of the sixties was soon to begin. Christopher Lasch explains this time as "a fatal conjuncture of historical changes: the emergence of a new social conscience among students activated by the moral rhetoric of the New Frontier and by the civil rights movement, and the simultaneous collapse of the university's claims to moral and intellectual legitimacy."[2] With regard to these changes, which would result in the social upheaval and chaos that helped to define the decade of the sixties and some of the seventies in America, author Elie Wiesel has affirmed:

> ... I remain convinced that the current wave of protest calls into question much more than the present. Its vocabulary takes one back a quarter of a century. Factories and university buildings are "occupied." The Blacks rise up in the "ghettos." ... The police use "gas" to disperse demonstrations. ... The Watts and Harlem riots are compared to the Warsaw Ghetto uprising. ... Political analysts talk of nuclear "holocausts." Racism, fascism, totalitarian dictatorships, complicity, passivity: words heavy with past significance ...[3]

It seems as if the language of the Holocaust and, therefore, the knowledge of the Holocaust, however superficial, had suffused the contemporary American imagination, with its newfound social awareness and concomitant social action.

Judgment at Nuremberg (1961), appearing two years after *The Diary of Anne Frank*, is the Holocaust film that opens the decade of the 1960s. Coinciding as it does with the Eichmann trial, and because of its wide impact as a film, *Judgment at Nuremberg* merits a close study. The approach is similar to that used for the analysis of *The Diary of Anne Frank*. We analyze the trend toward universalization and democratization (in the sense of equalizing) of the Holocaust along with the film's relation to current events in America. *Judgment at Nuremberg*, as Lawrence Langer indicates,[4] deals with principles rather than individuals. It is principles of justice that would dominate the next fifteen years in America, especially in relation to the black struggle and the war in Vietnam. In addition, we must ponder the image of the Jew: if and how it changes and what influences these changes. The film's use of history, too, is examined, and a new element is introduced, the use of documentary footage in a fictional story.

Once establishing the historical context of *Judgment at Nuremberg*, we can proceed to analyze several other popular films in order to continue to trace the cinema's contribution towards the integration of the Holocaust into the American imagination. These films are *The Pawnbroker* (1965), *Ship of Fools* (1965), *Cabaret* (1972), *Voyage of the Damned* (1976), and *Julia* (1977).

Increasingly, the Holocaust was becoming an established standard against which other catastrophes were measured or compared. The comparisons are at times outlandish, even grotesque. In 1960, for example, blacklisted writer Dalton Trumbo wrote a letter to Governor Edmund Brown of California pleading for the life of convicted mass murderer Caryl Chessman. In it he urged:

> . . . I must beg you to remember that only eighteen years ago the first gas chambers were installed at Auschwitz—and they were legal; that three million men, women, and children were suffocated in those chambers—and each death was legal; that the commandant of Auschwitz had no choice under the law but to carry those executions through. . . . Three million or one, the difference is merely quantitative: man again has taken his brother's life.
>
> Somewhere, sometime, somehow, we must break this chain of death which binds all of us together in a compact for murder. I hope you will be able to find a way . . . to smash the first link by sparing the life of Caryl Chessman.[5]

Essentially Trumbo, like many other well-meaning liberals,

equated the Holocaust and its victims, the Jews, with all others who kill and all who are killed, including convicted murderers.

Such painful distortions began to pierce the soul of the Jew. Survivors especially resented these parallels drawn in the name of liberty, equality, and justice. For the survivor, the Holocaust is sacred; it is unimaginable, therefore unknowable. Herein lies the crux of the paradox: If the event is unknowable, then to most people it might also be irrelevant. The Holocaust becomes meaningful to large numbers in both an historical and human context only through attempts to make it understandable, either by comparisons or by universalization.

Alongside this continuing tendency toward universalizing the Holocaust, the 1960s witnessed the eruption of a controversy within the Jewish community concerning the guilt of the victims. Did they contribute to their own destruction by complying with the Nazi machinery, be it by way of the Jewish Councils, by not fleeing, or by "marching to their deaths like sheep to slaughter," as Hannah Arendt, Raul Hilberg, and Bruno Bettelheim have argued? Many argued against such interpretations, from historian Jacob Robinson to author Elie Wiesel. But on a popular level, the arguments of the former predominated: the Holocaust became the ultimate tragedy even while its victims bore the guilt for their own victimization.

Bruno Bettelheim, in particular, contributed to both general trends. He espoused a universalistic approach to the Holocaust and at the same time blamed the Jews for complicity in their own destruction. He castigated the Jews for their history of "ghetto thinking"—ignoring the outside world with the idea that what happens to the Jews is unique. "Usually I meet with unbelieving astonishment when I remind American Jews of what should be known to them," he writes, "that Hitler also destroyed millions of Russians, Poles and the entire Gypsy population of Europe . . . "[6]

Bettelheim's use of the Holocaust as the referent for his thoughts on ghetto thinking further advanced the idea of Holocaust as metaphor for many facets of contemporary American life. Regarding *The Diary of Anne Frank*, he claims he was not being critical of the Franks or Anne, "but of the universally positive reception given her *Diary* in the western world. . . . I'm highly critical of the ghetto philosophy that seems to have pervaded not only the Jewish intelligentsia but large segments of the free world." Bettelheim poses—and answers—an interesting question: Why was Anne Frank's story such a success in comparison with stories of those who resisted and survived?

> This acceptance of the fate of the Franks is part of a ghetto thinking that derives a reality which would otherwise compel us to take action. It suggests how widespread is the tendency to deny reality among Jews and Gentiles alike, in the Western World, and this though her story itself demonstrates how denial can hasten our destruction.[7]

Bettelheim's (simplistic) interpretation of Jewish actions during the Holocaust also implies a generalized behavior that was perhaps applicable to segments of American society during the 1950s and into the 1960s: Americans who accepted McCarthy and Americans who had yet to make their creed one with their practice. America was on the verge of awakening from social indifference and in so doing would free itself of its ghetto mentality.

And for many Americans, especially Jews, the Holocaust proved a major ingredient in the creation of a more active and radical America. Writer Paul Cowan, a left-wing activist in the sixties, has explained his and his family's involvement in liberal American causes as stemming from the fact that they were Jewish. "Everything we did," Cowan says, "we did because we were Jewish, from fighting anti-Semitism to working in the Civil Rights movement. We did those things on behalf of the six million as well as because they were just causes."[8] Cowan's colleague at *The Village Voice*, Jack Newfield, also connects his own commitment to social change to his Jewishness: "We all referred to the sense of Jews as victims, Jews as underdogs, and the sixties, and at least for me, of blacks as victims and blacks as underdogs."[9] Professor Jacob Neusner believes that the concern with Auschwitz in the 1960s and 1970s was more rooted in America's problems of the period than a desire to comprehend and understand the phenomenon of the Holocaust per se:

> What happened, I think, was the assassination of President Kennedy, the disheartening war in South East Asia, and a renewed questioning of the foundations of religious and social polity. "Auschwitz" became a Jewish codeword for all the things everyone was talking about, a kind of Judaic key word for the common malaise.[10]

Whether the Final Solution influenced behavior, as it did for Paul Cowan and Jack Newfield, or whether the concern with the Holocaust came as a response to changing conditions in America, as Professor Neusner asserts, the event itself and its language, as Elie Wiesel points out, were very much connected to the period of the 1960s and 1970s. It provided the metaphor for those involved in the changing social scene in America.

If the Holocaust was becoming the metaphor for contemporary tragedy and injustice, one might expect films on the subject to follow suit. In the play and film of *The Diary of Anne Frank,* the Holocaust becomes a personalized symbol, a springboard for viewers, especially the young among them, to identify with Anne. Their problems are reflected by Anne. The films of the 1960s and 1970s, as well, do not explore the process of the European destruction in order to enhance comprehension of it, a point that lends credence to Professor Neusner's position. Rather, the Holocaust usually provides a moral lesson for the present. *Judgment at Nuremberg* (1961) reminds us of what can happen when justice loses its meaning; *Julia* (1977) voices the guilt of the modern liberal. In other words, in the paradox of the unknowable trying to become known, the Holocaust can function only as a standard whereby the extremes of evil of which man is capable can be measured and thus serve as a warning of the result such extremes can bring. The more visible the event becomes, the greater are its chances of being internalized in the American psyche. This brings with it a tendency toward Americanization. In a bizarre way, the Holocaust becomes part of the American tradition, albeit as a 'refugee.'

At this time, much in the traditional, "American way of life" seemed to be dissipating. Perhaps the overriding change of the times took place in the realm of American justice, with the enactment of measures that promised civil rights to all Americans. In this way, the "American way" came to include minorities. Their Americanization was a process that had begun after the war and that would be realized in the law of the land in the 1960s. And as minority groups were entering into the mainstream, other, related, changes in the character of the American population were discernible. In 1960, due to a decline in immigration and a natural population increase, only one in twenty-four Americans was foreign-born. In 1930, approximately one in nine Americans was foreign-born. And by the 1960s, according to questionnaires at the time, those asked whether Jews had changed for the better answered that "they have become more like ordinary American citizens. You might say they *have* become Americans."[11]

In fact, according to Alan Spiegel in his article on the Jew in contemporary American film, throughout the 1960s and to some extent in the 1970s, there was in America a fascination with the personality, manners, anxieties, hungers, ecstasies, and follies of the American Jew. By the 1960s, Jewishness had become a mass cultural concept,[12] due, in part, to the interest in the Jewish intellectual—Philip Roth, Norman Mailer, Joseph Heller, Mort Sahl—who helped define the cultural scene in America. This fascination with "Jewishness" was also influenced by the sheer amazement people felt at the Jews' ability not only to survive but also to rebuild their ancient land into a modern country. Besides, as Ben Halpern observes, "Hitler's attempted 'final solution of the Jewish problem' has cast extremist anti-Semitism into deep and lasting disrepute in the Western Christian world,"[13] which signaled a decline in anti-Semitism in America.

In the 1960s, then, the Jew was viewed less stereotypically, and Americans found more admirable qualities among Jews than objectionable ones. Moreover the positive qualities had no latent negative connotations attached to them as they had in the 1930s.[14] What notions came to replace the old, commonly accepted stereotypes? Or, otherwise, what constituted the "idea" of Jew? Certainly new stereotypes, such as the Jewish mother, did appear, but they did not reflect negatively on the general Jewish character. With Americanization came two factors that would enhance the Jewish image—the Holocaust and Israel; and, as the decade opened, both factors converged. This occurred when Israel's Prime Minister, David Ben-Gurion, made worldwide headlines on 24 May 1960 with the announcement that Adolf Eichmann had been found and would be tried in the Jewish homeland for his crimes against the Jewish people. The dramatic capture of Eichmann, including his secret abduction from Argentina, "had all the excitement of a detective or spy thriller; it is hard to imagine anyone remaining totally indifferent to this real-life story of undercover agents and their adventures."[15] Even at the Nuremberg trials no special emphasis had been placed on the Jew. Here was a unique opportunity to present before the international community the details of the Final Solution.

Susan Sontag identifies the political trial as one of the un-acknowledged art forms of our time, created to help resolve our great historical tragedies; she includes the Eichmann trial as one of the most moving examples of this art. Not only Sontag, but others as well, have pointed out that Eichmann the man stood trial for his own crimes while Eichmann the symbol was tried for the destruction of European Jewry, if not also for the entire history of anti-Semitism: "The trial was thus an occasion for attempting to make comprehensible the incomprehensible."[16] In other words, the Eichmann trial represents the persistent attempt to use the media to try and teach, even to popularize, what no one could understand. We have engendered a situation whereby information on the Holocaust, the ultimate example of an event shaped by horror and inhumanity, is disseminated using the tools of popular culture. Critics decry this popularization; even worse, according to some, the Holocaust has been trivialized. It is a "no win" situation. When attempts are made to assist the public in trying to understand the Holocaust, as in the case of the Eichmann trial, unavoidably the process begins: popularization, universalization, or any other epithet, for that matter, that profanes the sacred. The riddle defies solution. Elie Wiesel has at times looked to silence, but much of his own work stands in repudiation of this. Popularization, it seems, is inevitable, and, equally inevitably, it will often result in universalization of the Holocaust.

In fact, the mass media in America, by their nature tending toward trivialization if only because of their inherent commercialism, gave sympathetic coverage to the Eichmann trial. The public was informed and its perceptions shaped, resulting in more understanding for the Jewish people in general. By the middle of 1961, the trial had already occupied the world's headlines for over a year. Four months before the trial ended, according to the Gallup poll, 87 percent of the United States population had heard about it. It was the subject of several national television programs and feature stories in mass circulation magazines like *Life* and *Time*. People might have been less aware of details because of the foreignness of the event, but, to a surprising extent, the trial won the sympathy of the apathetic majority.[17] For, "unlike the trial itself, the central concern of the trial is not destined to die so quickly."[18]

With regard to film, the immediate response came in the merging of the real-life drama of the Eichmann trial with the fictionalized account of the last Nuremberg trials of the Nazi judges, *Judgment at Nuremberg*. Murray Schumach wrote in *The New York Times*:

> In a somber courtroom set in Hollywood, genocide is as current these days as it is in the Beit Haam, in Jerusalem, where Adolf Eichmann is being tried for responsibility for the deaths of six million Jews. In Hollywood, however, cameras and actors are working in a replica of the courtroom of Nuremberg, where civilized nations set the legal precedent that made a special crime of genocide.[19]

In a sense, the Eichmann trial was but a continuation of the trials that had taken place in Nuremberg some twelve years earlier. There was, to be sure, a difference: The Nuremberg trials were legally established, whereas the Eichmann trial was surrounded by controversy owing to his abduction by Israeli agents and the question of the legality of trying him in Israel at all. In retrospect, there is something almost bizarre about the two trials taking place concurrently—one, history being transmitted live, the other, filmed history, but both, to an American audience, films. The Eichmann trial must have lent authenticity to producer-director Stanley Kramer's film and helped to make it so successful as well.

The première of *Judgment at Nuremberg* also happened to coincide with the sentencing of Eichmann on 14 December 1961. One can discern in this an unintended irony: Written on screen at the film's end was the information that, of those sentenced in the last Nuremberg trials, not one was still serving his sentence, whereas Eichmann was sentenced to hang in a country where capital punishment was anathema. That is to say, *Judgment's* ending vindicates Israel with regard to the accusations of the illegality of the trial, for only in Jerusalem could justice be found.

Fate brought together elements conducive to enhancing *Judgment's* appeal to a general audience. An article in *Variety* in March 1961 questions whether a nonspectacular treatment of a serious subject dealing with moral principles could succeed as a "hard ticket offering." Stanley Kramer, according to the article, "is convinced of the public interest in the subject matter, as evidenced by the conflict over Berlin, the upcoming Eichmann trial in Israel, and the success of William L. Shirer's *The Decline* [sic] *and Fall of the Third Reich*."[20] But this had not been the case when scriptwriter Abby Mann first began writing *Judgment* in

Judgment at Nuremberg (1961). Judge Haywood (Spencer Tracy), presiding judge in the film.

Judgment at Nuremberg (1961). Filmed against the backdrop of war-torn Germany, *Judgment* became the first American film dealing with the Holocaust to combine fiction and history, incorporating U.S. Army Signal Corps footage of the liberation of the concentration camps.

1957 for television's *Playhouse 90* (produced in 1959 by Herbert Brodkin, later the producer of *Holocaust*). According to Mann, it was not yet acceptable either in America or Europe to speak of German guilt or the victims of Nazi Germany.[21] In effect, by 1960 certain events had occurred that in 1957 were not yet foreseeable. With 1960 came the end of the injustice of the McCarthy era, the media penetration of the Eichmann trial, and the rise of the civil rights movement in America. So in spite of what was indeed the foreign nature of *Judgment*, its metaphorical content on the discourse of justice, so very relevant to Americans, created an atmosphere of what Pierre Sorlin calls "readiness"[22]; Americans were indeed ready to deal with German guilt on the level of metaphor for much of what was occurring in contemporary society.

Regardless of opportune timing, or "readiness," business instincts and commercialism influenced the casting of the movie. Film critic Pauline Kael quotes Gavin Lambert's cynical, black humor in describing the cast as "an All-Star Concentration Camp Drama, with Special Guest Victim Appearances."[23] However, film critic Hollis Alpert justifies the use of such a cast as insurance at the box office, the best means of attracting large audiences to Kramer's picture.[24] Stanley Kramer explains his choice of actors:

> ... do you think United Artists wanted to make that thing about the trial? They weren't interested at all in war guilt and those people in the ovens and crooked judges. ... I studded it with people to get it made as a film so that it would reach out to a mass audience ...[25]

Undoubtedly, his perception was on target, for, as Christopher Lasch observes, there is a "cult of celebrity" associated with mass media that includes attempts to surround it with glamor and excitement and that makes America a nation of fans.[26]

Film, regardless of the import of its content, must appeal to the public's imagination. *The Apathetic Majority* shows that details of even the most publicized and international events elude the majority of the public; that "only when an event has deep personal meaning for a population is lack of interest and concern overcome."[27] On some level, then, it becomes essential to create the impression that the subject corresponds to American problems, concerns, or needs. This means, even, that the "Jewish-

Judgment at Nuremberg (1961). Colonel Lawson (Richard Widmark), chief prosecutor at Nuremberg in the film, pores over Nazi files.

ness" of the Holocaust must be muted if the event is to have meaning in an American context. In *The Diary of Anne Frank,* Anne is transformed into an almost saintlike, universal symbol of youth and goodness. Yes, Jews suffer, but so do all other peoples. No death camps intrude upon this image. In the hands of the diary's adapters, the Holocaust opens up the possibility for the viewer to remark to himself, "It might have been me." In *Judgment,* the Jew, no longer a symbol, becomes a partner in suffering along with Czechs, Poles, Communists—in other words, with the rest of humanity, which leaves an opening for viewer identification beyond the specific Jewish issue. *Judgment* makes the Jew a victim among victims; universalizing becomes shared history; the Holocaust is not a uniquely Jewish event.

The film conveys its sense of shared history in several scenes. In one, a witness, a former judge, is asked about changes in the criminal law during the Nazi period. He replies: "Sentences were passed against defendants just because they were Poles or Jews, or politically undesirable."[28] Or, from the two major cases discussed during the trial—one dealing with the crime of racial pollution for which a Jew was sentenced to death, the other concerning the sterilization of a Communist—one may infer that Communists and Jews suffered equally under German law. One might argue, further, that the film, concerned as it is with the trial of judges, is not specifically about the Holocaust. Therefore, it is reasonable to refer to other ethnic or political groups who suffered under the Nazi judicial system along with the Jews, especially during the 1930s prior to the outbreak of war.

However, in the sequence showing documentary footage of the camps, which includes images of corpses as well as emaciated survivors, the idea of shared history and common fate is especially striking. Once documentary footage of Bergen Belsen and Buchenwald is introduced and there is talk of gassing and crematoria, then the subject becomes a specific one, one very closely connected to the Jews. Nevertheless, during the showing of the footage, there is no mention of Jews but of "these people—90,000 Slovakians, 65,000 from Greece." Only when the footage finishes does the prosecutor, Colonel Lawson, ask: "Who were the bodies? Members of every occupied country of Europe. Two-thirds of the Jews of Europe were exterminated. More than six million according to reports from the Nazis' own figures." Certainly, Colonel Lawson mentions the Jews, but along with members of "every occupied country of Europe." In so doing, *Judgment* obscures the reality of Nazi policy against the Jews and, in turn, by means of shared history, universalizes the Holocaust.

At the time the film was made, Telford Taylor, chief prosecuting judge at the original Nuremberg trials, criticized Israel's trial of Eichmann. His argument, presented in *The New York Times Magazine*, echoes the one in *Judgment* that a deliberate program of extermination of a race should be regarded as crimes not against a particular country or people "but against the international community." He continues:

> Nuremberg was based on the proposition that atrocities against Jews and non-Jews are equally crimes against world law. To define a crime in terms of the religion or nationality of the victim, instead of the nature of the criminal act, is wholly out of keeping with the needs of the times and the trend of modern law.[29]

In other words, the chief prosecutor at Nuremberg believed that the crime and not the victim is the issue, that the victim becomes all victims. Since *Judgment* is indeed based on the actual Nuremberg trials, it is no wonder that the film mirrors the message of the trials, the universalization of the victim during World War II, the inclusion of all war victims as having suffered equally under Nazi law.

Writing at the time *Judgment* premiered, Harry Golden of the *Carolina Israelite* makes the following observation: "[T]he Eichmann verdict helped alleviate [German guilt for] the Nazi crimes. For most Germans have been insisting since the end of the war that it was Hitler, Goebbels, Goering and Eichmann who perpetrated these crimes, not they."[30] *Judgment* offers a similar suggestion. After the documentary footage is shown in the courtroom, there is a cut to the Nazi judges in the prison dining room. One of them, Lammpe, says to another prisoner: "Pohl, you ran those concentration camps, you and Eichmann." The mention of Eichmann as a symbol of German guilt in this scene presents an opposing view to the film's main thrust of collective guilt.

Actually, *Judgment at Nuremberg* is the first American film that simultaneously points the finger of guilt at Germany and universalizes this guilt, two opposing tendencies. Stanley Kramer, asked about his intent in *Judgment*, said he wanted the viewer to think: "[W]ho among us may judge others; who among us is so innocent if we are so sure of the guilty?"[31] This same attitude is espoused by Rolfe, the lawyer defending one of the judges, Janning, who at one time had been considered a great jurist. In his defense of Janning, Rolfe says that if Germany is guilty, so is the rest of the world for allowing such events to occur. Later Rolfe speaks to Janning in prison, insinuating that Hiroshima and Nagasaki are equal in scale to the Holocaust. "I could show you a picture of Hiroshima and Nagasaki. Thousands and thousands of burnt bodies! Women and children! Is that their superior morality?" Clearly, it is members of the accused nation speaking to each other. And at a time when the nuclear threat is a present reality, reference to Hiroshima easily elicits sympathy. Rolfe, of course, ignores the different rationales for each of these contemporary tragedies, which, again, universalizes guilt and therefore mitigates German responsibility.

In light of the above, it is interesting to note that there are no Jewish characters in the film. As mentioned, two cases form the core of the trial: the sterilization of a member of the Communist Party and a case of racial pollution. With regard to the latter, the Jew Feldenstein, an elderly gentleman and family friend of the much younger Irene Wallner, does not appear in the film because he had been executed for having had sexual relations with Irene. Irene, then, is the witness at the trial.

The Feldenstein case had actually occurred and was important enough to have been singled out in Raul Hilberg's *The Destruction of the European Jews.*[32] (In the film, the names are changed.) Hilberg views the case as symptomatic of attempts to break friendly relations between Jews and Germans, thereby isolating the Jewish community. However, Irene Wallner, and not this aspect, is the central focus of the case. She wins our sympathy as she is victimized in the courtroom: frightened, in obvious pain as she is forced to relive the trial, she is intimidated by defense attorney Rolfe who hints strongly that she had had intimate relations with Feldenstein. Feldenstein is virtually forgotten, except for the lingering doubt that the Nazis manage to instill that he probably was a lecherous old man. The injustice of his execution and the proper understanding of the laws of *Rassenshande* as they applied to the Jews are glossed over. Rather, Irene's present suffering commands our attention. Thus, it evolves that in both cases our sympathies are extended to the Germans who suffered. Ultimately, the Jew exists in name only as "the Feldenstein case." The viewer may believe this film is about the Holocaust, espe-

cially because of the Eichmann trial, but the Jew has been removed from his own history to become a prop for suffering Germans.

With regard to this, Judge James Brand, one of the American
judges during the actual Nuremberg trials, was sent a copy of
the script before it was filmed. In a letter to Stanley Kramer from
attorney Gunther Schiff describing Schiff's and Abby Mann's
meeting with Judge Brand, Schiff writes that Judge Brand had
suggested including the testimony of one of the German judges
on trial re the Katzenberg (Feldenstein) case at Nuremberg to
the effect that evidence of an Aryan girl sitting in the lap of a
Jew was sufficient to warrant the death penalty for the Jew.[33]
Such a point would have been an important clarification of Nazi
policy toward the Jews. Judge Brand's advice was essentially ignored.

Only one scene in the film includes Jews and clearly indicates
the policy of destruction: the showing of the documentary footage. It is at the end of Colonel Lawson's narration of the film,
after he has referred to other victimized nationalities, that mention is made of the six million Jews; and then, nothing is said of
their planned systematic destruction. We are never enlightened
as to what policy caused their death. Our final memory of these
images, is of six million dead Jews—an overwhelming number
to any viewer—expressed for the first time in the film (and, of
course, mentioned repeatedly at the Eichmann trial).

With this image in mind, we return to Bruno Bettelheim's
question: How was it possible for six million Jews to die? Hannah
Arendt poses a similar question in her book *Eichmann in Jerusalem*, written as a response to the Eichmann trial. Her answer
is not unlike that given by Bettelheim. Indeed, Jewish scholar
Gershom Scholem wrote to her with the following accusation:
"At each decisive juncture . . . your book speaks only of the *weakness* of the Jewish stance in the world."[34] The documentary footage in the film combined with the knowledge of the horrors of
the camps that emerged from the Eichmann trial yield a portrayal of passivity, one that is heightened by the stark contrast to
the new image created by the fighting Israeli. Undoubtedly an
unintended result, such footage leads the viewer to wonder, along
with Bettelheim and Arendt, how six million Jews allowed this
to happen.

In any event, documentary footage of the Holocaust is problematic.[35] Such film comprises two kinds: German filmed footage meant to be used for anti-Semitic propaganda, and footage filmed in the concentration camps by the liberating armies. These filmed images, though truly horrifying, can also effect a negative response in that they are simultaneously pathetic, possibly resulting in an ambiguous vision. Additionally the limited content of the footage imposes restrictions as to its function in authenticating the Holocaust. Nazi anti-Semitic film, when used, requires explanation for obvious reasons, whereas liberation footage is already post-Holocaust film, not part of the concentration camp experience. To the viewer, such footage appears shocking regardless of the opinion he forms of the victim. But for the confused victim in the film, it is, paradoxically, 'joyful.' It signifies the beginning of freedom. It is a 'truth' that is actually a partial truth; it is not the Holocaust.

103
Chaos and
Social
Upheaval:
The 1960s and
1970s

Much of the documentary footage seen in *Judgment at Nuremberg* is film shot by the U.S. Army Signal Corps after the war; the army wanted its own film record to show what had happened in Germany. A great deal of narration from the army film is utilized by screenwriter Abby Mann and put into the mouth of the fictional Colonel Lawson. In both, as discussed earlier, the Jews are hardly mentioned, the fact of the Final Solution is obscured, and an idea propounded by the army—the equalization, or democratization, of the victims of Nazism—is perpetuated. It is clear that Kramer and Mann want to specify the loss of six million Jews, two-thirds of Europe's Jews. Mann includes this in the narration; but the centrality of the Nazi Jewish policy is lost. The historical materials themselves—the Nuremberg trials and the army film narration—reflect this bias, which, therefore, surfaces in the film.

Whereas a certain degree of historical exactness is pertinent to *The Diary of Anne Frank*—it is, after all, a document—the overall intent of *Judgment at Nuremberg* is to create the mood of the era. Telford Taylor was originally approached to be an adviser on the film but refused because he was dissatisfied with historical inaccuracies in the script (especially with regard to himself). Attorney Gunther Schiff explains in a letter to Taylor what in fact was the goal of the film:

> I know that you will realize . . . that the script is not meant to portray with historical accuracy, or at all, precisely the persons or events who

were involved in, or which occurred at, the Nuremberg Trial. Rather it was Abby's (Mann) desire . . . to depict in a fictionalized manner the essence of what occurred at Nuremberg. Accordingly, Lawson represents not General Taylor but rather a composite picture of a fictional prosecuting officer who need not necessarily have been the chief prosecuting officer; Haywood is not a Judge Brand but is rather a judge who presides at this fictional trial and whose attitudes, rulings and deportment are not intended to, nor do they, depict any actual person. Finally, the evidence which is presented—as you know—is based upon factual evidence presented at the trial although, for dramatic reasons, there have been changes made.[36]

Schiff's account, written on behalf of Kramer, pinpoints some objectives of historical fiction films in general. In the same vein, Pierre Sorlin argues that a historical film is not a historical work: "[E]ven if it appears to show the truth, it in no way claims to reproduce the past accurately. So I think that when professional historians wonder about the mistakes made in an historical film, they are worrying about a meaningless question."[37] Nonetheless, *Judgment* falters in its inability to separate the individual aims of the director and writer—to specify the death of six million Jews—from previously established attitudes.

Much of the commercial and critical success of *Judgment at Nuremberg* can be attributed to an unprecedented volume of publicity, culminating in the world première in Berlin. The film was completed in May 1961. In August an international group of journalists was selected to be flown to Berlin for the première as guests of United Artists. Approximately seventy-five journalists were invited from twenty-seven key cities in the United States and Canada; altogether, including Europe, two hundred received invitations.[38] They were supplied "with a continuing series of stills, stories, layouts and developing information on the première . . . continuing up to the time of their departure for Berlin."[39] The première took place in the Berlin Kongress Halle on 14 December 1961. Besides the press, the guest list included members of the Berlin Senate, Allied commanders (among them General Lucius Clay, President Kennedy's personal representative), and other celebrities. Television covered the event. And West Berlin Mayor Willy Brandt agreed to sponsor the première and the party afterwards.

In his welcoming speech, Brandt called the occasion "an important political event," true on several levels. In the broadest sense, the film shows what happens when any country strays from justice: "This is a subject on a grand scale, perhaps the greatest problem in the world."[40] On another level, according to Nathan Broch of *The Los Angeles Mirror*:

> West European editors attending the Berlin première felt the historic impact of the Kramer film. French, Belgian and Dutch spectators praised the movie as a fundamental effort to explain to their own peoples how the "justice" of German wartime occupation of their countries had been corrupted at its civilian roots.

Although some felt it was wrong to première the film in the shadow of the Berlin Wall, Broch demurred on the grounds that the German people were building a wall in their hearts and minds against their own history, which *Judgment at Nuremberg* might succeed in breaking through.[41] Applause at the end of the screening came mainly from the foreigners in the audience; the Germans were silent, reflecting what *Variety* correspondent Harold Myers perceived as a reaction of shame. Stanley Kramer was asked at a press conference if he did not think it was time for the Germans to tackle the subject; he agreed, but, he said, they had not yet.[42] And finally, the film premiered (coincidentally, the day the Eichmann verdict was announced) at what had been the seat of the Nazi government, in its correct context.

There was a didactic aspect to an American film dealing with the Nazi past premiering in Germany. Stanley Kramer sets up America as the exemplar and guardian of justice. In a letter to Kramer concerning aspects of the script, Justice Michael Musmanno, a former judge at Nuremberg, writes: "America stepped into the European arena and held high the banner of integrity and humanity—and justice."[43] *Judgment at Nuremberg* attempts to re-create this ambience—America teaches Germany and the rest of the world a lesson in democracy; the courtroom depicts justice at its best. A former Nazi officer, prior to viewing the film, said he could not understand why Americans would want to dig up old bones.[44] The reason, of course, was to chastise and accuse those who neglected to carry out justice, with America synonymous with justice.

At the same time, however, the film asks: Who among us can judge? Even as American justice is touted, questions are raised regarding the guilt of America and the rest of the world—for their inaction during the war and for other acts as well. In this sense, the film also functions as a metaphor for contemporary history. Whereas it follows the Eichmann trial and reminds us of the evils of National Socialism, it also comes on the heels of the McCarthy era, when American justice was perverted. In fact, the blacklist had only recently been broken when Otto Preminger hired Dalton Trumbo to write the script for *Exodus* in the spring of 1961. Then, too, America was beginning to acknowledge its own brand of racial injustice. Did not American justice also apply to Americans? Even the Feldenstein case had its contemporary parallels, albeit on a less drastic scale, with blacks in the South. Incidentally, in Germany, *Judgment at Nuremberg* had an immediate impact with regard to the Feldenstein case. Student demonstrations forced the early retirement of Judge Hermann Markl, the first judge who heard the actual (Katzenberg) case (though he did not sentence him).[45] Nonetheless, despite an initial burst of success, the film played largely to empty houses in Germany.

Elsewhere, however, the film was an enormous success, highly lucrative at the box office as well as the recipient of a long list of awards, both national and international. Eleanor Roosevelt said of it: "[I]t must have taken courage to produce this film at this time—a time when most of us have forgotten what went on in Germany before and during World War II."[46] Senator Jacob Javits called it one of the most "eloquent documentaries of our time."[47] And the press was almost unanimous in its praise. Critics claimed: "[F]ew films are important. *Judgment at Nuremberg* is"; or "To evade this film is a weakness in courage. . . . This picture is a voice like a clarion call for peace, fair dealing, mercy, and absolute justice."[48]

In summary, *Judgment at Nuremberg* serves several functions and makes a number of, at times contradictory, points. It finds the Germans guilty of war crimes yet claims we are all guilty. It weakens the image of the Jew without having a single Jewish character in the film. In attempting to show the uniqueness of the Holocaust to the Jews, it instead universalizes the event by portraying the Jews as victims among victims. *Judgment* also becomes a metaphor for all injustice, especially in America in the 1960s. Finally, it is the first American film to combine fiction and history in the text of the film by its use of documentary footage of the liberation of the camps. Too, the film coincides with the Eichmann trial in Jerusalem, an odd merging of fiction with history in the public imagination. Film critic Andrew Sarris offers a fascinating observation: ". . . almost from the moment the ghoulish spectacles of the exterminated were projected on the screen, a self-conscious satanism began to spread through our society,"[49] a point borne out by events of the 1960s—the loss of America's innocence followed by years of violence and chaos. We must wonder whether much of what took place in America was in some way influenced by the shadow of the Holocaust.

107
Chaos and
Social
Upheaval:
The 1960s and
1970s

America in Flux: Reflections Through Holocaust Film

A merican culture—literature, film, art—was influenced by World War II and the Holocaust. One perspective as to why is enumerated by Morris Dickstein in an essay on black humor novels of the early sixties: ". . . it's because the unsolved moral enigma of that period and that experience most closely expresses the conundrum of contemporary life fifteen years later."[50] During the 1960s, especially, Americans began to take notice of artistic activities in great part because of the media obsession with news. The "happening" was a product of the 1960s, understood by Susan Sontag to be a new genre of spectacle, one of its most striking features being the abuse of the audience. Happenings took place in an "environment," generally extremely crowded and messy, constructed of materials chosen for their abused, dirty, and dangerous condition. Sontag offers the following description of one happening:

> . . . the spectators were confined inside a long box-like structure resembling a cattle car; peep-holes had been bored in the wooden walls of this enclosure through which the spectators could strain to see the events taking place outside; when the Happening was over, the walls collapsed, and the spectators were driven out by someone operating a power lawnmower.[51]

Even without explicit mention of the Holocaust, could one doubt the intent of simulating the experience of deportation? This type of reenactment, regardless of its particular audience, was at best a crass attempt to try to "experience" the Holocaust. It could only trivialize the Holocaust and, at the same time, demonstrate that those in the avant-garde of American culture had feelings of being victimized by violence and disdain for human beings.

Violence was indeed infiltrating the American scene. For Americans, the assassination of John Kennedy was to begin a cycle of ferment that would continue into the early 1970s. Richard Walton, author of *Cold War and Counter-Revolution*, writes of Kennedy's death: ". . . the saddest thing of all about Kennedy's death was the meaninglessness of it all. It had no real significance. If some one had succeeded in shooting Hitler, it would have changed the course of events . . ."[52] Meaningless violence was increasing, exhibiting a disregard for humanity that was seen as a legacy of fascism and the Holocaust. This environment stimulated artists to create "abusive" art; an assassin gunned down a president. And it was only the beginning.

Violence would play a major role in the civil rights movement. What began as a nonviolent attempt to win equality eventually exploded into confrontations between blacks and whites in the South, the deaths of civil rights leaders and civil rights workers, and the eruption of violence in the black ghettos. Black cultural leaders like James Baldwin and Leroi Jones vented their anger through theater, and the notion of social guilt was on its way to becoming part of the cultural scene. In ancient drama, masks functioned as a quick means of identifying vice and virtue. A contemporary parallel in the theatre of the 1960s is found in the figure of the Negro, as Susan Sontag observed:

> Once a grotesque, a figure of folly—childlike, lawless, lascivious— "the Negro" is fast becoming the American theatre's leading mask of virtue. For definiteness of outline, being black, he even surpasses "the Jew," who has an ambiguous physical identity. (It was part of the lore of the advanced position of Jewishness that Jews didn't have to look like "Jews." But Negroes always look like "Negroes," unless, of course, they are unauthentic). And for sheer pain and victimage, the Negro is far ahead of any other contender in America. In just a few short years, the old liberalism, whose archetypal figure was the Jew, has been challenged by the new militance, whose hero is the Negro.[53]

In a period of changing attitudes, the American Jew retained his liberal face in continuing to work with black civil rights groups, while many blacks began to reject the Jew both as aide and as friend. Paradoxically, at a time when the Holocaust and its language was often appropriated to describe black suffering in America, many in the forefront of black militancy resorted to anti-Semitic rhetoric in their fight for black equality.

Although black writers had earlier expressed negative feelings toward Jews, it was during the summer riots of 1964 that black anti-Semitism became a public issue. Rioters aimed at stores owned by Jews. The press reported hearing cries of "let's get the Jews." Much of the anti-Jewish feeling on a popular level in the black community resulted from what blacks saw as economic abuse against them by the Jews. As has been pointed out in Selznick and Steinberg's study of anti-Semitism: "Ironically, in accepting anti-Semitic beliefs Negroes bear witness to their participation in Western culture and its symbols."[54]

109
Chaos and
Social
Upheaval:
The 1960s and
1970s

A short time later, in 1965, events were taking place whose effects would ease discrimination for both Jews and blacks. In America, President Lyndon Johnson's Voting Rights Act (preceded by the Civil Rights Act of 1964), the most sweeping in American history, was passed, bringing with it, among other things, voting rights, antipoverty programs, and other elements geared to help blacks and other minority groups.[55] And the Second Vatican Council repudiated anti-Semitism and denounced the notion that the Jews as a group are collectively responsible for the Crucifixion. Similar declarations were also adopted by many Protestant groups. Prejudice against Jews seemed to be ebbing, and blacks were beginning to make gains in American society.

During this time, the black situation was often compared with Jewish conditions during the Holocaust. Screenwriter Abby Mann used the parallel in a speech he gave at Temple Israel of Hollywood in 1965, at a meeting to press for an extension of the Statute of Limitations for Nazi war crimes. Mann said to the gathered crowd: "We are meeting here tonight (because) we want it to be established in Germany that it is a crime to put a baby or an old lady into a gas furnace. It is as important to establish in Germany as it is for us to establish in this country that the murder of [black leader] Medgar Evers is a crime."[56] His words are indicative of a trend that sees the Holocaust in relation to another concept of universalization, that of comparative tragedy: a black shot in Alabama is like a Jew gassed in Auschwitz. The Holocaust is in this way demystified, available for all groups to use as needed in order to interpret specific events. The unknowable becomes knowable.

Director Sidney Lumet's film *The Pawnbroker* (1965) plays upon this theme of juxtaposing those who suffered during the Holocaust with blacks and Puerto Ricans struggling to survive in Harlem. *Boxoffice,* a film industry magazine, suggested the following "catchline" for advertising the film: "A Memorable Motion Picture Dealing with Today's Tumultuous Times and Yesterday's Horrifying Experiences ... "[57] MGM Studios had originally planned to produce the film. It seems, however, that the studio demanded too many script changes, among them, an upbeat ending, so the film was taken over by independent producer Ely Landau.[58]

The Pawnbroker tells the story of a survivor of the Holocaust, a former professor, who now runs a pawnshop in Harlem. He lost his wife and children in the camps, scenes of which we are shown in flashbacks. Film critic Penelope Gilliat neatly sums up the core of the film:

> The shame of surviving the concentration camps where his wife and family died has numbed him to present reality, including the fact that he takes money for his relatives from a Negro who lives off tenement rents. The analogy between the German in the war who didn't want to know and the Jew now who doesn't want to know either is made with fair crassness, like the visual puns between the cattle trucks and the New York subways, or the pawnbroker's grill and the wire around the camp.[59]

Or, in the words of *The New York Times* film critic Bosley Crowther:

> By counterpointing the memories of the hero against the withdrawn and sterile life he lives amid the wretchedness of Harlem, it brings him—and us—to realize that his unwillingness to commit himself to helping others is, in a sense, comparable to the unwillingness of the German people to involve themselves in trying to stop Hitler's rise.[60]

Whereas Penelope Gilliat sees the film as a vulgarization of the Holocaust, Bosley Crowther views it as a contribution to understanding the problems of contemporary society. Both critics agree

The Pawnbroker (1965). Rod Steiger plays a survivor of the Holocaust, now running a pawnshop in Harlem.

on the goals of the film, however: to evoke parallels between the Holocaust and Harlem. American society is responsible for the suffering of the blacks; and the Jew, himself so recently a tragic victim, is guilty of complicity, not unlike the Germans responsible for the pawnbroker's suffering and the death of his family. The Jew is portrayed as having learned nothing from the Holocaust, while the viewer, from his "objective" standpoint, understands the lesson.

Another dimension of the Jewish character is reflected here, as it is shown in *The Diary of Anne Frank* and alluded to in *Judgment at Nuremberg*: that of the Jew as a weak, almost feminine, figure, dependent upon the Christian/gentile as symbol of maleness. This dependence "is on the surface rather obvious in light of the position of the Jew as victim during the Holocaust. However, implicit here is an image of the Jew as being incapable of saving himself without the aid of the strong, male Christian."[61] In effect, the Jew cannot survive alone. Now, in *The Pawnbroker* the Jew is alive but his soul is dead. He is saved, restored somewhat to the ranks of humanity by his Puerto Rican helper, Jesus, who is himself shot. So with *The Pawnbroker* another dimension is added to the image of physical weakness: spiritual weakness.

Inasmuch as *The Pawnbroker* attempts to juxtapose the Holocaust with Harlem, the Jewish victim indirectly becomes a victimizer because of his inability to rise above his own suffering. There is a sense that Judaism, too, is indicted for its failure to provide spiritual sustenance. Indeed, can it be coincidence that the name of the Puerto Rican savior is Jesus? Judaism, it is intimated, lacks that essential ingredient of "love thy neighbor" found in Christianity.

Like *The Pawnbroker*, *Ship of Fools* accuses the Jew and blames him for having not anticipated the Holocaust. Even after the Eichmann trial, this film attempts to equate the suffering of the Jews with other victims of Nazism during the war. Working together again as a team, Abby Mann wrote the script for *Ship of Fools*, based on Katherine Anne Porter's novel, and Stanley Kramer directed the film. Once again, Kramer would cast his film with stars who would surely arouse public interest.

The film follows a ship sailing from Mexico to Germany in 1933. On board is a cross section of humanity, from a dwarf who introduces and ends the film, to Nazis, a Jew, Mexican peasants, and American pleasure-seekers. Their involvement in their per-

The Pawnbroker (1965). A visual pun—the pawnbroker's grill and the wire around the concentration camp.

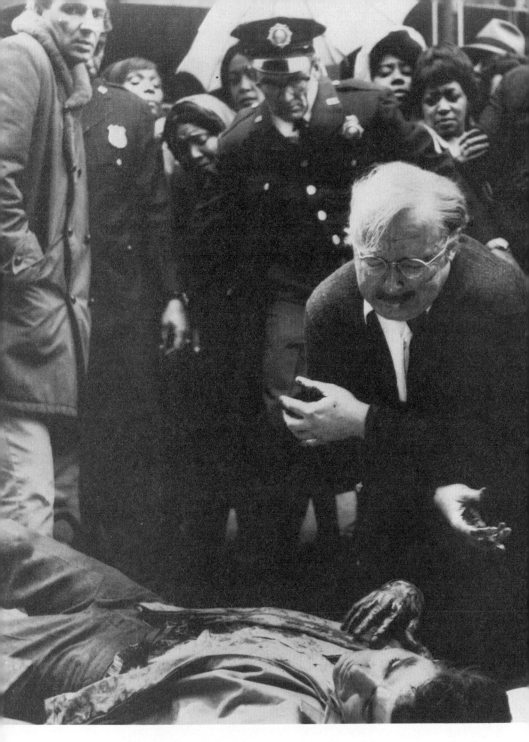

The Pawnbroker (1965). Rod Steiger mourns over the body of his Puerto Rican helper, Jesus (Jaime Sanchez).

sonal affairs leaves them oblivious to the world that surrounds them, a world on the verge of exploding. This "ship of fools" is a microcosm of the world in general as well as a metaphor for America in 1965.

In his introduction and epilogue to the film, the dwarf, Glocken, clearly delineates its contemporary message. In the beginning: "If you look closely, you might even find yourself on board." And at the end: "I can hear you say, 'what has all this to do with us?' Nothing." He laughs aloud and walks off. (Glocken, by the way, means bells in German, seemingly an allusion to John Donne's "Do not ask for whom the bell tolls, it tolls for thee."[62]) This unsubtle accusation warns the viewer that he, too, is a fool, for the world still sits on a live volcano ready to erupt as we meanwhile engage in the pettiness of daily existence. It requires no great insight to tell an audience in 1965 that people in 1933 were foolish for not foreseeing the Holocaust to come. The film's warning is more significant in telling us that we must be ever on our guard because the threat of danger is always present in society. In 1965, this danger was perceived in the black struggle, increased involvement in Vietnam, and the nuclear threat.

115
Chaos and
Social
Upheaval:
The 1960s and
1970s

As an example of the misuse of hindsight in the film, we see the anti-Semite reading a newspaper article on extermination of the unfit (in 1933?), including defective and useless children and the elderly. The same measures will be enacted for Jews, too— and for the Negroes and Chinese. Again, the uniqueness of the Holocaust is denied for the sake of universalizing suffering. And an extra message is added—the inclusion of Negroes and Chinese—which gives the film its contemporary tone and sets up the parallel between Nazi anti-Semitism and American racism. In response to the article, the ship's captain offers the reassurance that no one could ever take Hitler or his party seriously. Are the film makers prescient, able to anticipate tragedy unlike the fools aboard ship in 1933?

The film is most pointed in its treatment of the Jew Lowenthal for, as we know today, he stood to suffer most from Hitler's policies. He shares a cabin with the anti-Semite and constantly complies with his demands. Only the Jew and the dwarf may not sit at the captain's table: The Jew is thus equated with deformity, which reflects a certain Nazi "truth." Author Katherine Anne Porter and film makers Abby Mann and Stanley Kramer clashed over the portrayal of Lowenthal. Mann felt that the book presented the Jew as one who deserves anti-Semitism, and so changed him.[63] Miss Porter responded to Stanley Kramer: "If Mr. Mann has changed Herr Lowenthal's entire nature, problem and situation, he has destroyed the point and meaning of that character, so that it is no longer mine, but his."[64]

Nevertheless Mann's Lowenthal, too, is problematic because of the thrust of the film: the blindness of Lowenthal and others aboard the ship. Mann summarized his view of Lowenthal in a letter to Allen Rivkin of the Jewish Film Advisory Committee. Rivkin had misgivings about the character and Mann assured him that he would be pleased with Lowenthal, explaining: "While he is still a fool, as is everyone else on the boat, I hope he is a human and understandable fool, and I hope that we have caught some of the real meaning and the real tragedy of the German Jew. That is . . . he considered himself more German than Jew."[65]

Several scenes in the film depict that very undying devotion to Germany. When Lowenthal hears German music he gets a "special feeling about being a German." Or, he refers to the by now banal paradox of a people who love Goethe, Beethoven, and Bach and yet engage in brutal, uncivilized behavior. Glocken the dwarf asks Lowenthal: "Don't you see what's going on?" To which Lowenthal replies:

> "The German is something special. We're Germans first and Jews second. We've done so much for Germany. . . . A little patience . . . It works itself out . . . Listen. There are nearly a million [sic] Jews in Germany. What are they going to do? Kill all of us?"

In other words we have a double charge: The Jew stands accused for not knowing about Auschwitz in 1933, and the Jew is guilty for feeling himself to be what he indeed was, a German citizen.

This very qualified image found growing acceptance in the popular imagination, as it was easier to blame the Jews for their own destruction than it was to understand the process and history that led to the Final Solution or than it was for society to accept the guilt. In this respect, Lowenthal is essentially Bettelheim's Jew: the Jew who degrades himself in order to survive; the Jew who ingratiates himself with his enemy in order to survive; the Jew who deludes himself and thereby avoids taking action.[66]

Ship of Fools (1965). The film follows the sailing of a ship from Mexico to Germany. The passengers disregard a world on the brink of war.

However, such beliefs only mitigate the pain of guilt, which belongs to society and not to the victims of the Holocaust. Pauline Kael astutely questions whether Mann knows what will save Lowenthal any more than we do. She comments with sensitivity: "It's a strange place to look for the reasons for Hitler's policies—in the hearts of the Jews."[67]

By ignoring his imminent danger, the Jew becomes a contemporary symbol. As the film is summed up in one review: ". . . this and other forms of racism are rampant today . . . giving *Ship of Fools* a pertinence that the passing of years and a devastating world war have not outdated."[68] When one passenger on the ship asks the Jew why he takes it, Lowenthal says that Jews already have for a long time. An American Southerner then asks another American on board what the Germans have against the Jews; he, for one, never saw one till he was fifteen. She replies that he had been too busy lynching Negroes to take time out for Jews—the point being that the Jews in Germany are the equivalent of the blacks in America. And whereas the Jew did not act then, it is up to us to act now.

In 1965, besides *Ship of Fools* and *The Pawnbroker*, *The Sound of Music*, a frothy musical about the Trapp family singers and the Nazis, was an overwhelming success. And the Czech film *The Shop on Main Street*, about the deportations of Jews in Slovakia in 1942, received an Academy Award for the best foreign picture. The "lessons" of the Holocaust were indeed being disseminated through film. The parallel has often been drawn between the 1930s, the setting of many of these films, and events occurring in the 1960s. In *Hollywood Films of the Seventies*, the authors note that ". . . the thirties and sixties were periods of deep social unrest and political activism. . . ."[69] Following this line of thinking, one young Jewish radical observes: "There was a time when sane men ought to have assassinated Hitler and destroyed the Nazi machine; such a time is upon us again, one says, albeit in insidious and seductive guise."[70] In other words, with the memory of recent history in mind, the blacks continued their struggle, becoming more violent. As America increased its involvement in Vietnam, student protest against the war machine took hold at the universities. Perhaps this was one way for America to deal with the history of National Socialism and of the Holocaust: it could apply its lessons to contemporary life. Americans would no longer stand by in the face of inequality; nor would they allow an unjust war to escalate. They questioned American policy. And in so doing, they put America on the defensive.

While America went on trial for its policies, Jewish historians and writers began to question America about its policy toward Jewish refugees during World War II. Works such as Arthur Morse's *While Six Million Died* (1967) and Henry Feingold's *The Politics of Rescue* (1969) provide some concrete historical answers as to why European Jewry could not save itself. Their studies contrast sharply with Bettelheim's muddy psychological theories. Jewish alternatives were limited by restrictive immigration policies that left no escape routes from Europe. So, the America of the 1960s and early 1970s was one of deeper political awareness, a country that stood accused for its recent past as well as its chaotic present.

119
Chaos and
Social
Upheaval:
The 1960s and
1970s

As a result of this challenge to American policy, the Holocaust and its symbols were used rather loosely by new young radicals to define their enemies; at the same time, those challenging the system often resorted to tactics of violence themselves. Robert Brustein, at the time dean of the Yale School of Drama, remarked that the activities of the Students for a Democratic Society (SDS) reminded him of the bully tactics used by the Nazis before they came to power.[71] Andrew Sarris understood this trend as a vulgarization of the Holocaust: "When radical journalists chose to describe the late Hubert Humphrey as a war criminal on a Hitlerian level, the Holocaust began to lose much of its sacred uniqueness."[72] Actually, as early as the immediate postwar era, when universalization of the Holocaust first began, the Jewish specificity of the event became diluted.

There was an inherent logic in the application of these various phenomena—universalization, democratization, vulgarization, popularization—to the Holocaust. The Holocaust has influenced and permeated our society in such a way that it stands outside other events. It is the quickest, easiest, and most reliable means for facilitating instant comprehension: from the Left to the Right, its vocabulary and images have entered the imagination of the people. When Leftists refer to Humphrey as a Nazi, we immediately know their intent. Right-wing groups use Nazi symbols to frighten American Jews. When words like genocide and extermination are used with regard to American Indians, we understand the precise implication. Body art becomes stylish; its aim being to mutilate oneself in the name of art, sometimes until death.[73] Poets such as Sylvia Plath turn to Holocaust imagery to define their personal suffering.

Many films whose focus is not the Holocaust use the event. *Time* magazine, for example, writes about Alfred Hitchcock's *Torn Curtain* (1966) that the "comparison of a murder in *Torn Curtain* with the Holocaust of Auschwitz betrays a pompous misreading of history."[74] Hal Ashby's *Harold and Maude* (1971), a cult film among college students, refers to the Holocaust once when Maude displays a number on her arm and speaks of her past. She also lives in a boxcar. Although Maude is clearly a survivor, the film is not classified as a Holocaust film. Maude, in her seventies, has an affair with young Harold, approximately eighteen. Might she be compensating for a youth lost during the war? She is a free spirit who lives by her own laws and wants to control her own destiny. Conceivably, her attitude stems from her experience in the camps when her fate was in the hands of the Nazis. And Woody Allen's films make reference to the Holocaust, as for example in *Annie Hall* (1977), in which the Allen character sees the film *The Sorrow and the Pity* for the eighth time and after seeing the film, Annie wonders if she could have withstood torture.

Yet the Holocaust has also been responsible for what might be termed oversensitivity to portrayals of Jews in film. Any remotely questionable portrayal, many Jews feel, might spark off a rash of anti-Semitic feeling in America. Apparently, America's Jews were still insecure, in spite of the decrease in anti-Semitism and the condition that Morton Keller calls asemitism, that is, an "indifference to, or unawareness of, their identity as Jews."[75]

In the 1960s and 1970s, a number of films appear whose portrayal of the Jew brings new stereotypes, as for example, the Jewish princess or the Jewish mother.[76] Allen Rivkin, head of the Jewish Film Advisory Committee, argues:

> We cannot afford this outpouring of pictures showing the Jews, warts and all, these caricatures which are brutal without being penetrating. . . . Whatever we may like to think, we are not solid enough, not secure enough in this country or anywhere else to strip ourselves bare on the screen.[77]

In August 1972, Dore Schary (of the Anti-Defamation League and the JFAC, and former head of production at RKO Studios where he produced *Crossfire*) and Robert Weil (Chairman of the Community Relations Committee of the Jewish Federation-Council of Greater Los Angeles) prepared a statement to be issued in response to several new films, among them *Portnoy's Complaint*, which they felt portrayed a negative image of the Jew. Schary and Weil wrote in their letter: "It seems so odd when we look back at what happened under Hitler, for young Jews to be so unaware of what these kind of stereotypes, ostensibly funny sequences can do to stimulate anti-Semitism . . ."[78]

Yet, somewhat in contradiction to his previous statement, Schary, along with other Jews, felt a certain sense of security as he suggested to the JFAC that the Jews were not in the same position as blacks and other minorities and did not have to approach Hollywood on a militant basis.[79] In fact, in the early 1970s several Jewish organizations wanted to withdraw their funding of the JFAC (which they did by the end of the seventies) because, according to Mort Yarmon of the American Jewish Committee, the project had outlived its usefulness: "There would seem to be no imminent danger today of the kind of embarrassing stereotyping of Jews that was so prevalent two or three decades ago."[80]

As a result of anti-Semitism and the Holocaust, the JFAC had come into being to try to eliminate negative portrayals of Jews in American films. Yet, paradoxically, because of the Holocaust life for Jews and other minorities in America was vastly improved. In other words, there was a contradiction between their misplaced fear of damaging film images and the constantly improving situation of America's Jews.

Life was good for the American Jew, but the society in which he lived was growing more violent. This culminated, as Christopher Lasch notes, with almost everyone, rich and poor alike, living in danger, from which there is little escape. This includes international terrorism and blackmail, bombings, hijackings, crime, gang wars and racial violence.[81] In the period under discussion it included student violence as well as the violent atmosphere generated by the war in Vietnam. A number of films paralleled this violent atmosphere. Examples that come to mind immediately include *Bonnie and Clyde* (1967), *A Clockwork Orange* (1971), and *Straw Dogs* (1971).

Also reflecting the mood of violence in America and its cinema is the film *Cabaret* (1972), directed by Bob Fosse. It is set in Germany of the early 1930s, prior to the establishment of

121

Chaos and
Social
Upheaval:
The 1960s and
1970s

Cabaret (1972). The film portrays the relationship of an English university student (Michael York) with a young American cabaret singer (Liza Minnelli) in Berlin of the early 1930s.

National Socialist rule. We observe Germany through the eyes of an English university student involved in a relationship with a young American cabaret singer. Their story evolves through a juxtaposition of scenes in the Kit Kat Club, the cabaret, and daily existence in Berlin and its environs. We are witness to the disintegration of the Weimar Republic as the Nazis begin their rise to power. Songs and dances punctuate the film and provide a social commentary on the period. The format is reminiscent of that of *Ship of Fools*. Life in the cabaret goes on, whereas outside things are on the verge of exploding. The film evokes a loose parallel with decadence and chaos in American society.

Just as an American politician like Hubert Humphrey was described as a Nazi, contemporary America is here compared with the early years of the rise of the Nazis. It has been suggested that events such as the Vietnam war and the My Lai massacre had greatly impaired the American public's belief in the future: "As Berlin of the thirties slid towards fascism, so did some Americans sense that they were entering an era in which specific horrors were beyond their control . . ."[82] Or, as director Bob Fosse explains his film:

> I was not out to make a factual film, a documentary. . . . All I wanted to present and to remind people of was the impending doom and to show the people involved in their personal problems, their relationships, and then, outside of them all hell was about to break loose. . . . I was not trying to do a documentary on that period.[83]

The parallel between the situation in Germany of the early 1930s and that in America of the late 1960s and early 1970s operates on two levels: the political and the cultural.

On the cultural level, German expressionism thrived in the 1920s. With its distorted and abstract images, it shocked contemporaries and was a form of protest. Hitler, as we know, outlawed expressionist art. By contrast in America of the 1960s and 1970s, the openly permissive atmosphere negated the artist's ability to shock. Art critic Barbara Rose delineates the problem:

> Inevitably the nature of the relationship of the avant-garde to its audience defines the types of protest available at any given time. When the audience has become as excessively permissive as the current American audience, there is no longer any art of aggression the artist can direct toward it, since these actions will not be inter-

Cabaret (1972). Sally (Liza Minnelli) sings in Berlin's Kit Kat Klub while the Weimar Republic is disintegrating and the Nazis are beginning their rise to power.

preted as aggression but as more diversion. The system of signaling
has therefore broken down, largely as a result of the communications
revolution which neutralizes information and deprives both art and
criticism of a role antagonistic to established culture. Through the
media, aggression is transformed into harmless entertainment.[84]

In other words, what could shock in, say, 1931 is in 1972 simply
diversion; decadence cannot succeed in a society where decadence is passé. This is why the art re-created in *Cabaret* is no
longer grotesque but rather nostalgic.

125

Chaos and
Social
Upheaval:
The 1960s and
1970s

The metaphor on the political level also does not work, regardless of popular radical conceptions that compared America
of 1972 with Berlin of the early 1930s. Perhaps certain general
phenomena were similar: violence, murder, social and political
chaos. The conditions from which they erupted, however, were
disparate. Briefly, the Weimar Republic was Germany's first attempt at democracy; America was founded on institutionalized
democracy. The elements that destroyed Weimar intended to
destroy democracy; in America, the political chaos was a means
to more fully legitimize the promise of America. The voices yell-
ing to end Weimar were anti-freedom, and in the end, anti-
human; the cries in America, though sometimes extreme, were
those of the people telling their leaders: Enough racism, enough
of Viet Nam! Bob Fosse speaks of a cultural flourishing in the
permissive Berlin atmosphere, out of which came the swing to
the right. He sees a similar trend in America: exciting movements
in art, an atmosphere of permissiveness, and a strong right
wing.[85] The implication is that decadence, or permissiveness,
leads to totalitarianism, or perhaps, as film critic Stephen Farber
suggests, "*Cabaret* may even be read as a warning that contemporary America, because of its new sexual freedom, is a sick
society, comparable to Weimar Germany . . ."[86] No, in spite of
the possibilities, America was not Weimar.

The film depicts the beginnings of the Nazi threat against the
Jews. The two Jewish characters seem at first to be gratuitous in
the context of the film. Natasha is very wealthy; Fritz is a poor
student hiding his Jewish identity out of fear. In one scene, a
dead dog is found against the door of Natasha's home—an omen
of danger. Although the two fall in love, Natasha will not marry
Fritz because he is not a Jew. Fritz admits he is Jewish and they
marry. What is their function in the film?

Perhaps they serve as counterpoints to the decadence of their

Cabaret (1972). The expressionist culture of cabaret life—outlawed by Hitler—is juxtaposed with the political turmoil outside the club.

friends. This accords with one commonly held contemporary stereotype of Jews as sober and steadfast types. Also, Natasha's prudishness in her relationship with Fritz stands in stark contrast to Sally and her bisexual ménage à trois. The Jew becomes almost a calming factor, a figure of continuity and stability in a world where everything is in flux and chaos—indeed a positive statement about the Jew and his miraculous ability to survive the Holocaust to come. The Jew, perhaps, signifies stability, which is what is at stake in these years of change, the early 1930s, and what seems to be at stake in America of 1972. The Jew in *Cabaret*, then, symbolizes the hope—in the midst of the confusion in America in the 1960s and early 1970s—that rationality and calm will prevail in the end.

From the political turmoil of those years of confusion, Christopher Lasch observes, America retreated to the purely personal preoccupations in what was the spiritual crisis of the 1970s. Many former radicals turned to what he calls the "therapeutic sensibility," "getting one's head together," be it through a guru, est, health foods, a psychiatrist, body building, or whatever else.[87] The period became one of obsession with self.

Young Jews seeking spiritual satisfaction followed similar patterns, some turning to drugs, some turning to Eastern philosophies and gurus. Many, though, turned to Judaism as a source of guidance. And many turned to that event that carries its own mystique—unknowable, unimaginable—the Holocaust. Because of its horrors, because of the depth of its mystery of experience, because it signifies death and redemption, and because as American Jews who grew up in freedom, it became even more difficult to grasp, many turned to the Holocaust as a means of identification—a return—and as a study of human evil.

Professors Jacob Neusner and Leon Jick both believe that the Jewish preoccupation with the Holocaust was influenced by the newly developing social and political consciousness in the broader American society of the late sixties and early seventies.[88] This concern intensified when Israel faced destruction in the days preceding the Six Day War in 1967. Around this time, Professor Jick points out, author and Holocaust survivor Elie Wiesel became an important figure on the Jewish scene. Wiesel wrote haunting accounts about his Holocaust experience as well as his moving testimony, *The Jews of Silence* (1966), about the harassment of Jews in the Soviet Union. As political turmoil gave way to the search for identity, Jewish youth were drawn to Elie Wiesel and his works and built a "cult of the Holocaust" around him.

At a time of spiritual neediness Wiesel—with his appearance of otherworldliness, his dramatic carriage, his mystique, his image as a man returned from hell, his tales of the Holocaust and of a world that no longer existed—personified a lost culture with a contemporary relevance that was irresistible. This aspect of cult was perhaps unintended but, nonetheless, unavoidable, given the man's charisma. Wiesel and those he inspired delivered the message of the Holocaust throughout the United States, establishing its reality, singling out its uniqueness as a Jewish event, even providing the rationale for the continuing decrease in anti-Semitism.

However, by 1973, after the Yom Kippur War in Israel and the pursuant Arab oil embargo, American Jewry worried about a resurgence of anti-Semitism. The JFAC remained concerned about the impact of negative film images. But, as we see from Allen Rivkin's questioning of Hollywood writers, some American Jews were feeling very secure. When Rivkin asked one writer if he didn't believe some of his screen images might add to anti-Semitism, the writer answered: "Let 'em go back to where they came from—Alabama, or Texas or one of those foreign countries." That is a sense of security. Or when Rivkin spoke with one of Mel Brooks' writers about *Blazing Saddles* (1974) and how some of the Jewish material offended him, the writer replied: "Dad, get with it. This is another century."[89] And indeed it is.

American Jewry was at a crossroads. There were those who still remembered an uncomfortable past; and there were those at ease with postwar American freedom and the security Israel provides. In December 1974, Richard Reeves, a gentile, published an article entitled "If Jews Will Not Be for Themselves, Who Will Be for Them?" in *New York Magazine*. In this response to the Yom Kippur War, Reeves captures the essence of the Jewish ethos at that time[90]: Jews are too self-conscious and therefore not sufficiently vocal in their support of Israel and in spreading this support beyond the main centers of America.

He suggests that, in fact, Jews are demographically "the best educated and most affluent group in the United States, and most Americans admire them for it." Jews are no longer victims. "One does not instinctively feel sorry for his dentist or for the chairman of CBS." He finds little value in publications put out by the Anti-

Defamation League, for example, that contribute to perpetuating the fear of anti-Semitism. Reeves writes: "It can't happen here, no matter how much oil the Arabs have or how tough they get."

Reeves cites Rabbi Wolfe Kelman who says that, despite what people say, America in 1974 is not like Weimar of 1932. The United States has no comparable history of anti-Semitism. "My son feels he owns as much of this country as you do," says Kelman. And finally, Reeves quotes Stephen D. Isaacs, author of *Jews in American Politics*:

"After decades of apologizing and deferring, they [Jews] are expressing themselves openly, enthusiastically, and brashly—as Americans are wont to do. That *is* the American way, and the thrust of their political activity is the ultimate proof of their Americanization."

In effect, Reeves contends, the Jew is at home in America in 1974. In a letter from Allen Rivkin to Charles Posner, Executive Director of the Community Relations Committee in Los Angeles, Rivkin writes that he has spoken to most of the Hollywood writers, of whom some 75 percent are Jewish, about Jewishness in their writings. The consensus was that "it's about time we came out of the closet."[91]

After the Yom Kippur War, it was apparent that American Jewry was one partner in a three-sided relationship that also included Israel and the Holocaust. They were independent yet interdependent. In fact, this triangle helped forge a strengthened Jewish identity in America. The Holocaust was becoming more identified as the unique Jewish experience it was, and Israel sometimes seemed like a fifty-first state, or an appendage of America.

As the Jews identified more openly with particular Jewish concerns, they only reflected a general trend in America. The desire to be unique was indeed keen. Various groups demanded their civil rights, from blacks to American Indians to women. Each group accused America of suppressing it, of disregarding its rights, of having persecuted it. In America persecution had not been part of the Jewish experience; elsewhere it had been a continuing motif. Like others, Jews were looking for their roots, which had been destroyed in the Holocaust in Europe. And so, like a latter-day refugee the Holocaust was brought to America's shores. Slowly, it was integrated into the American scene. And as the event became part of the American Jewish memory, it also became part of the memory of the country. America would relate to the Holocaust in terms of its experience, that is, through the refugee problem. The United States was guilty of aiding the Final Solution because it failed to open its doors to European Jewish refugees.

Guilt, as a matter of ·fact, was an important theme in this period of American history. America had lost much of its innocence and naïveté, especially in the aftermath of Vietnam and Watergate. It was a period of self-analysis, including a new look at America's record regarding American Indians, blacks, and the treatment of the Jewish problem during World War II.

The history written in books like those by Morse and Feingold is also reflected in films: American guilt, collective or individual, is the theme of two major films. (By contrast, we recall that *Judgment at Nuremberg* introduces the idea of collective guilt within a universal framework.) *Voyage of the Damned* (1976) deals with collective guilt, its advertising manual calling it "the incredible story of the ship that shamed the world." *Julia* (1977) deals with the individual guilt of the liberal who twenty years later tries to atone for her inaction during the war. Allen Rivkin of the JFAC read Steve Shagan's script of *Voyage* and tried to find a producer for the film. Rivkin wrote to Joel Ollander of the National Jewish Community Relations Advisory Council telling him he had sent the script to producer Sherril Corwin. Rivkin writes: "This is an important opportunity for us to present . . . a *positive* image of Jewish humanity and our incredible survival in the face of unbelievable odds."[92] Corwin rejected the script, reasoning: "I cannot appraise its commercial potential . . . and I don't know what appeal this would have to non-Jewish audiences."[93] In order to ensure this appeal *Voyage*, like several of its predecessors, has an all-star cast, as the reviewer in *Newsweek* comments: ". . . it [the cast] seems to have been put together as an international business venture. The enormous cast is of the sort that prompts you to whisper, 'Isn't that Jose Ferrer?' "[94]

Voyage of the Damned is the first post-Holocaust American film to focus on the Holocaust from a purely Jewish perspective. It is based on the story of the ship *St. Louis* that sailed with its cargo of Jewish refugees from Germany in 1939. Refused entry by both Cuba and the United States, the ship was forced to return to Europe. Several European countries finally agreed to take many of the passengers, but, as the film informs us at the end, 600 of the 937 on board ultimately died in concentration camps.

Although the film is about the Jews, the real hero is actually the Christian captain of the ship, a man who refuses to join the Nazi party. When two former concentration camp victims attempt to mutiny, the captain convinces them to call off their assault; he, of course, will forget the incident. At one point, he plans to run the ship into the rocks and set it on fire in order to get the passengers ashore. The captain is always a perfect gentleman to his passengers, guests not refugees. This in contrast to the antagonism of the crew members. In Cuba, the captain cancels shore leave for the crew because his passengers cannot disembark. In Germany, the captain, a hero from the beginning, orders away SS cameramen who are there to film religious Jews for propaganda purposes. The film informs us that because he had been in command of the ill-fated *St. Louis*, the captain was tried for war crimes after the war. Thanks to the testimony of surviving passengers, he was acquitted and later awarded a medal for his role in helping to save Jewish lives.

131
Chaos and
Social
Upheaval:
The 1960s and
1970s

The film clearly distinguishes between Nazis and Christians. When the passengers mutiny, the captain gives his word "as a Christian" that they will not sail back to Germany. That is to say, Christians, as opposed to Nazis, do attempt to save Jews. As the title tells us, however, the Jews are inevitably "damned." The Jews have a look of elegance; they may be fleeing for their lives, but not without caviar, gowns, and dancing, their way of dignifying themselves despite their deep sadness. Their morale is weakened. We see suicides and Jews dying of "broken hearts." And they are victims—but not because they do not resist or because they do not face reality, as Bettelheim and others have argued. The Jews are victims because the world allowed them to be; they are a people damned in the eyes of the world. The film informs us that the Germans allowed the *St. Louis* to sail with the knowledge that Cuba and America would not receive its passengers. With this example before the eyes of the world, the Germans knew they would then be free to do as they wished to the Jews.

Nonetheless, as in *The Pawnbroker*, the Jews in *Voyage* are spiritually weak. The captain's sensitive dignity permeates the film; the Jews act as if they are damned. Their relationship to the *Christian* captain is one of dependency. They need his strength. The ship is the vehicle of the modern wandering Jew, doomed to wander because of his role in the Crucifixion; the Jews are damned for the past and damned in the present, eternally weak. As portrayed in *Voyage*, the Jews need the Christian captain for their survival; their function is to help bring out the "goodness" incumbent upon good Christians. On a theological level, as well as that of reality, the captain fails if he loses his Jews, and the Jews cannot survive without the captain.[95]

On another level, the one that focuses on guilt, the Jews are lost because America reneges on its promise to be a haven for the oppressed. It must bear responsibility for the death of Jews during the Holocaust. As a metaphor for the present *Voyage* reminds us of refugees from Southeast Asia, as well as from Cuba, Haiti, and other countries. America could atone for its guilt over the Holocaust by allowing other victims of oppression to enter the United States.

Personal guilt and self-analysis form the core of *Julia* (1977), Fred Zinnemann's film based on Lillian Hellman's memoir in her book *Pentimento*. This story of the friendship of two women takes place against the backdrop of the rise of Nazism. It claims to be autobiographical truth. Throughout the film most of the characters, including Lillian, retain their true identities (although the film feels like fiction masquerading as history). It can be read as a story of personal guilt, the desire of a political liberal to exonerate herself.

The story concerns two people very important to Lillian Hellman—Julia (the only major character in the film whose real identity is not revealed) and Dashiell Hammett. The film revolves around the friendship with Julia, an upper-class socialist, gentile, elegant, and brilliant, who studies at Oxford and with Freud in Vienna. In Austria, Julia, involved with a resistance movement, is severely beaten by Nazi hooligans at the university and loses a leg as a result. Lillian, in the meantime, becomes the toast of Broadway and spends her time in Paris, in Russia, and in search of Julia. When Julia does reach Lillian in Paris, through a contact, it is to request that she deliver $50,000 into Nazi Germany for use by the underground. Despite her fear, Lilly agrees and successfully completes her mission. In the end, Julia is murdered because of her political activities.

It is unfortunate that a film appearing thirty years after the war still insists upon universalizing the suffering of the Nazis' victims. Certainly, in Nazi Germany of the early 1930s, political prisoners as well as Jews were in jeopardy. Nonetheless, anti-Semitism formed a central core in Nazi ideology. To imply an equality of suffering gives a false picture of Nazi reality. Nevertheless, when Lilly asks Julia if the $50,000 is to help save Jews, Julia tells her it is for Jews and for political prisoners—not unlike what we hear in the film of *The Diary of Anne Frank* when Anne says that Jews are not the only ones to suffer. (Meyer Levin and others point to the phrase in *Julia* as proof of Hellman's influence and contribution to *The Diary of Anne Frank*.) Still, despite the similarity, the two films are quite different in this regard. Anne does not equate the suffering of the victims of World War II but, rather, places her own suffering in a broader historical framework—people have *always* suffered. In *Julia*, however, the intent is to equate the Jews with other victims of Nazism. Andrew Sarris points out the absurdity of this way of thinking:

> To this day Lillian Hellman reflects '30s leftist attitudes on the Jewish Question when she quotes the martyred Julia on wanting to help not just the Jews, but all sorts of political prisoners. One would have thought that the perception of the outside world changed traumatically and irrevocably with the first exhibition of the death-camp footage in 1944 and 1945.[96]

In an earlier Hellman story, the film *Watch On the Rhine* (1943), the word Jew is not mentioned at all, although the film bears a striking resemblance to *Julia*. *Watch On the Rhine* is the story of Kurt, a hero of the resistance who arrives in America with his adoring American wife to visit her prominent and wealthy family. He leaves his safe haven to return to the imbroglio in Europe. Kurt and Julia are very similar characters—aristocratic and devoted to freedom. Kurt's wife and Lilly resemble each other in their adulatory love of husband and friend.

There are also several scenes resembling each other, which suggests that *Julia* is derivative of *Watch On the Rhine*. For instance, a Warner Brothers synopsis of *Watch On the Rhine* states that Kurt is in the United States with $23,000 collected from the pennies of the poor in order to fight fascism.[97] In *Julia*, it is Julia's $50,000 that Lilly must bring to Germany, but the idea is the same. Kurt must bring the money himself to Germany; Lilly will deliver the money to Julia. (Perhaps Lillian Hellman assigned herself the deed in order to be counted among those who helped in the fight against Nazism.) Kurt works in Europe with the leader of the underground movement, Max Friedank, who has been taken captive; Lilly is a friend to Julia, who is eventually murdered in Europe because of her underground activities. Kurt's hands are smashed; Julia loses her leg. One scene in Dashiell Hammett's final version of the script, which does not appear in the film, places Kurt in a German hotel room with a young man. In the script's directions it says: "The young man's attitude towards [him] is one of great respect." There is money on the table, to be used to buy prisoners out of camps. The young boy wants to help Kurt, but Kurt says: "No. Whatever happens, I wish no one else to be involved." Kurt speaks of children and tells the young man: "If you should ever meet my boy, and I . . ."; he breaks off because someone is coming. Kurt tells the boy to go quickly. The boy runs for the back door and looks back to see Kurt smiling.[98]

There is a similar scene in *Julia*. Lilly, on her mission, arrives in Berlin. She is brought to a little café across the street from the train station where Julia awaits her. Lilly, adoring as always, passes the concealed money to Julia, who assures her that she has done something important, that they can save some five hundred to one thousand people with it. Here is when Lilly asks if they are Jews, and Julia replies, Jews and political prisoners. Julia then reveals that she has a baby and wants Lilly to take care of her. Julia tells Lilly she must leave. Lilly goes as we see Julia smiling at her.

Such remarkable similarities cannot be a result of coincidence. (There are other examples as well.) What can we deduce from this? Apparently, *Julia*, supposedly an autobiographical memoir, is as much a fiction as *Watch On the Rhine*. In fact, several writers have questioned the integrity of Lillian Hellman's work—Michael Billington, for example, in *The Illustrated London News*, who writes: ". . . the film has the ring of fiction rather than that of truth." Author Clive James says: "For the truth is that the Julia chapter (in *Pentimento*), like all the others, happens in a dream." Sidney Hook says of Miss Hellman: "She has spun a myth about her past that has misled the reading public of at least two countries." And author Mary McCarthy, in a quote from an interview on the Dick Cavett Show, proclaims: "She's a . . . dishonest writer . . . every word she writes is a lie, including 'and' and 'the.' "[99] In fact, in a book that appeared in 1983, *Code*

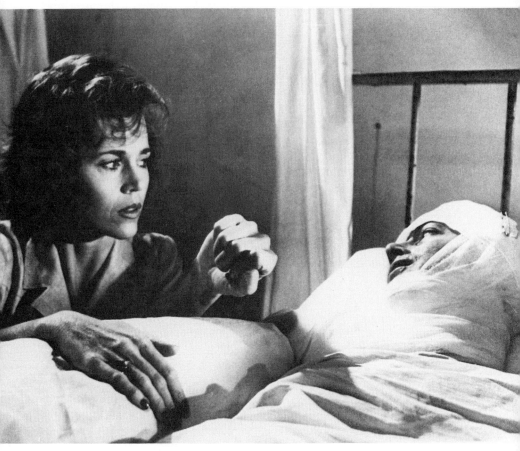

Julia (1977). As a result of her involvement with a resistance movement in Austria, Julia (Vanessa Redgrave) is severely beaten by Nazi hooligans at the university.

Name "Mary" by Muriel Gardiner, Miss Gardiner intimates in the introduction that she is in fact the prototype for Miss Hellman's Julia.[100]

Why did Lillian Hellman conceive Julia in the landscape of her memoirs? Could it have been guilt? The heroine of the McCarthy trials, who with such ease condemned those she thought lacking in moral strength, the Lillian Hellman who knew so clearly the right responses, was silent about the persecution of the Jews during the Holocaust. *Watch On the Rhine*, which does not mention the Jews, is telling proof of this. Through Julia she is able to involve herself. In some way, even the choice of the name Julia is indicative of her fantasy: Julia sounds like Jew. Julia is the alter ego of Lillian, the Lillian who never was but should have been. It is appropriate that Julia studies with Freud in Vienna; for Julia is the creation of Miss Hellman's wish fulfillment. Only, pen and ink replace the psychiatrist's couch.

If, as suggested, *Julia* is contrived, then the story must be understood differently. Lillian Hellman needed to justify her past during a period of renewed awareness of the Holocaust, when accusations were made against those who "did nothing" to help the Jews during the war. Miss Hellman implies that only in the 1970s could she tell her story, for she had been on a secret mission to which even her dear friends were not privy. In other words, she did do her share, and *Julia* is the proof. Oddly, of course, Julia's identity is still a closely guarded secret, in spite of the fact that she has been "dead" for thirty years. More important is our awareness of Lillian Hellman's bravery during the war; and that she absolves herself of guilt.

However, despite Lilly's heroics, she projects a weak image in contrast to Julia, as Bonnie Lyons points out: "In Miss Hellman's eyes Jewishness often seems to be associated with weakness."[101] Thus we have the weak Jew in worshipful relation to the strong, protective gentile (although it is noteworthy that Muriel Gardiner is part Jewish). Lilly is a frightened soul in contrast to the fearless Julia.

Within the context of the Holocaust, the relationship is further complicated. A rich aristocratic American gentile literally gives her life to save mankind in the fight against Hitler, working in an underground organization to rescue political refugees (Jews incidentally included). At the same time, while her brethren are about to be destroyed, the American Jew works on a play, attends

Julia (1977). In a Berlin cafe, Lilly (Jane Fonda) gives Julia (Vanessa Redgrave) money that will be used to save Jews and political prisoners.

a theater conference in Russia, and plays in Paris. In fact, Julia saves Lilly's moral soul by allowing her to participate, albeit briefly, in underground activity. In the light of the heroics of her friend Julia, Lilly is indeed weak and self-seeking.

On another level altogether, the choice of Vanessa Redgrave to play the role of Julia introduced a political element to the film. Because Redgrave had backed an anti-Israeli film called *The Palestinians*, the Jewish Defense League threatened to picket theaters where the film was playing. Twentieth-Century Fox refused a request made by the JDL to repudiate Redgrave's politics. Given the extremist nature of the JDL, it is a wonder that Fox replied, which they did, in an overly liberal response, perhaps an answer to McCarthy politics. They said they would not be "blackmailed into any policy of refusing to employ any person because of his political beliefs."[102] In answer to the JDL threat, the producer of the film, Richard Roth, said: "No movie could be more pro-Jewish than this one."[103] Even though Roth was more or less incorrect, the JDL was, in fact, not questioning the film's content but rather Miss Redgrave's political persuasion.

On the night of the Academy Awards, the JDL was picketing Vanessa Redgrave outside the auditorium. Redgrave won an award for best supporting actress as Julia and used the occasion, on one of the most popular television shows of the year, to make a political speech in which she referred to the JDL as "Zionist hoodlums." John O'Connor, television critic for *The New York Times*, wondered:

> What are we to make being left with the words "Zionist hoodlums," words that constitute a code phrase for Communist and terrorist anti-Semitic propaganda throughout the world. Miss Redgrave's performance must be deemed either irresponsibly thoughtless or viciously calculating.[104]

For Vanessa Redgrave, this was to be the beginning of a series of occurrences in which roles she would play would have repercussions because of her anti-Zionist position.

Julia brings to conclusion a series of American films on the Holocaust that began with *Judgment at Nuremberg* in 1961. These films, we have discovered, all serve a specific function both in relation to the Holocaust as well as to the society that produced them. With the exception of *Voyage of the Damned*, none of them succeeds in broadening our knowledge of the Holocaust. Rather, they reflect a growing tendency to see the Holocaust in the context of American society; that is, these films all serve a dual function. On one level, they deal with the Holocaust itself. On another level, they are a mirror of American society in the 1960s and 1970s. *Judgment at Nuremberg* turns to collective guilt for the Holocaust and focuses on justice, very much an issue in the 1960s. *The Pawnbroker* brings the Holocaust into Harlem, where it functions as a backdrop for the black struggle. *Ship of Fools* reflects a trend toward violence and chaos in America and resorts to anachronisms in order to develop its metaphor. *Cabaret* reflects America in chaos, while the Jews symbolize the hope for stability and continuity. And *Voyage of the Damned* and *Julia* represent a period in which the Holocaust becomes a contemporary issue: Why did America fail to help European Jewry?

At every level—daily speech, politics, culture, Jewish life—the influence of the Holocaust is felt. It is part of the American vernacular. The event has indeed been universalized, democratized, vulgarized, and popularized. It is a metaphor for tragedy as well as a valuable lesson to prevent further tragedy. American films on the Holocaust reflect much in American society and contribute to the Americanization of the Holocaust. And by Americanization, we mean the adopting of a "refugee" event by the American public to the point where it belongs to the American conscience—not to be forgotten.

139
Chaos and
Social
Upheaval:
The 1960s and
1970s

Four

Television and the Effects of *Holocaust*

In his article "The Holocaust in American Popular Culture," Alvin Rosenfeld affirms: "The eye and ear remain hungry for visual and mental representations of the Hitler period and apparently are far from being sated." In his analysis of the popularization of the Holocaust through movies, popular literature, popular parlance, and television, Rosenfeld begins with television, for, as he observes: "Television is primary and, with respect to present concerns, one turns first to a review of the NBC docu-drama *Holocaust*."[1] Professor Rosenfeld begins his discussion with *Holocaust* (1978) because of its role in helping to popularize the Holocaust. We therefore conclude our analysis with the same film, the climax of the process of the Americanization of the Final Solution.

Television, as critic Michael Arlen indicates, has become the major source of our perceptions of the world at every level, be it news, sport, talk, or social values.[2] Whereas the cinema is limited in its ability to disseminate information, television offers an all-encompassing world view that is available to an audience any time, day or night. Often, television's position on an issue will help shape the issue in the popular consciousness. David Dortort, the producer of *Bonanza*, seen at one time by 350,000,000 people in ninety-three countries every week, says about television: "Its penetration is total, pervasive and all-encompassing. No one is left out, but no one."[3] In essence, television is a crowd phenomenon: The viewer is alone in his living room but is mesmerized along with the rest of the crowd. Suggestibility becomes all-powerful, establishing, as Gustave Le Bon writes, "the state of fascination in which the hypnotized individual finds himself in the hands of the hypnotizer." Television levels its audience so that the individual, whether intellectual or uneducated, becomes part of the whole.[4] The crowd watches, not together but simultaneously. Martin Esslin describes the power of television:

> . . . not the educational system or religion or science or the arts—is so all-pervasive, so influential, so totally accessible to and shared by all individuals in society as is the world presented by television. . . . Television is the *one* factor that practically all the individuals in this society have in common. It is the unifying substratum of experience. In this sense television—and above all the fictional world that informs it—is a dominant ingredient shaping our consciousness of reality.[5]

In addition, Esslin notes that "American popular culture has become the popular culture of the world at large. American television is thus more than a purely local phenomenon. It fascinates—and in some instances frightens—the whole world."[6] Television has increasingly surpassed film as the dominant communicator of American culture.

In light of this, the pattern we have followed with regard to the role of specific films in influencing and reflecting the Americanization of the Holocaust now gives way to the influence of television. And the show most characteristic of this change is NBC/TV's *Holocaust*. Televised for the first time in April 1978, it appears to have served as a catalyst for a resurgent fascination with the World War II era. *Holocaust* has furthered the penetration of the event into the American popular consciousness and has stirred the conscience of the European audience.

Many of the issues to be raised in this discussion parallel those in our analysis of films focusing on the Final Solution. So, for instance, we have seen how the Holocaust develops from a universal symbol for the suffering of mankind in *The Diary of Anne Frank* to a universal symbol for contemporary suffering in *Judgment at Nuremberg*. In *Holocaust*, universalization implies focusing on the centrality of Jewish suffering during the Final Solution and applying its lesson to modern evil. The issue of the Holocaust as a contemporary metaphor is raised again in this context. And once again we consider the image of the Jew. *Holocaust* offers a wide range of Jewish characters and types, perhaps altering the stereotyped images in order to create a vision of the Jew as an individual.[7] At the same time certain images persist, in particular, those of the weak Jew and his new counterpart— the Israeli. The merging of fiction with history, and the attendant question of the authenticity of the material presented is a point first addressed in *The Diary of Anne Frank*. It becomes more pertinent in *Judgment at Nuremberg* with the introduction of documentary film. Finally, we must deal with the issue of the trivialization of the destruction of European Jewry, one of the major accusations aimed at *Holocaust*. The debate over this matter has at its heart the dilemma of mass appeal versus a more intellectual, therefore selective, approach. This controversy moved beyond America's borders to Europe, where many intellectuals bemoaned the fact that so melodramatic an American show should receive the credit for stripping away the mask of the recent European past.

The raison d'être for *Holocaust* came about as a result of the success of *Roots* (1977). Both programs reflect the resurgence of "ethnic consciousness" in the United States, the strengthening of ethnic identification that renewed itself in American life during the days of the black struggle for civil rights in the early 1960s.[8] *Roots* traces the history of a black American family from its African beginnings through the time of slavery in America. At the time of its airing, it garnered the largest percentage of viewers in the history of American television. Jacob Neusner correctly sees *Holocaust* as the television counterpart to *Roots*, and he writes: "Unstated in this simple equation, "Roots" = "Holocaust," is the idea that being Jewish is an ethnic, not primarily a religious category."[9] While it would be closer to reality to assume that *Holocaust* appeared because of the popular reception given to *Roots* as the story of black suffering rather than as television's Jewish ethnic answer to *Roots*, nonetheless there is truth in Professor Neusner's assertion. Clearly, in recent years, many Jews have affirmed their Jewish identity through the Holocaust. In an interesting twist, at least on the level of popular culture, the Holocaust has often served as a metaphor for the black struggle, and black history provided the precedent for *Holocaust*.

The Holocaust is indeed the source of much of American Jewish ethnic identification. Originating in the "cult of the Holocaust" initiated by American Jewish youth, the movement grew to encompass much of organized American Jewry. Author Elie Wiesel played a leading role in this development. Holocaust study centers and museums were created under the umbrella of Jewish federations. In addition to viewing American Jewry's new-found interest with the Holocaust as "a way of feeling ethnic distinctiveness, of rescuing out of a 'heritage' of unspeakable suffering a kind of collective pride," Jacob Neusner continues, "what we have done is to make the murder of the Jews of Europe into one of the principal components of the civil religion of American Jews."[10] For the major establishment leaders directing this renewed interest in the Final Solution, the goal is "to strike a balance between universalism and particularism, defending Jewish claims of persecution while pleading for a politics of conscience that will protest genocide or the denial of human rights wherever they occur."[11]

American Jewry was easily able to voice its concern about the tragic past, for at no other time in contemporary history was American society so free of anti-Semitic content. Stereotypes were disappearing; extreme anti-Semitism was not a major factor in America. On the contrary, what concerned some Jews was a new attitude: because Jews had "made it" in America, there was no need for the non-Jewish community to fight anti-Semitism.[12] Anti-Zionist attitudes were replacing anti-Semitism as a major concern of organized Jewry in the United States.

Inevitably, the relationship between the Holocaust and Israel, so inextricably bound together, came to dominate American Jewish concerns and has often been invoked to arouse the American public. Senator Rudy Boschwitz of Minnesota, himself a survivor of Nazism, comments: "It's a hard way to obtain support. Yet it is the recognition by the American people that Israel was born out of the ashes of the Holocaust and that many of its citizens are survivors, which generates the support that Israel needs. Only the most fanatically anti-Israel advocates can fail to appreciate the connection."[13] The Holocaust, then, accounts for the importance of Israel and serves to explain Israel's political and military actions.

In searching for reasons for American television's revived interest in World War II, which began with *Holocaust, New York Times* columnist Drew Middleton suggests that Americans feel nostalgia for what they perceive to have been a time of unprecedented unity: an unquestioned evil was loose and the enemy was clearly defined.[14] Since the 1960s, following the Kennedy assassination and into the black struggle and the war in Vietnam, American society has been seriously divided. Perhaps so many undertook "spiritual journeys" in the 1970s in a quest for a peaceful existence. But they did not find the unity they might have craved. Many came to believe that perhaps too much freedom had caused social chaos. Conservative politicians began to gain strength, hoping to influence the moral fiber of the nation. A weakening economy and a shortage of jobs forced students to take their studies more seriously rather than indulge in the luxury of campus upheavals. By the late seventies, there were indications that those born during the "baby boom" tended toward conservatism in all aspects of life, from their feelings about sex to drugs to child rearing.[15] Therefore, in conformance with the general conservative trend in society, television, through World War II imagery, could harken back to a period in which Americans were one and in which harmony more or less prevailed because Americans shared the same goal of defeating the external enemy.

But while Americans may yearn for tranquillity at home, as reflected in television's new emphasis on World War II, they are simultaneously exposed to suffering and upheaval on an international scale. Film critic Andrew Sarris observes in this regard:

> The nationalism, xenophobia, and anti-Semitism that Hitler exploited so adroitly are still powerful crowd-pleasers in most countries of the world. Troops in East Germany are now goose-stepping with gusto, and the Ayatollah Khomeini can achieve unity in Iran only by promising a jihad against Israel. The Chinese have been described as the Jews of Viet Nam, and religious, racial and tribal troubles circle the globe with a river of blood. Hitlerism is therefore alive and well, and feeding on fresh corpses in a bewildering variety of location.[16]

In other words, in a world informed by advanced technology in diverse areas, from communications to military weapons, it is difficult to ignore turmoil outside of the United States. A war in the Middle East, as we found out in 1973, upsets the American economy and has an impact on the average American citizen. Television notifies us daily that the world is not as serene as we might desire.

Vietnam, for example, was the first American war to be fought on the television screen. Photographer Cornell Capa asks: "What did the visual image do? It ended the war. Never mind that it did it by choking you, by making you so sensitized that you threw up your hands and shrieked 'Enough! I don't want anymore.' "[17] On the other hand, the question of the opposite response, desensitization, was raised in respect to *Holocaust*. Milton Shulman writes in the *BBC Radio Times* that "before the advent of television the mere sight of documentary films showing mounds of human bodies in the camps raised a storm of protest. We have now advanced morally to a situation where we can accept such infernal visions as a fictional nightcap." These two opposing notions signify a relevant problem concerning the impact of visual horror in the media as a daily diet. Shulman himself asks the question: "Does the capacity to brutalize offset the good done to society by information about these terrible times?"[18]

With regard to the function of war images, one might suggest that perhaps audiences are fascinated by horrific images, but never bored by them; viewers are not immune to their tragic message. Therefore, the moral lesson of *Holocaust* helps us confront contemporary issues, albeit at a certain cost. *Holocaust* may, ultimately, influence popular responses, so that the Boat People, for example, find refuge in America. But, as contemporary images of horror and suffering are taken for parallels of the Holocaust, they often blend into one giant world disaster. The average viewer equates burning bodies in Vietnam with the crematoria at Auschwitz. Or Cambodian refugees are compared with Jewish refugees. One mutilated body, after all, resembles another.

Moreover, even when transmitting images of war and disaster, television is subject to its own limitations, namely, that it is perceived as an entertainment medium. As James Oliver Robertson writes in *American Myth, American Reality*: "News, advertising, commentary, non-fiction as well as fiction, are personified and dramatized in order to provide human meaning and human impact."[19] Frank Rich of *Time* magazine finds *Holocaust* fascinating precisely because it is a product par excellence of orthodox television: created by veteran showmen; interspersed with commercial breaks; produced according to a soap-opera-like format—guaranteed to keep an audience for four nights. As Rich sees it:

> ... TV's built-in limitations ... can make difficult material more accessible to a mass audience. It is hard to imagine *Holocaust* being so effective in another format. Were the show exhibited in movie theatres, no one would sit still for its 9½-hour running time. Were it produced for PBS [public television], *Holocaust* would probably be drowned in a sea of historical minutiae. By creating their show for NBC, the authors have forced themselves to be equally responsive

to the demands of both primetime show biz and historical accuracy. They prove that such a marriage of commerce and art can bear remarkable fruit.[20]

It is precisely this belief that frightens and angers the intellectuals while satisfying millions of viewers.

Holocaust was among the first popular American films to focus on the Final Solution as a specifically Jewish event. Producer Herbert Brodkin had been drawn to the subject as early as 1959, having produced the original televised drama of *Judgment at Nuremberg*. Gerald Green, whom Brodkin asked to write the script, had previously authored *The Artists of Terezin* (1969, which he seems to have used as the basis for several scenes in *Holocaust*).

Here, it is germane to review recent events that made the focusing on the Holocaust and its Jewish particularity feasible in the eyes of a major television network. For the Jewish community, the Six Day War in 1967 and the Yom Kippur War in 1973 triggered fears of yet another Holocaust—this time in Israel—awakening in them a new consciousness of the Final Solution.[21] The coverage of these two Middle East wars by the American media, followed by the daring Entebbe rescue in 1976 (preceded by the "selection" of Jewish passengers at Entebbe) emphasized the importance of survival for Israel, which had risen out of the ashes of the Holocaust. Given the disproportionately high visibility in the media accorded Israel since the Six Day War, the Holocaust and Israel have been inextricably intertwined, once again reaffirming what following the war and the emergence of Israel had become veiled in universalized images—the Holocaust as a Jewish event.

This new awareness of the Holocaust brought with it many related activities. Conferences are being convened on the subject. One such example, sponsored by the Institute of Contemporary Jewry of the Hebrew University, brought together sixty scholars in New York City, and was covered daily by Israel Shenker in *The New York Times*.[22] The 1970s saw the rise of Holocaust centers, beginning with Rabbi Irving Greenberg's National Jewish Conference Center in New York and a Jewish Federation–sponsored center in St. Louis, Mo. There was an increase in academic courses offered at American universities, as well as a surge in academic publications, including Lucy Dawidowicz's very successful *The War Against the Jews* (1975). Christian theologians, among them Professor Franklin Littel of Temple University in Philadelphia, insisted that churches accept the moral responsibility of confronting the issues raised by the Holocaust. To the preceding we include the rise of ethnicity in America, with Jewish ethnicity, in Jacob Neusner's view, so closely tied to the Holocaust, and we might say that the environment was ripe for a film like *Holocaust*.

Gerald Green realized the difficulties he faced in his dramatization. He said in a publicity synopsis of *Holocaust*: "Neither 8 nor 80 hours would be sufficient to detail and document the entire story of the implacable Nazi assault upon Europe's Jews." The idea, as conceived by producer Herbert Brodkin and Green, was to create a fictional Jewish family swept up by the war of destruction against the Jews of Europe.[23] Both were aware of the limitations of their format yet firm in their goals. Not since Chaplin's *The Great Dictator* has an American film been so unequivocal in portraying what was a core of Nazi ideology—the battle against the Jews. Jewish history is not compared, shared, or universalized. Even the title, in spite of criticism leveled against it, conveys to the public imagination the notion of the Holocaust as a Jewish tragedy.

Since in *Holocaust* the Final Solution is identified as a Jewish event, there was concern that it might be dismissed as *merely* a Jewish event and, therefore, of limited relevance to an American audience. The viewer had to be given the impression that *Holocaust* pertains to him. Rabbi Jordan Pearlson of Toronto, Canada, one of the advisers on the script, thought the answer was to "broaden the base to avoid the usual 'It's only a Jewish problem' response as a turn-off in the early episodes. The facts are there. No mention of projected death of Slavs. No reference to Freemasons, of whom your audience will include many."[24] Rabbi Pearlson, in suggesting the inclusion of other nationalities, only adds a wider variety of ethnics; they do not, however, create a broadly based appeal to the average American. If, as Martin Esslin believes, "the identity of a culture, the self-image of a nation, is formed by the concepts, myths, beliefs, and patterns of conduct that are instantly recognized by the members of that social entity as being peculiarly theirs,"[25] then by necessity, *Holocaust* would have to function as a paradigm or as a metaphor.

Holocaust as a paradigm had to exist on a moral plane. Rabbi Marc Tannenbaum of the American Jewish Committee, also one of the show's advisers, feared that *Holocaust* would be termed a "Jewish obsession." Therefore, he felt, it must function in "raising the consciousness and deepening the moral commitment of the American people 'not to stand idly by' while hatred, prejudice, verbal violence, and actual murder are being unleashed against Jews, and against any other human beings."[26] Toward this end, the Weiss family was created. Gerald Green explains:

> I wanted a real German family, the equivalent of American Jews who think of themselves first as Americans. We didn't want to do *Fiddler on the Roof* Jews, although they were prime victims of the Holocaust. We were afraid they would vitiate what we were trying to do—appeal to a broad audience.[27]

Green did not expect the audience to identify with the Weisses but rather to sympathize with them, to understand that they were not "foreign," but the equivalent of middle-class American Jews whose lives were destroyed only because they were Jewish. The moral, of course, is evident: the bystander—the neighbor—is often as guilty as is the perpetrator, be it in Nazi Germany or contemporary America.

The goal of *Holocaust* was simplified because it fit in with the mood of historical revisionism that was becoming important in America, a mood that was reflected in film. For example, *Little Big Man* (1970) makes heroes out of the American Indians slaughtered during "Custer's last stand."[28] *Voyage of the Damned* (1976) portrays the real picture of American policy toward Jewish refugees fleeing Nazi Germany. Within this revisionist context, history comes to include and validate a search by minority ethnic groups for their own past. On television, as we have already seen, *Roots* established the pattern for this type of program. In academics, minority studies became the vogue—for blacks, for women, for American Indians, and for Jews. Here again, we face an interesting paradox. For the American Indian and blacks, the search for roots begins with a noble past only to end in degradation, defeat, and destruction in America. For the Jews, on the other hand, Europe was the site of their suffering, where ultimately, their culture and roots were destroyed; for them, America signifies regeneration. Therefore, the Jew functions as a true American symbol—in the popular sense—of hope and the promise of America.

Yet, it is in regard to immigration—the failure to allow Jews in—that America is guilty. As we recall, John Higham indicates that anti-Semitism in America must be seen in relationship to immigration. Because of restrictive immigration laws and the State Department's unnecessarily excessive zeal in enforcing them,[29] many Jews who might have survived safely in America were destroyed during the Holocaust. Therefore, in the context of historical revisionism, America's relationship with its Jews is perceived to be a function of the broken promise of America as a land of refuge. This may have been a factor in the abolition of the quota system in the Immigration Act of 1965: new refugees seeking safety would not be turned away as the Jews had been. A film like *Voyage of the Damned* reflects America's guilt toward its Jews.

America has chosen to carry the burden of the Holocaust more than any nation apart from Israel. Ben Halpern has written of the Holocaust, with regard to how it changed American attitudes toward Jews: "Other atrocities have produced revulsion in their time and left their mark on history; but none would seem to have stirred such pervasive, enduring, profound feelings of guilt."[30] The Holocaust, in the American idiom, signifies a lapse of conscience in the American psyche, which may, in part, explain America's embrace of the Holocaust. Perhaps America could make amends for a broken promise. Metaphorically, it reflects an American desire to rediscover its own lost past—a past that saw America as a land of refuge.

History, and its cousin memory, then, are essential components of *Holocaust*. In a culture that renders an event important one day and forgotten the next; at a time when new technologies force themselves daily into people's lives; in an environment in which established values are questioned and often left to die; in a society in which everything is in flux—history provides a source of continuity, a means by which we confirm our immortality. Christopher Lasch identifies the relationship between the chaos of contemporary life and the necessity for history:

> The propaganda of death and destruction, emanating ceaselessly from the mass media, adds to the prevailing atmosphere of insecurity. Far-flung famines, earthquakes in remote regions, distant wars and uprisings attract the same attention as events closer to home. The impression of arbitrariness in the reporting of disaster reinforces the arbitrary quality of experience itself, and the absence of continuity in the coverage of events as today's crisis yields to a new and unrelated crisis tomorrow, adds to the sense of historical disconti-

nuity—the sense of living in a world in which the past holds out no guidance to the present and the future has become completely unpredictable.[31]

For society, then, popular history provides a needed structure as well as values.

In this context we must ask: What role can *Holocaust* play in a society that did not experience the event? What problems does this pose for the viewer? Wolfgang Ernst addresses these issues in *The Journal of Contemporary History*:

> A credible evocation of history by means of film can only take place where there is a continuity in people's minds between the past and the present, as in the United States with its mere 200 years of history.... A film like *Holocaust* ... creates an illusion of past reality, a deceiving intimacy with history instead of revealing the gap between present day understanding and past meaning.[32]

Therefore, Ernst would argue that *Roots* has a logical place in the discourse of American history, whereas *Holocaust* cannot—an assumption that robs America's Jews of their roots. And can it not be argued that much of American history is refugee history? Moreover, since there are no longer viable Jewish communities in the countries with which *Holocaust* deals, it is incumbent upon America to tackle that history because, in fact, it belongs to mankind. It is true that *Holocaust* does reveal a "gap between present day understanding and past meaning"; it does not assume an intimacy with a foreign history. This gap is the result of the problems inherent in attempting to understand what cannot be grasped. True, *Holocaust* deals with history, and on one level this history is understandable as a series of events; nonetheless, at the same time it stands outside of the historical discourse. Michiko Kakutani writes in *The New York Times* in her article on artists struggling with the Holocaust that "as far as some scholars are concerned, the Holocaust represents the first time in history that reality exceeded the imagination . . ."[33] Susan Sontag, in confronting the Holocaust through the Eichmann trial, has observed: "There was a fundamental paradox in the Eichmann trial: it was primarily a great act of commitment through memory and the renewal of grief, yet it clothed itself in the forms of legality and scientific objectivity."[34] In a way, any study of the Holocaust must parallel Sontag's claim: it is a study of grief and terror clothed in the science of history. Even in the context of film as history, of film as a document of history, one cannot evade the struggle between history and the unimaginable. Historian Isaac Deutscher explains the problem of "the Jewish Tragedy and the Historian" in the following manner:

> I am sure that it is not my personal involvement in the Jewish cat-astrophe that would prevent me, even now, as a historian, from writ-ing objectively about it. It is rather the fact that we are confronted here by a huge and ominous mystery of the degeneration of the human character that will forever baffle and terrify mankind.[35]

But since we must deal with the event, *Holocaust* is surely very relevant as a metaphor that helps us deal with contemporary tragedy and avoid future disaster. The Holocaust is the paradigm for contemporary tragic history. In the absence of the attempt to give it meaning—even in an American context—the historical discourse itself is meaningless.

History aims to revive memory. We cannot—must not—forget the Holocaust. At the same time, we cannot remember what we did not experience in our own personal history. For Elie Wiesel is perhaps correct when he asserts that "Auschwitz cannot be explained nor can it be visualized. Whether culmination or aber-ration of history, the Holocaust transcends history."[36] In this sense, memory belongs only to a select few—the survivors. Therefore, history as a metaphor is the key to the solution for the rest of us. If we are to remember the Holocaust, it is chiefly through programs such as *Holocaust* that this task will be achieved. A letter written to Herb Brodkin from the Anti-Defa-mation League in Los Angeles says: "We are indebted to you for having participated in presenting this powerful statement to tens of millions of Americans in a way which conveyed what the Holocaust meant then and what it means now."[37]

Holocaust as a metaphor teaches a contemporary lesson. As America again becomes a nation of immigrants, *Holocaust* re-minds us not to renege on America's principles, as happened when lack of concern for the Jews paved the road to Auschwitz. Or, in Rabbi Jordan Pearlson's opinion:

> As one of the rabbinic consultants who carefully checked the early script with survivors and scholars of the Holocaust, I am intensely committed to everything that would give this presentation the strong-

est credibility and the broadest viewing public. The times call for a confrontation with the issue of dehumanization and there is no greater text than the record of the Holocaust.[38]

Herbert Brodkin, producer of *Holocaust,* was sensitive to the enormously complicated issues involved in the project. As mentioned, he had first produced *Judgment at Nuremberg* for television in 1959 (and, after *Holocaust,* he produced *Skokie* for television). It was up to his company, Titus Productions, to present a completed program to NBC. At one point Brodkin pleaded with Herbert Schlosser of NBC not to treat *Holocaust* like a Universal Studios novel; that no money should be withheld, for *Holocaust* "will perhaps be the greatest drama ever done on TV."[39] In choosing Gerald Green to write the script, Brodkin selected someone already familiar with the subject. As bibliography for research on the script, Green listed as his general historical references such standard works as Gerald Reitlinger's *The Final Solution* (1953), Raul Hilberg's *The Destruction of the European Jews* (1961), and Lucy Dawidowicz's *The War Against the Jews* (1975).

Even so, one can question the apparent absence of a historian as an adviser to the show. Among those who read the script in its early stages were Rabbi Marc Tannenbaum of the American Jewish Committee in New York and Rabbi Jordan Pearlson of Toronto, Canada. Rabbi Pearlson showed the text to eminent Holocaust philosopher Emil Fackenheim, who, according to Pearlson, "read the text and criticized it." Rabbi Pearlson's findings, with Fackenheim's criticisms in mind, were that "the script is powerful and essentially it rings true. The guilding is great. Some sandpapering is in order."[40]

Initially, permission had been granted by Eastern bloc countries to film there. It was, however, withdrawn due to "Zionist" elements in the script.[41] Instead, filming took place in Germany and Austria, with Mauthausen serving as the locale for the concentration camps. There was a conscious decision not to cast big stars in the major roles. According to NBC programming chief Paul Klein, people will either want to see the show or they will not.[42] Many cast members, most of them unknown to the viewing public, were recruited from the New York Shakespeare Festival and the Royal Shakespeare Company in England. Without stars to attract an audience in our society that worships in the "cult of celebrity" (and given the depressing nature of the material), the producers were taking a major risk. For, alongside their desire to create a fine work, they were also committed to bringing in a profit for the network. The choice of cast, then, indicates the sincerity with which those involved approached their topic.

It was the avowed intention of Gerald Green and the producers to focus on the Final Solution. In his proposal for the show Green writes:

> . . . but it should be developed slowly, never losing sight of the fact that the *persistent, unchanging ultimate* goal of the Nazi movement was the destruction of the Jews. (A later scene can dramatize the astonishing, yet verifiable, fact that even when the program of annihilation threatened Germany's war efforts, the murder of the Jews was given the highest priority).[43]

Green's statement might be perceived as an historical exaggeration, but having utilized *The War Against the Jews*, perhaps he was influenced by author Lucy Dawidowicz's contention that the destruction of European Jewry was Hitler's uppermost priority. She writes of Hitler: "He never swerved from his single-minded dedication to the goal of their (the Jews') destruction." And further: "The destruction of the Jews was inextricably associated in Hitler's mind with the war he planned and finally initiated." And finally:

> Even after the German government, its army, the Nazi party, and the SS had murdered six million European Jews, and even when the very foundations of Berlin were crumbling under the Russian and Allied assault, the Jews remained uppermost in Hitler's mind.[44]

It seems that Green conceived the Nazi party and Hitler as one and the same, their goals coordinated. In the script, Dorf, the symbolic mastermind of the Final Solution, says that when the Italian ambassador raised objections to the Nazis' Jewish policies, Hitler told Mussolini that in 500 years he, Hitler, would be "honored for one thing—having wiped the Jews from the face of the earth."[45]

In order to achieve his goal of portraying the centrality of the destruction of European Jewry to Nazi thinking, Green structured his script in what he calls a simple contrapuntal style, the object being "to bring the story down to human scale, to make it understandable—insofar as it is understandable—in terms of individual lives and not to present a mass of statistics."[46] Consequently, *Holocaust* presents two parallel dramas: the unfolding of the Final Solution as experienced by the Weiss family and the stages of planning of the annihilation of the Jews by the Nazi hierarchy. In his original proposal, Green emphasized that in the German characters there should be no "ranting or raving, or foaming at the mouth. The plan to annihilate the Jews was precise, calculated, and thought out ... it was *central* to Nazi theory." He includes the role of the Church in sponsoring anti-Semitism, the participation of Ukrainians in the destruction, and a picture of resistance groups fighting the Nazis yet ready to betray or kill Jews.[47]

Green achieves considerable success with his portrayal of the German characters. They are not the stereotypes to which we have become accustomed in film and television. There are no phony German accents, for example. Rather, the image of the Nazi reflects a popularization of Hannah Arendt's notion of the banality of evil. Thus, Eric Dorf is not bad. He is simply out of a job and so joins the Nazi party. Eichmann, Dorf, Heydrich and others are rather businesslike as they formulate plans for the Final Solution. The script attempts to make "the Nazis as three-dimensional and interesting as the Jewish family."[48]

Nevertheless, the portrayal of Dorf, in particular, was the target of a good deal of criticism. The character was based on Otto Ohlendorf, a handsome lawyer and economist, who during the Nuremberg trials admitted to the murder of ninety thousand Jews in the Crimea.[49] In *Holocaust*, Dorf surpasses the feats of Ohlendorf in that he actually masterminds the Final Solution. Lance Morrow, for one, in his criticism of *Holocaust*, points to "the story of Erik Dorf, a prissily murderous family man and SS officer around whom nearly all the horrific deeds of genocide have been densely crowded."[50] One can draw some insight on this matter from the Eichmann trial. The Israeli government turned Eichmann into the symbol of all those who planned and executed the Final Solution. Eichmann stood trial for the destruction of European Jewry (which, in fact, may have assured him a larger role in history than might otherwise have been accorded him). In like manner, the figure of Dorf becomes symbolic of all those who attempted genocide against the Jews. The viewer understands that this is a structural device to involve him in Dorf's life as well as to expose the Nazi system. Dorf is a fictional

Holocaust (1978). The high Nazi command, including Heydrich
(David Warner, far left), Erik Dorf (Michael Moriarty, standing)
and Eichmann (Tom Bell, third from right), meet to solve the
Jewish question.

version of what Eichmann came to represent; and in this vein, the Weisses are the symbol of the Jewish families who were destroyed by the various Dorfs during the Holocaust.

Structurally *Holocaust* focuses on the battle between the German and the Jew, and in so doing, omits most of Western Europe from consideration. This simple device allows us to follow the battle from its earliest stages. And the details of the tragic destruction of the Weiss family at the hands of the Nazis is indeed plausible. Many families were separated in a similar manner: some sent to work camps, some to death camps, some escaped into the forests. It was not unusual for each family member to have experienced a different facet of the Final Solution.

Holocaust as it relates the step-by-step process of destruction also raises issues pertinent to the post-Holocaust discourse: resistance versus passivity, the role of the Church, the role of various minority groups in aiding the Nazis, and German reaction to the Nazi program. The Jewish characters give voice to a variety of responses: Mrs. Weiss believes in her rights as a German citizen; Dr. Weiss wants to remain in Germany to help Jews who need him; Rudi, his son, wants to resist; Helena, Rudi's wife, is a Zionist. Together, the characters represent the many possible Jewish responses to the war. In so doing, as Frank Rich of *Time* points out, "*Holocaust* attaches human faces to the inhuman statistics of mass murder."[51]

Lawrence Langer, who has written extensively on Holocaust literature, is bothered by the Americanized quality of *Holocaust,* by which he means the upbeat finish to a program that of necessity demands a gloomy ending. To do otherwise, according to Langer, is to negate the impact of all that precedes it as well as defeat the reality of the Final Solution.[52] One can counter this with the fact that all of the Weiss family, except for Rudi, are destroyed. Furthermore, in life just as in the film, there is despair and there is hope after Auschwitz. Perhaps the difficulty for Langer is with American popular culture (even serious popular culture), to which *Holocaust* belongs. It is therefore unimportant whether the ending is overly sentimental, for the film must appeal to a mass audience. Rudi's survival does not negate the fact that almost every person the viewer has cared for throughout the nine and one-half hours is dead; and in every instance we have witnessed the brutal manner of death. The truth is, illusions are necessary for survival. Illusions sustained the Jews who experi-

Holocaust (1978). Michael Moriarty won an Emmy Award as Best Actor in a Limited Series for his portrayal of Erik Dorf.

enced the Holocaust, and they are important for the mass audience watching the film. The ending does not signal delusion
or avoidance of reality; rather, it is that which makes survival a
possibility—hope. Jacob Neusner writes along these lines about
theologian Abraham Heschel's affirmation of life after the Holocaust. Heschel, Neusner explains, had himself barely escaped
destruction, though he lost his entire family. Surely, writes Neusner, there is

> a contrast between the dignity and hopefulness of Heschel, who had
> suffered and lost but endured, and the bathos and obsession of those
> who, thirty-five years later, want to speak of nothing but transports,
> gas chambers, a million abandoned teddy bears, and the death of
> God.[53]

There is certainly no intention here to compare the profound
theology of Heschel with the message of *Holocaust*. Still, *Holocaust*, in its peculiarly American ending, does indeed capture the
spirit of Heschel's beliefs in that it, too, defies despair.

The series consists of four segments. The first, entitled "The
Family Weiss," has an interesting background. In Gerald
Green's first proposal for the script, the story was based on a
lower-middle-class Polish Jewish family named Levin that
ranged from an elderly Orthodox grandfather to young Zionist
children.[54] The Polish Levins were replaced by an upper-middle-
class, assimilated German family, so that Americans, both Jewish
and non-Jewish, could more readily identify with them. In America, Jews are not usually identified with the working class. The
Weiss family, on the other hand, is not much different from its
American counterpart. The viewer, watching the insanity of the
tragedy, can recognize his neighbor. As noted previously, Green
himself realized that he needed the German equivalent of an
American Jewish family who see themselves first as Americans,
this to broaden the show's appeal. Additionally, the change to a
German family allows the story to depict the early, prewar Nazi
anti-Semitic policy. Last, in selecting a family like the Weisses
the script alludes to the dangers of assimilation. For it is their
mistaken belief in the rights of their German citizenship that
leads to their destruction. The remaining segments are titled as
follows: "The Gathering Storm," "The Final Solution," and
"The Saving Remnant," which identify the process taking place
in Europe.

Holocaust (1978). Berta Weiss (Rosemary Harris) tries to comfort her husband, Josef (Fritz Weaver) to offer him some hope after their arrival in Auschwitz.

Holocaust leaves no doubt that the Jews are victims. Only one scene vaguely suggests a possible explanation. The film opens in August 1935 at the wedding of Karl Weiss and Inga, his Catholic bride. Inga's working-class family, the Helms, are juxtaposed to the wealthy, aristocratic Weisses. During the wedding toasts, Inga's father says: "Our family is not so famous as yours, Dr. Weiss,"[55] referring to the fact that Weiss is a well-known physician, a profession that generally signifies position and money. In other words, there is a hint at an economic basis for the German hatred of the Jew, an idea that falls prey to two stereotypes: that all Jews were wealthy and that all Nazis came from the working class. Even Eric Dorf, the prototypical Nazi, joins the Party because he is jobless. Certainly, however, this scene does not serve to justify minor anti-Semitic persecutions, much less Auschwitz. The intent, perhaps, was to show the roots of Jew hatred in the German psyche.

The image of the Jew as victim has two components: his relation to the Christian and his passivity. We have noted that in other films, such as *The Diary of Anne Frank* and *Voyage of the Damned*, Christian themes are important because of the notion that Christianity too is a victim—of its own failure—during World War II. In *Holocaust*, some Christians save Jews; the majority do nothing. Among the good Christians is Father Lichtenberg, based on a true figure, who dies at Dachau for preaching publicly against the persecution of the Jews. Karl's wife Inga sells her body for her husband and finally has herself interned in a camp in order to join Karl (an act that was almost impossible).[56] Oddly enough, it is her child, by Jewish law a Christian, who is one of the surviving remnant.

The confrontation between Father Lichtenberg and Eric Dorf leads to a most damning attack on Christianity. After Father Lichtenberg publicly prays for the Jews in church, Dorf approaches the priest and tells him he is misinformed. Father Lichtenberg tells Dorf he knows what is happening to the Jews. Dorf replies: "Father, Pope Pius concluded a Concordat with Hitler. The Vatican regards us as the last bastion between Christian Europe and Bolshevism." Dorf warns Father Lichtenberg not to let his conscience lead him astray: "You must be aware, Father, that almost to a man, Church leaders are either observing a discreet neutrality toward our policies—or actually supporting them." Father Lichtenberg replies: "Then I am obliged to draw

Holocaust (1978). The series begins in August 1935, at the wedding of Karl (James Woods, center) and Inga (Meryl Streep), his Catholic bride.

a distinction between what Christianity really is—and how men can distort and betray it." His statement indicts the Pope as well as informs the largely gentile audience of the failure of Christianity—an unequivocal warning to the viewer.

The relationship between Inga and Karl fits the pattern of the weak Jew in need of protection by the Christian.[57] Inga constantly reassures Karl of his talent, that he is not a failure at his work. And when they kiss, according to the description in the script, "she is clearly the aggressor—a strong, passionate woman." Inga is the good Christian who attempts to save the Jew, in contrast to her parents and other Germans. Inga and Karl live with Inga's parents. After Karl is arrested, Mrs. Helms says to Inga: "You make trouble for us." And as Karl is marched down the stairs, tenants peek out of partially opened doors and watch. According to script directions, they are "fearful, relieved, uncommitted." They are the bystanders who allow the Holocaust to happen. They are the symbol of the lapse in Christian conscience, ignoring the basic Christian tenet of "love thy neighbor as thyself." They are the people about whom it is written: "For Christians, Auschwitz, geographically and symbolically located in the heart of Christian Europe, suggests the moral disorder of the 'Christian' civilization that permitted the Nazi philosophy to grow in its midst."[58]

The Nazis themselves perceived this failure of Christianity. In the film Dorf says to Heydrich, who worries about international reprisals after *Kristallnacht*: "Few governments will stick their necks out for the Jews. Jews have always been fair game. It's almost as if there's a moral precedent for punishing them . . ." A similar idea is repeated in a scene at the Terezin concentration camp. After the Red Cross pays a visit to this "model" camp, one of the artists remarks: "What confounds me is that no one asks—what right did the Nazis have to imprison us at all? They seem to assume that it is all right for Jews to be jailed provided they aren't murdered." In still another instance, during the Wannsee Conference, 20 January 1942, which confirms the plan for the Final Solution, someone expresses concern about a possible Vatican and Church response similar to the cries against the euthanasia program. Heydrich replies: "No one will raise a finger to protect the Jews." In other words, we have an almost unqualified vision of the relationship between the Christian and the Jew. As mentioned in the discussion of *The Diary of Anne*

Holocaust (1978). A scene depicting Kristallnacht, "the night of broken glass," when German mobs raged through the streets of Berlin beating up Jews and destroying their property.

Frank, the Final Solution was predicated on a breakdown in the practice of Christian principles.

The second component of the image of the Jew as victim holds him responsible for his own weakness and blames him for both his failure to resist and his complicity in his own death. Bruno Bettelheim remains one of the chief ideologues in this debate. In an article written for *Encounter* in December 1978, which was intended to coincide with the televising of *Holocaust* in England, Bettelheim pursues his argument on the danger of denial in the face of destruction—a notion endemic to the ghetto thinking of the Jews. Bettelheim persists in his opinion that, based on Hitler's speeches, the Jews should have known that the Nazis sought a *Judenrein* Europe[59]; and by their behavior they contributed to their own destruction. Several scenes in *Holocaust* corroborate Bettelheim's position by presenting that response as one among the many that constitute the scope of Jewish reactions. For every Jew in the film who wants to comply with Nazi demands in the hope of forestalling danger, there is another who demands resistance. Among those who obey are the kapos and Jewish "police," prisoners with authority over other prisoners in the ghettos and camps. But even their reaction is geared toward survival. For, as one Jewish policeman says to Dr. Weiss after dismantling the doctor's illegal clinic: "Don't blame me. They'll get around to me one of these days." The point is made that it is impossible to judge one's fellow, for under such dehumanizing conditions survival often becomes the ruling passion.

Frequently the Jews are put in the position of simultaneously complying and resisting. Both Dr. Weiss and his brother Moses are on the Warsaw ghetto Jewish Council. As Dr. Weiss says: "I hate this business of deciding who gets so much to eat . . . who gets a place to sleep . . . who will live, who will die . . ." Yet both he and his brother are also members of the underground resistance in the ghetto.

The head of the Warsaw Jewish Council, Dr. Kohn personifies the dilemma of how to respond to the Nazis. He represents the stereotypical Eastern European Jewish leader who tended to compromise with the gentile authorities. His comment that resistance isn't the Jewish way has its basis in fact. For centuries Jews survived by making accommodations. Dr. Kohn is portrayed as in constant opposition to the Zionist response. Mordecai Anilewicz, leader of the ghetto resistance movement, informs him

Holocaust (1978). Many refugees are forced to leave Germany and deported to Poland in the early days of the war.

that they are not dealing with politicians or cardinals but with mass murderers, that if the Jewish Council is too cowardly to give orders, the Zionists will. In essence, according to the film, the confrontation is one between the weak diaspora Jew and the new Jew—the Israeli (Zionist). This portrayal becomes more of a contemporary image rather than an historic one, for in fact, several of the Jewish council heads were Zionists, including Adam Czerniakow of Warsaw. In postwar historiography, however, the general image of the leaders of the Jewish councils has often been one of compliance with the authorities (as we see in Hilberg and Arendt),[60] whereas the Zionists are accepted as the fighters. It is this broad perception on which the scene is based rather than on a precise historical depiction. Clearly, Green did not intend to condemn Dr. Kohn; he did want specifically to call attention to the heroic behavior of Mordecai Anilewicz and the Zionists—a position, as we see, that is hardly a minority one.

Another scene reinforces this appreciation of the Zionist at the expense of the diaspora Jew. Kovel from Vilna (based on the Zionist poet Abba Kovner) visits Warsaw, where he reads his (Kovner's) famous manifesto in which he uses the phrase, "Let us not go to our deaths like lambs to the slaughter," the phrase that encapsulates the central myth of Jewish reaction during the war. In his script emendations, Rabbi Pearlson suggests that "Kovner's manifesto is worth quoting exactly." Yet in the same letter, he warns the producers to "be careful of the phrase 'sheep to slaughter'—it is loaded."[61]

The Kovner manifesto, in fact, gives voice to a most damaging image of the Jew, which survives into the present. Worse, in terms of this film, is that the Nazi characters themselves are allowed to speak of Jewish passivity. Dorf, for example, tells Eichmann that there is no need for violence because, to his amazement, the Jewish leaders cooperate with them. Himmler intimates that the Jews are intent on aiding them in their own annihilation. Dorf says at Babi Yar: "It's astonishing how they cooperate." Another Nazi says: "No protest, no fight, nothing. Himmler is right. The bastards are subhuman." By contrast, Rudi captures the true horror of the situation as he and Helena watch the execution of the Jews in open pits: "No one will believe any of this. They'll say we lied. Because nobody could do this to other people." But instead of emphasizing such comments, the

Holocaust (1978). Arms expert Mordecai Anilewicz (Murray Salem) instructs young Aaron (Jeremy Levy) in the use of one of the weapons the boy smuggled into the Warsaw Ghetto in preparation for the revolt against the Germans.

script gives the Nazis ample opportunity to denigrate their victims.

Gerald Green's script strengthens the Zionist viewpoint that Jews can fight and resist but that weak, passive diaspora Jews usually do not. In the ghetto, Anilewicz says: "We'll teach the young Zionists to obey orders and be soldiers . . . then we'll get guns." During the uprising, the resisters unfurl the Zionist flag from a window. Rudi Weiss is a partisan. He and Helena greet the Jewish partisans with "shalom." "Jews with guns," Rudi comments. Helena wants to go to Palestine where no one can jail or beat or kill them. Rudi participates in the uprising at Sobibor. At war's end, when Rudi meets Inga, he tells her to teach her son "not to be afraid." And even early in the story, Rudi says to his family: "They mean to kill us all, but they won't kill me without a fight." "That perhaps," says Green, "is the moral—if there need be one—of *Holocaust*."[62] The only member of the Weiss family to survive, apart from Karl's Christian son, is Rudi: Rudi who marries the Zionist; Rudi who at the war's end departs for Palestine; Rudi, the bridge between the Holocaust and Israel. The Jew who fights back is the Jew who survives. Rudi is the prototype of the new Jew—the Israeli.

Rabbi Irving Greenberg perhaps best sums up the flaw in the Zionist argument of *Holocaust*, writing in a letter to *The New York Times*:

> . . . the program conveyed a typical beginner's reaction: why did they not resist? Out of sympathy, it then focused on military resistance. But survivors and those who have "worked through" the Holocaust realize the overwhelming force and cruelty that made death inescapable and often a relief; the collective responsibility and the way family and children tied the hands of those who would have fought. More important, they realize that just living as a human being, refusing to abandon family or religion or dignity was the true, incredible everyday heroism of millions who died and the few who survived.[63]

In truth *Holocaust* does not completely overlook the nuances of resistance, for, as Dr. Weiss exclaims: "Wait till you see the children of Warsaw! Nothing in the stomach half the time . . . but those kids give concerts and plays!" This is a tribute to the humanity of the Jews during this period.

The title of the program, clearly suggesting fire and war, met

Holocaust (1978). Moses Weiss (Sam Wanamaker, far left) and the other resistance fighters of the Warsaw Ghetto are captured by German soldiers.

with criticism. Elie Wiesel was especially disturbed because it distorts the meaning of the event. In his words: "Holocaust, a TV spectacle. Holocaust, a TV drama. Holocaust, a work of semi-fact and semi-fiction."[64] Gerald Green himself also had hesitations about using "Holocaust" as a title. Among his other suggestions was "The Family Weiss: A Story of the Holocaust."[65] Yet, given the history of universalization of the Final Solution during the previous thirty years, and considering the film's particular Jewish focus, then perhaps "Holocaust" was a wise choice for the title. It becomes an aid to memory. Through the combined impact of publicity, commercial breaks, and four nights of viewing, *Holocaust*, as the title of a show, becomes synonymous with the Jewish tragedy. When people say "Holocaust," they think of Auschwitz.

Critics of *Holocaust* were also disturbed by the merging of documentary with fiction, not a new problem by any means. Jerry Kuehl, associated with Thames Television's *World At War* series, observes that the earliest films employed the style of docu-drama. There are films about the Dreyfus trial and the mutiny aboard the battleship Potemkin, both of which deal with real events by showing what the camera did not record at the time.[66] More recently, this form appears in novels such as E. L. Doctorow's *Ragtime* (as well as the film), the stage production of *Evita*, and Woody Allen's film *Zelig*. One might say that the so-called docu-drama, as old as film itself, is eminently suited to television—an entertainment medium that provides us daily with living history. As James Oliver Robertson observes:

> The reality of events occurring in a machine which can be turned off at will is difficult to determine. At the same time, modern mechanical media tell stories of unreal, made-up people—heroes and heroines who are played by actors—but present them and dramatize them in exactly the same way as they do stories of real people. The difference between play and reality, between mythical and real person, between an actor who plays a part or a role in a made-up drama (which might well be a drama about real people) and an actor in a real role in a news broadcast—the difference between metaphor and reality, image and reality, is all but lost in the modern telling of a tale.[67]

Thus the distinction between fiction and reality can be blurred on television. What is important is that the ambience of history

Holocaust (1978). Inga Helms Weiss (Meryl Streep) becomes hysterical as her husband, Karl Weiss (James Woods), is taken off to a concentration camp.

is accurately conveyed in the context of what could have happened. According to television critic Michael Arlen:

> Generally speaking a docu-drama is a story whose energy and focus has shifted from fiction to what is supposed to have actually happened. Although the word itself is split down the middle and neatly hyphenated, the weight of a docu-drama is not spread evenly between the two forms. The message of these stories is that they speak the truth.[68]

Holocaust, in employing fictional characters against the backdrop of history, is very much of the genre of the historical film. We must credit the audience with some ability to distinguish between actual historical events and the plot devices used to explain them. In an article on politics and film, Robert Sklar observes:

> In movies as in the wider political world, Americans seem to prefer to grapple with social issues in the context of individual and family concerns, rather than the larger units of classes or social groups— and filmmakers have followed this preference as a dramatic dictum.[69]

And in film the narrative structure—the story—is of central importance because the viewer cannot refer back to these images as he can in a book. It is the device that fosters memory of the film and its content.

Indeed, the question of what is real and what is unreal can be equally problematic in the documentary, or nonfiction film, although, because of its form, it almost always passes for the "truth." Witness the vicious Nazi anti-Semitic "documentary," *The Eternal Jew* (1940), a film that deals with perverse racial stereotypes and the Jewish world conspiracy. Still, its statistics, maps, and facts, which purport to be authentic, are tedious and hard to remember. A film based on history and aided by fictional characters can very effectively relate the same ideas. The Nazi anti-Semitic feature film *Jew Suess* (1940) is a case in point. Using the framework of history, it had a far greater impact than *The Eternal Jew*. German audiences could absorb anti-Semitic ideology at the same time as they were emotionally involved and entertained.

Veracity, or authenticity, it seems, is not necessarily a function of the form in which a subject is portrayed. Documentary can be

Holocaust (1978). Heydrich (David Warner, left) and Himmler (Ian Holm), historical figures in this docu-drama of the Final Solution.

as false as fiction can be true, that is, either can be true and either can be false. The essential element is to portray the historical context, which is possible even in a docu-drama that combines fact with fiction. It does not matter whether the viewer ignorant of history believes Dorf or Heydrich were real. What does count is that he comprehends the reality of the events. *Holocaust* tries to further this end with the addition of actual photographs, utilizing a technique similar to that of *Judgment at Nuremberg* (as we remember, Herbert Brodkin produced *Judgment at Nuremberg* for television). *Judgment at Nuremberg*, however, uses movie footage that is often problematic in nature. It is necessarily either German propaganda film or footage shot by the liberating armies. *Holocaust* employs mainly stills that were not necessarily photographed for propaganda purposes. Sometimes a soldier happened to have a camera with him; or perhaps a Jew had a hidden camera in the ghetto, as happened in Lodz. Nonetheless, the use of stills also raises complex issues.

Susan Sontag, in *On Photography*, recalls accidentally coming across photographs of Bergen-Belsen and Dachau in a bookstore in 1945: "Nothing I have seen . . . ever cut me as sharply, deeply, instantaneously." Yet, she is aware that: "At the time of the first photographs of the Nazi camps, there was nothing banal about these images. After thirty years, a saturation point may have been reached."[70] But even thirty years later, one wonders how many people are indeed familiar with these photographs. A large number probably first viewed them in *Holocaust*. More likely it is those immersed in the history of the Holocaust, already familiar with its photographed images, who are saturated and seek alternative methods for translating the Holocaust into the language of memory.[71]

Even so, many remain of the opinion that authentic photos of the horrors are more effective than fictionalized re-creations. Lawrence Langer concurs with Lance Morrow of *Time* that two or three black and white photos from the camps displayed by Dorf in *Holocaust* are more powerful and heartbreaking than two or three hours of the dramatization.[72] Yet there is a paradox here, for many who criticize *Holocaust*, Langer included, contend that one cannot portray the unimaginable. But the stark reality of the stills does just that: it visually authenticates what cannot be imagined. Therefore, the photographs are in a sense an illusion of reality, a falsity, because they delude us into believing that we understand what happened.

The use of photographs raises moral questions as well. Referring to *Holocaust*, Elie Wiesel has written: "To use special effects and gimmicks to describe the indescribable is to me morally objectionable. Worse! It is indecent. The last moments of the forgotten victims belong to themselves."[73] But if the last moments are sacred, does this not hold true for authentic photos as well as for re-creations? Following from Wiesel's notion, we must ask whether we have any right at all to project these photographs of the victims being hanged, executed, or marched naked into execution pits.[74]

In discussing photographs of the Holocaust, Sybil Milton informs us of the importance of knowing, for historical purposes, who was the photographer, what year was the picture taken and where was it photographed.[75] Who snapped the picture becomes a central concern in deciding how to utilize such pictures. When Mendel Grossman recorded daily life of the Jews in the Lodz Ghetto with his camera, he provided a visual document, just as Emmanuel Ringelblum and other diarists in the Warsaw Ghetto did with the written word.[76] They felt a consuming urgency to record a history that they might not, and did not, live to tell. Using these testimonies today would, we believe, comply with the wishes of the Jews to have their history remembered.

On the other hand, many of the pictures of Jews being executed—including the few we see in *Holocaust*—were shot openly by Nazi photographers or secretly by German soldiers. Given the Nazi propensity for recording their "deeds," might we ask if using these photographs does not become a travesty of a people's suffering. Susan Sontag observes:

> To photograph people is to violate them, by seeing them as they never see themselves, by having knowledge of them they can never have; it turns people into objects that can be symbolically possessed. Just as the camera is a sublimation of the gun, to photograph someone is a sublimated murder—a soft murder, appropriate to a sad, frightened time.[77]

In this case, there is a compelling truth in Sontag's comments, in that the object of the camera's eye, the Jewish victim, prior to being photographed had purposefully been violated and dehumanized as part of an overall plan. Does not such an exhibition

Holocaust (1978). Referring to the re-creation of scenes such as this, Elie Wiesel has written: "To use special effects and gimmicks to describe the indescribable is to me morally objectionable. . . . The last moments of the forgotten victims belong to themselves."

of the Jews in their total and final humiliation perhaps add to the crime? Is there a perverse parallel between carrying out the acts of the Final Solution and the desire to capture these events on film and in photos? This allowed the Nazis the opportunity, even the pleasure, of reliving their deeds, to commit them over and over again at their discretion simply by turning on a projector or thumbing through an album. Indeed, the contemporary audience sees many of these pictures exactly as the Nazis intended them to be seen, that is, as anti-Semitic propaganda or as a record of the Jews' dehumanization and degradation. Are we not then their accomplices?

As it happened, the producers of *Holocaust* found themselves in a dispute with NBC over the use of authentic photographs of naked women being led to the gas chambers. NBC yielded to pressure from affiliate stations to delete the nudity.[78] (Strangely, the stations objected to the nudity because they perceived it as erotic.) The Reverend Frederic A. Brussat, television critic for the two largest Protestant family magazines in the United States, was dismayed at the network's decision to delete the four seconds in question. He sums up Brodkin's and Gerald Green's position when he writes:

> In the context of Gerald Green's story of the dehumanization of Jews in concentration camps, it is entirely appropriate and historically correct to portray the nudity of the victims. For many of these righteous Jews, nudity was the final humiliation.[79]

But by what right do we expiate our guilt by witnessing naked Jews, when, as Rev. Brussat points out in the same letter, it is "in total disdain of the Jewish religious tradition of physical modesty?" This complicated question promises no simple answer. Perhaps it is often best to rely on dramatization. For, although a re-creation of Babi Yar is melodrama, we at least are watching actors and actresses portraying the condemned Jews. The victims themselves are thus spared posthumous humiliation.

To carry the idea of using photographs one step further, we return to the question of the veracity of the documentary picture. Again, we look to Susan Sontag: "Although there is a sense in which the camera does indeed capture reality, not just interpret it, photographs are as much an interpretation of the world as paintings and drawings are."[80] What then does the viewer understand when looking at photographs of the Holocaust? Is the odious nature of the crime—photographing the process of murder—evident? In *Holocaust* the dramatization of Nazi cameramen filming destruction in the Warsaw ghetto reflects their inhumanity, an image generally unseen but crucial in aiding our understanding of photographs of the annihilation of the Jews. An article in the National Catholic News Service acknowledges that "the photographs of the Nazi death camps are ubiquitous icons of 20th Century 'civilization'—how many have meditated on their meaning?"[81] How neatly this sums up what seems to be the inadequacy of the documentary photos in helping to penetrate the meaning of the Holocaust.

Historical accuracy is another controversial aspect of *Holocaust*. Henry Feingold, in his review of the program, criticizes its simplistic manner of dealing with history or, as he calls it, "fictionalized history": "There are . . . incidents in which the plot is distorted, complex incidents are oversimplified and basic facts inaccurately portrayed."[82] Others agree with Professor Feingold in finding *Holocaust* not authentic enough: Jewish refugees crossing into Russia were not set free but were arrested; inmates at Auschwitz did not keep suitcases, family pictures, and music sheets; Jews do not wear prayer shawls at night, as we see in the wedding scene; Hitler youth members did not wear summer uniforms in the middle of winter. And, no doubt, these and other errors could have been eliminated with more detailed research. However, more significant than the presence of what often seem to be minor inaccuracies is the degree to which *Holocaust* succeeds in picturing the actual event. Although the film is a drama, it is grounded in history and comes as close to depicting the actual event as any film that precedes it. One might disagree with its style, but its content imparts the "truth" about the horrors of the Holocaust to a mass audience.

In *The Apathetic Majority* it is written:

> . . . people rarely take the trouble to inform themselves about the details of current issues. Nevertheless, most of them form opinions even when they know very little. These opinions may not be profound, but they do establish the framework within which people think and when the occasion arises, act.[83]

Keeping this in mind, a program like *Holocaust*, with its authentic historical mood (granting that it is not an historian's history) provides historical knowledge as well as a lesson for the future. According to an article in the German press, it is pointless to dwell on the details of misinformation in the production; they do not "detract from the fundamental veracity of the film. . . . The sum total of what was true is far larger than that of what was not." As the writer suggests, even better history at school or stories told by parents are not singularly adequate to the task. "It needs a film like *Holocaust*, complete with the features it has in common with soapbox [*sic*] opera, to try and make the period understandable."[84]

In which areas does *Holocaust* attempt to reveal history? With regard to locale, it is sufficiently authentic, having been filmed in Austria and Germany and at the Mauthausen concentration camp. The obvious innocence of the Jewish victims is always contrasted to the evil nature of the Nazi crimes. Jews are burned to death in a synagogue because they are "saboteurs," according to Nazi parlance. Several scenes depict operations of the *Einsatzgruppen*—the mobile killing squads. Postmortem discussions among the Nazis revolve around numbers and statistics: they "handled" forty-five thousand Jews in the Minsk area in five months, or they handled thirty-three thousand Jews at Babi Yar in two days. *Holocaust* portrays the early gassing operations, which took place in trucks. The Nazis complain of the lengthy time it takes to gas the victims—ten to twelve minutes—and the need for more permanent installations. Dorf is taught the utilitarian aspects of the gas Zyklon B as a replacement for the outmoded vans. Rudolf Höss, commandant of Auschwitz, describes with the aid of a diagram how the Auschwitz gas chambers operate. Several Nazis watch a gassing operation. And so on. Perhaps, as Elie Wiesel argues, this is an invasion of the privacy of the victims' last minutes; but it also serves to remind us of Kurt Gerstein's account of the gassings he observed, including the horror of the Nazis' ability to witness mass murder. In a scene in the Warsaw Ghetto, the Jews speak of transports of six thousand people a day; Mordecai Anilewicz, leader of the Warsaw Ghetto resistance, exclaims: "The crime is so huge, no one believes it." *Holocaust* wants to portray the unbelievable truth. Accurate history, if not always precise detail, permeates every scene. Whether or not the Weisses, or even the Dorfs, are true characters is unimportant, for they could have been—and that is what counts.

In an undertaking as ambitious as *Holocaust,* complaints were inevitable. These included not giving enough attention to other categories of victims such as gypsies, Poles, Russians, and Communists (which would have reduced *Holocaust* to another attempt at universalization). The Boston Chapter of the Lithuanian-American Community complained to the producers about false slander concerning the participation of Lithuanians in the Final Solution. Robert Berger, co-producer of *Holocaust,* answered them with quotes from Dawidowicz and Reitlinger citing examples of Lithuanian participation.[85] Letters arrived from as far away as Australia accusing *Holocaust* of unfairly indicting the Poles for having helped the Nazis against the Jews in the Warsaw Ghetto. Gerald Green was aware of the numerous problems involved, as we see in a letter he wrote to Herbert Brodkin: "I think maybe we are reaching point [*sic*] of no return in these endless changes and corrections. Someone can ask us, what about the Pope? Or what about the way the French betrayed the Jews? Or what about Roosevelt?"[86]

The Apathetic Majority, a study of the results of the Eichmann trial, reports that the less sophisticated the viewer, the less he was aware of the trial. In spite of the enormous media coverage, on one level, then, Israel's objective of bringing the crimes of the Final Solution to the attention of the world might be called a failure. Thus it seems evident that those who desire to make the Holocaust and its lesson part of the public consciousness must be ready to accept, within reason, the means that make this possible, most notably commercial television, with all its inherent problems. *Holocaust* has succeeded in conveying the message of the Final Solution as no other show before it. Is this a positive achievement? Or was the result simply to trivialize the event? Would it have been better left unmade?

Any consideration of these questions must examine the controversy spurred on by Elie Wiesel, *The New York Times* television critic John O'Connor, and others regarding what they considered to be a blatant trivialization of the Final Solution. Trivialization has perhaps become one of the more overworked words in the contemporary intellectual discourse for criticizing popular culture. Sometimes there is truth to the accusation, as when Christopher Lasch refers to the trivialization of our everyday lives and of our personal relations.[87] That is, in the light of too much freedom, the cult of self, the manner in which our leaders approach politics, the shadow of the nuclear threat, our lives seem insignificant. Daily existence is devalued. But there is a difference between this type of daily diminishment (which we bring on ourselves) and the concept of popular culture,[88] which is not by definition trivializing. So if indeed *Holocaust* resembles a soap opera, it is by no means necessarily trivial.

What, then, is trivial? When the process of destruction—starvation, beating, gassing—becomes commonplace, it becomes trivial. When the death of millions of Jews becomes unimportant in the eyes of the murderers and the bystanders, it is trivial. The "banality of evil" is trivial: when insignificant public functionaries, without passion, carry out daily the details of the Final Solution, they exemplify the trivialization of humanity.

It may be that there is too much interchangeability (and this might be the fault of the media) of trivialization and those other concepts that are intrinsic to the media—demystification, commercialization, and popularization. For instance, in a review of a book on conductors, the reviewer considers what might happen were Toscanini to reappear today: He would be on talk shows; they would ask him about his love life; he would be asked to explain his rages or other temperamental quirks; he would be forced to stop harassing musicians.[89] He would, in the best style of the modern talk show, be demystified, or popularized. But neither he nor his work would be trivialized. However, an example from public television, viewed by some as a haven from the perils of commercial television, brings us a program we should treat as trivialization: a look at the new trend (a word that intimates a move toward the commonplace) of "dying with dignity." *Joan Robinson: One Woman's Story* (1980) relates a woman's struggle with cancer. We are invited to observe all: chemotherapy, psychotherapy, "intimate" conversations, even death itself. Joan Robinson was, naturally, cognizant of the camera. Knowledge of the presence of a camera generally forces some kind of posturing on the part of those being filmed. One's inner self is concealed from the camera, forcing one to act, in this case, to "act" out dying and death. Death as voyeurism. Death as spectacle. Death as entertainment. What is the point? To confront death? To immortalize Joan Robinson's death? To teach us how to die? The inevitability of death never escapes us. What we must cherish is the uniqueness of an individual's life as well as his death. In filming death, we automatically cancel the attendant human and very intimate moments between loved ones, moments that were meant to be private. To exclaim, "Watch me die!" only emphasizes how ordinary, how trivial death is in our self-indulgent society.

Without any thought of comparing two such dissimilar events, there is a similarity in the act of "watching": be it the slow death of one woman transmitted into our homes or Nazis photographing and observing Jews executed in pits or gassed in the "showers" of Auschwitz. The more one observes death, be it natural death or genocide, the more ordinary it seems. In both instances, the intrusion of the camera brings with it a concomitant degradation of dying. Certainly, this substantiates a case for dramatization, in which the meaning of life and death can be explored rather than trivialized.

In assuming the role of voyeur at a person's death, we also participate in the demystification of dying. To confront actual images of Jews suffering unimaginable horrors would constitute a similar act. Perhaps Lawrence Langer is mistaken when he writes about *Holocaust*:

> The failure of *Holocaust* is a failure of imagination. The vision which plunges us into the lower abysses of atrocity is not there. We do not know what it was like in the Warsaw Ghetto and elsewhere, to have been reduced to eating dogs, cats, horses, insects and even, in rare unpublicized instances, human flesh . . .[90]

If we could be made to know "what it was like" through visual images, would that not indicate a step toward trivializing the horror? *Holocaust,* in its attempt to confront the destruction of the European Jews—even by means of popularization and commercialization—means to prevent us from devaluing our own lives. It does this through its somewhat sentimental, but accurate, depiction of the tragic repercussions of trivializing Jewish life: All of human existence is trivialized.

With regard to commercialization, included among the complaints against *Holocaust* was the intrusive, some felt offensive, use of commercials. It must be remembered that television is a profit-making industry in the United States. "The commercials are more than a mere marginal ingredient in American television," observes Martin Esslin. "They are in fact the lifeblood

and the *raison d'être* of all the other commercial programming."
Esslin continues: "They are the most costly and most elaborately
produced ingredient on TV and its most ubiquitous element. All
other programs exist to attract viewers to the commercials."[91] In
fact, within this framework, *Holocaust* was an advertisement for
itself. Advance advertising on NBC included some sixty-five commercials—more than NBC had ever done for a single event.[92] In
a letter to *The New York Times*, former head of production at
RKO Studios Dore Schary writes that he appreciates the complaints about the bothersome, sometimes outrageous intercut of
commercials. "But," he adds, ". . . we are living in a television
world which offers us occasional meaningful programs for the
price of being offended by ads for deodorants, soap, beer and the
like."[93] As was brought out by T. Fabre in the National Catholic
News Service:

> The criticism of "Holocaust" on the grounds of "trivialization" and
> "commercialism" might seem justified if the series were considered
> only as another TV entertainment. NBC, the producers, religious
> and civil groups all worked together to make the broadcasts an oc-
> casion for further discussion and reflection by their particular con-
> stituencies.

Mr. Fabre continues: "Far from demeaning the memory of all
those murdered by the Nazis, 'Holocaust' paid them tribute by
touching the heart and conscience of Americans."[94]

In essence, the key to confronting television is to understand
that "in our age, even the members of the intellectual elite are
routinely exposed to TV and are expected to adapt to its level if
they want to communicate through it."[95] As T. Fabre so correctly
explains:

> To insist that the Holocaust can only be treated by the historian or
> the artist is to limit its meaning to a specialist audience. Dismissing
> the NBC effort for not being done well enough or completely enough
> is really beside the point. "Holocaust" intended to bring these events
> to the consciousness of the large contemporary television audience.
> It has apparently succeeded where scholarly dissertations and artistic
> interpretations have not.[96]

Siegfried Zielinski, in his research on the effect of *Holocaust*
in West Germany, points out a functioning contradiction in the
film in which an historical theme has been commercialized while

simultaneously stimulating relevant discussion: "The discussion is wrenched away from its confinement in intellectual circles and placed firmly in the area of everyday public debate."[97]

Again we ask: Is *Holocaust* a trivialization of the destruction of European Jewry? Or is a film like *Holocaust* more a secularization of what for so long was treated as a holy subject? But even on the level of the holy—the artistic and intellectually respectable—the Holocaust is "trivialized" in much the same manner as others accuse NBC of having trivialized. That is, it is popularized, and in a particularly American style—commercialized. Elie Wiesel points out in *Legends of Our Time* (1968) that the Holocaust has become the vogue—at cocktail parties, theaters, and so on. Various speakers, often not survivors, give talks throughout the country relating the most gruesome details they can conjure up, essentially as a dramatic device to capture the attention of the audience. One is hard put not to see the commercial aspect of the proliferation of Holocaust study centers in America, necessitating use of the Holocaust to gain funds for these institutions. Are we not witnessing the "selling of the Holocaust"? And then, how do we respond to those involved in the study of the Holocaust who say that Anne Frank's diary has been overused, that it is not interesting any more? The intent here is not to criticize but, rather, to call attention to the realities and pervasiveness of the American system. Instead of being disturbed by the commercial aspects of *Holocaust*, we must place it in the context of the society that produces it and praise its accomplishments. Clive James, writing in *The Observer*, underscores the contribution of *Holocaust*:

> There is no hope that the boundless horror of Nazi Germany can be transmitted entire to the generations that will succeed us. There is a limit to what we can absorb of other people's experience. . . . Besides, freedoms are not guaranteed by historians and philosophers, but by a broad consent among the common people about what constitutes decent behavior. Decency means nothing if it is not vulgarised. Nor can the truth be passed on without being simplified. The most we can hope for is that it shall not be travestied. "Holocaust" avoided that.[98]

We have seen how the Holocaust became part of the avant-garde in "happenings" of the 1960s. Today the Holocaust no longer stands outside of society; it has become an integral part of society. Television generally offers sentimentalized, middle-class versions of lessons and morals related to history—reflecting the rejection by the masses of the contemplation of the depth of every horror through an act of anguish—each day's living, each day's hurt, every natural death, every violent death, the despair of torture, death by cancer, the horror of Auschwitz. Indeed it would be a futile exercise. For the inescapable truth is that all tragedies have within them moments that go unwritten in order to spare us, to allow us to continue living. This is especially true of Auschwitz. Few of us could tolerate the ultimate reality of the Holocaust. When one suffers the loss of a close one, the agony of the moment is mitigated by recounting the suffering to a friend. So begins the act of sentimentalizing (and we shall avoid the notion of trivializing)—the repetition to a listener who has not shared the experience. Rather than chastising, we must accept that only the few are artists, that it remains for the rest of us to attempt to use the lessons of history as a lesson for the present and a memory of the past. *Holocaust*, in its own way, achieves this goal.

NBC made every attempt to avoid tasteless promotions of *Holocaust*. They spent weeks lining up and circulating recommendations from civic and religious leaders. Advance screenings were offered to Christian and Jewish groups, including religious writers and the religious press. Study guides were prepared by various organizations to provide the audience with background material on the TV presentation as well as bibliography for further study. The Jewish Welfare Board Lecture Bureau sent out speakers to various Jewish communities throughout the United States to prepare for *Holocaust*.

The day of the airing of the first segment, Sunday, 16 April 1978, was unofficially proclaimed "Holocaust Sunday" and was to begin a week of thought and reflection. In many churches and public places, ecumenical services were held. Sunday newspapers, for example *The Chicago Sun-Times*, carried a special twelve-page section on the Holocaust. It was prepared by the Anti-Defamation League, which distributed it to public school children in Chicago. In public schools, colleges, universities, temples, and churches, *Holocaust* was the topic of the week. NBC also distributed study guides to facilitate discussion, as did several major Christian organizations, including the National Council of Churches, and education magazines. *TV Guide*, with its enormous circulation, featured *Holocaust* as its cover story. The *New York Daily News* serialized Green's story. *Holocaust's* pre-broadcast promotion was probably unprecedented in television history.[99]

Holocaust was viewed by approximately 120 million Americans, or 50 percent of the population. On the whole, reaction was favorable. Many Holocaust survivors were moved by the show. One survivor writes that no one can understand the anguish of Auschwitz, yet she thanks those involved in the production for bringing the tragic events closer to society and the younger generation.[100] Another letter came from the 1939 Club, Inc., a group of survivors who dedicate their lives to bringing events of the Holocaust to the attention of mankind in the hopes of preventing any repetition of them. On behalf of their members, the author of the letter writes: "We think you will agree with us that survivors of the Holocaust are entitled to be the film's toughest critics, and their favorable response to the film is a compliment of the highest regard."[101] Reference has been made to Elie Wiesel's extremely negative criticisms of the show chiefly in the battle fought in print in the pages of *The New York Times* between Wiesel and Gerald Green. Wiesel called *Holocaust* "untrue, offensive, cheap."[102] Letters from the famous and the unknown came pouring into the *Times*. One of these, the letter from Joseph Papp, director of New York's Public Theater and an outstanding innovator in contemporary drama, captures the essence of *Holocaust*. Papp's letter acknowledges the flaws in *Holocaust*—its melodramatic dialogue, the abject acceptance of death with a smile, and so on. He also agrees with many points raised by Elie Wiesel and the *Times* TV critic John O'Connor. Nevertheless, despite its flaws, Papp argues: "No one, except an unregenerate fascist, could come away from this series without sympathy for the Jew and hatred for the Nazi." He continues: "These are minimal accomplishments, but on the tube, that wasteland of mediocrity, they loom large." And further:

> Considerable taste was in evidence: It spared the audience from close-up horror, but did not compromise on the bestiality of the Nazi. . . . The cumulative effect of the experience was powerful, and as much as I dislike paying tribute to a network, I think NBC deserves some recognition for undertaking the series.
>
> The series has opened up on a broad front the entire racist issue and its meaning to us today. "Holocaust" should not be dismissed

for its limitations. To do this is to deny its effect, however small, on Americans who haven't heard of the Holocaust at all, on those who know about it vaguely and on those who choose to forget it.[103]

The American Jewish Committee, in selecting Herbert Brodkin and Robert Berger to receive its Institute of Human Relations Media Award for 1978, writes: "It is the judgment of our AJC leadership that 'The Holocaust' has been without question the most effective dramatization yet presented on national television of the meaning of the Nazi Holocaust for the whole of mankind."[104] Writing more generally about television and World War II, *The New York Times* columnist Drew Middleton sums up the importance of *Holocaust*: "Television programs alone can not tell us how to avoid future catastrophe. But they can spell out what it means to live with evil."[105] And film critic Molly Haskell, in her review of *Holocaust,* raises the question:

> And even if *Holocaust* were a more impressive work, even if it informed a new generation of Hitler's evils, what evidence is there for supposing it might do what greater art has failed to do, i.e., translate awareness into moral action?[106]

Herein lies the amazing aspect of the phenomenon of *Holocaust.* Perhaps more than any previous work dealing with the Final Solution, it brought results, both moral and political, both nationally and internationally.

Holocaust has taught a contemporary moral lesson. At least in the evolution of American film of the Holocaust, the event is no longer a universal symbol or part of shared history or even compared history but, rather, a universal metaphor. The destruction of European Jewry is the frame of reference for contemporary suffering; its lesson, a lesson for today. Newspapers reflect this change in their reports of events in Southeast Asia. One reports: "US says Vietnam engaging in brutal activities like the Nazi treatment of Jews"; that the exodus of refugees from the Communist regime in Vietnam parallels the "thousands of Jews in the late '30s who couldn't find an open port . . . who went from port to port trying to find safe haven." Or, an article on refugees in Cambodia says: "One relief worker said that the scene reminded him of Auschwitz and German Jews marching to their deaths in gas chambers." Yet another refers to Vietnamese Boat People being turned back to sea as evoking memories of Jewish refugees under the Nazis. And finally, in an article on diplomatic efforts seeking relief for the Boat People, Vice-President Walter Mondale evokes the Evian Conference: If every nation at Evian had taken in 17,000 Jews, all the Jews in the Reich could have been saved.[107] The Holocaust has clearly become a powerful metaphor for contemporary evil.

Holocaust has other achievements to its credit as well. It conveys information. It answers those who have attempted to delegitimize the Final Solution. Publishers were hoping that millions of Americans, their interest aroused, would buy paperbacks telling more about the Holocaust. They were moved by commercial interest, of course, but the result will be a better-informed public. Bantam, for example, had seven books ready for the occasion, including John Hersey's *The Wall*, Lucy Dawidowicz's *The War Against the Jews*, and Gerald Green's *Holocaust*. Dell Publishers reissued Howard Sachar's popular *The Course of Modern Jewish History*.[108] The National Archives in Washington, D.C. received so many inquiries requesting further information after *Holocaust* that they mounted an exhibit in the lobby of the Archives building of documents recording how the Nazis planned and executed the near extinction of European Jewry.

The Holocaust was rapidly becoming institutionalized in American society. Only five months after *Holocaust* was televised, President Jimmy Carter established the Carter Commission, calling for a national memorial and museum to keep alive the memory of victims of the Holocaust. A thirty-four-member panel was selected, and the commission was officially established in November 1978. It was also up to the commission to suggest ways in which America could commemorate a day of remembrance for the victims of the Holocaust. In another area, generous funding, both private and from Jewish Federations, was made available for Holocaust centers and courses to be offered in universities. According to literary critic Robert Alter, in nearly half of the universities offering a course on the Holocaust, it is the only course on Jewish history or culture.[109] An article that appeared on 3 January 1979 in *Variety*, the journal of the entertainment business, sums up the Holocaust phenomenon: "At home, hardly a week goes by without hearing in the press and on the air, at mass rallies or kosher chicken dinners—about the holocaust, as if the event had just been discovered. Candidates in the recent election campaign found it to be a choice subject."[110] Along with institutionalizing the Holocaust into the American social and political structure, the culmination of its popularization came with the presentation of an Academy Award to the film *Genocide* (1981), produced by the Simon Wiesenthal Center in Los Angeles.

The importance of the Holocaust to America's Jews, along with the relevance of the Holocaust to America in general, grows more evident. For America, the Holocaust becomes a moral imperative: a reminder of the recent past when the country refused to raise the quotas for Jewish refugees; and a reminder to fulfill its promises in the present—to uphold the values on which it was founded. For the Jews, the triangular relationship between America, Israel, and the Holocaust is strengthened. *Holocaust*, especially with its Zionist emphasis, aids Israel by fostering a sympathetic attitude among gentiles. Columnist Harriet van Horne pointed out in her column on *Holocaust* that Christians can now understand "the passion behind Jewish sentiment behind Israel."[111]

The international repercussions of *Holocaust* were overwhelming. Whereas in America this confrontation with the past had at its foundation a moral response, in Europe *Holocaust* brought with it political tensions. Europeans, especially Germans, were forced to confront their own history. So once again American perceptions of the Holocaust were carried overseas to the source of the horror; an American interpretation of the period upset the European status quo with regard to World War II, and again American popular culture became the arbiter of morality.

What is striking about the enormous impact of *Holocaust* in Europe is that in spite of the criticism of American television on the part of Europeans, *Holocaust* was a huge success. A quote from the German magazine *Der Spiegel* perhaps sums up the power of *Holocaust*:

> An American TV series of a trivial sort has done what hundreds of books, plays, films, and TV broadcasts, thousands of documents, and all the concentration camp trials in more than three decades of postwar history never succeeded in doing: It presents to the Germans so strong an image of the crimes against the Jews performed in their name, that millions were shocked.[112]

That is to say, *Holocaust* is the first show to confront the process of the destruction of European Jewry in all its enormity; and, indeed, it is shocking.

In Germany, the airing of *Holocaust* in January 1979 turned into a political happening. The series ended for millions of Germans a thirty-five-year taboo on discussing Nazi atrocities. It emerged, in *Der Spiegel's* words, as "the topic of the nation."[113] In fact, even the decision as to which channel would broadcast *Holocaust* became a political one: it was buried on the regional channel in order to minimize its impact. Some right-wing extremists bombed lines in several viewing areas as a warning not to watch the show. The series was endorsed by West German Chancellor Helmut Schmidt, and, in the end, it was seen by more than double the expected audience. There was an unprecedented telephone response to the headquarters in charge of the regional hookup. Many German teachers required that students view the show as a part of their homework. The last part of the show, in which Rudi, the sole survivor of the Weiss family, is seen en route to Palestine, was deleted, apparently to avoid any intimation of Zionist propaganda. According to Heinz Kühn, acting board chairman of the West German TV network that aired *Holocaust*: "Any apologetics for the Jewish homeland would have been undesirable."[114]

Holocaust precipitated a shock that had immediate repercussions: many West Germans began denouncing suspected Nazi war criminals; Nazi hunter Simon Wiesenthal was flooded with calls from West Germany; the statute of limitations, due to expire on 31 December 1979, was cancelled; exhibitions on Jewish history were mounted, and plays with Jewish themes were performed. There was a large increase in the number of visitors to Dachau. In sum—"the 'week of the Holocaust,' as it is now called, proved to be a catalyst."[115] The subject of the extermination of the Jews was introduced in Germany, finally, by an American television show.

Holocaust was aired throughout Western Europe, where it continued to cause controversy. In France, *Holocaust* was at first refused a showing on grounds of poor artistic quality and historical inaccuracies. It was finally purchased because of a series of protests led by Health Minister Simone Veil, a survivor of the Holocaust—and as a result of an interview with Darquier de Pellepoix, named France's Commissioner-General for Jewish Affairs in 1942, who continued to claim that the Jews exaggerated the horrors of the camps and that the gas chambers were for exterminating lice. Following the airing of *Holocaust*, in February 1979, magazines and newspapers gave front-page coverage to the period, especially to the deportation of the French Jews. Actually, one government official admitted that he was relieved that *Holocaust* deals with the extermination in Poland and does not touch on the French Jews. Valery Giscard d'Estaing's party felt that perhaps the televising of *Holocaust* was not timely. Accusations that *Holocaust* was soap-operaish, a product of Hollywood, were dropped after the screenings, the results of its successful impact. Critics reacted strongly and emotionally. Those particularly sensitive to this painful period resented the "implication that France is being given a lesson from the U.S."[116]

Yet another myth was shattered with the showing of *Holocaust*. In Switzerland, the myth of Swiss opposition to the Nazis was replaced by the facts. Of the two hundred thousand refugees allowed to enter Switzerland, only twenty-nine thousand were Jewish. At the Evian Conference in 1938, Switzerland refused to join any campaign to save the Jews. Swiss police officers sent Jews back into occupied France. Whereas German Jews were required to have visas to cross into Switzerland, Nazi Germans could come and go at will. "While none of this appeared in the TV series 'Holocaust,' it reminded many Swiss of their country's complicity."[117] So we see that in countries like France and Switzerland, and especially Germany, an American television show created an uproar and forced Europeans to confront their past, that is, their participation in the destruction of European Jewry.

Holocaust was rebroadcast in America in the fall of 1979. Prior to its airing, NBC asked three religious leaders to write letters on the lesson of the Holocaust. The three were Rabbi Marc Tannenbaum of the American Jewish Committee, Monsignor George G. Higgins, Secretary for Special Concerns, the U.S. Catholic Conference, and the Reverend Billy Graham. All three chose to draw a contemporary lesson from the Holocaust. The Rev. Monsignor Higgins felt that Christians must not fail to counter the Ku Klux Klan and the Nazis marching in Skokie; that Christians must always aid Jews threatened by anti-Semitism. He suggests that the Holocaust might not have happened had Christians learned this earlier. Rev. Graham's letter also refers specifically to the Holocaust and the role of Christian guilt. Rabbi Tannenbaum sees in the Holocaust a metaphor—for the

Boat People, for Cambodians, for those murdered by Idi Amin. In his words: "The world is in the Jewish condition today. The vulnerability and feeling of abandonment is paradigmatic for what is happening to hundreds of thousands of human beings in Asia, Africa ... in Latin America ..."[118] *Holocaust*, in other words, provokes a confrontation with Christian guilt and provides a paradigm for contemporary tragedies as well. It has made the history of the destruction of European Jewry a part of the American consciousness, both Christian and Jewish. The memory of the event belongs to the American people, to be refreshed annually, to be commemorated in the nation's capital, absorbed as part of its own history.

In a letter to Herbert Schlosser, Executive Vice-President of NBC, Herbert Brodkin writes: "Too bad it doesn't open more programming eyes."[119] But, indeed, that is exactly what happened, for, inevitably, greater knowledge aroused curiosity and a desire to better understand the event—even among television audiences. Thus television viewers soon saw the controversial *Playing for Time* (1980) starring Vanessa Redgrave, which, because of her political affiliation with the PLO, signified the politicization of an American entertainment show on the Holocaust. There was a made-for-television version of *The Diary of Anne Frank* (1980), in which, oddly enough, Anne still espouses the line the writers created in order to universalize the *Diary*, that is, "We're not the only people who have had to suffer. ..." Herbert Brodkin produced *Skokie* (1981) about the Nazis' march in Skokie, Illinois, which introduced a debate on civil liberties in America. And there was *The Winds of War* (1983), second only to *Roots* in the size of its viewing audience. Its major theme is not specifically Jewish, but through its Jewish characters it depicts the antipathy of the U.S. State Department for the Jewish refugees. More recently, there was *Wallenberg: A Hero's Story* (1985), which detailed Swedish diplomat and hero Raoul Wallenberg's frantic efforts to save Hungarian Jewry. And—thanks to the precedent set by *Holocaust*—there will likely be others.

Holocaust is the culmination of a trend that, since the end of World War II, has seen the Holocaust evolve in various ways, finally to enter into the consciousness of mainstream America and to be institutionalized into American life. *Holocaust* views the Final Solution primarily from a Jewish perspective, but its lesson as a Jewish event is paradigmatic for all men. The film offers a variety of Jewish characters and responses, some stereotypes; and its thrust is essentially Zionist. History is its primary metaphor—a need to search the past in order to calm the present. And finally, despite opinions to the contrary, *Holocaust* does not trivialize but, rather, popularizes the Holocaust in such a way that its message is available for all to share. As Rabbi Marc Tannenbaum sees it:

> NBC-TV's "Holocaust" has brought that message—as nothing else has, neither books, nor lectures, nor documentaries—to some 220 million people in 50 countries throughout the world. It is a message on which the very survival of the human family depends in a nuclear missile age, an age which for the first time is able to conceive of a global Auschwitz.[120]

Holocaust warns us. At the same time, America confronts the Holocaust with a certain innocence, for apart from those survivors who came to America after the war, the Holocaust is an event tied *only* to memory. An editorial in the *International Herald Tribune* sums up this paradox:

> The war is over. I do not wince when crowds of demonstrators shout "Hitler" or "Sieg Heil" at Lyndon Johnson or Richard Nixon or Ronald Reagan. This is another continent, another generation, a new world. The swastika is recycled as a junk button; Auschwitz is a metaphor. And "Holocaust" is a television series.[121]

Indeed, it is the luck of most Americans that they can confront and memorialize the Holocaust without having had to experience its tragedy.

Conclusion

According to James Oliver Robertson, "American destiny was informed, in myth, by one central principle: America is a fresh place, a new beginning, an opportunity; it *is* the New World."[1] Indeed, America continues to symbolize the notion of a new beginning, a kind of eternal hope, or optimism. Even today, refugees dream of America. It is in the context of this myth that the Holocaust, a foreign event, a "refugee" event, arrived on American shores to be absorbed into the "New World." After the liberation of the concentration camps, Jewish survivors, not wishing to return to homes and memories destroyed by the Nazis, were placed in displaced persons camps throughout occupied Europe. At that time, survivors were led surreptitiously across Europe and by sea from Italy to Palestine, in defiance of the British White Paper. Author Meyer Levin captured this moving journey in his unique filmed document *The Illegals* (1948). In his review of the film in *Commentary* in October 1948, Robert Warshow comments about the couple around whom Levin built the "story" of his film as they stand silently in the ruins of the Warsaw ghetto:

> The main characters, Sara and Mika, have one possession, a camera: they use it only to photograph each other in stiff poses standing on a heap of rubble; it is a way of saying all they have to say: we have survived. This is not even a statement of triumph; it is simply, for this moment and these people, the one fact of their experience that they are ready to absorb and make use of. Some day they may be willing to say more, but not in Europe and not *for* Europe.[2]

In his observation, Warshow captures the initial impetus that made it possible for the Holocaust to be assimilated into the American tradition: the need to preserve the memory of the event far away from the countries in which Jewish life had so recently become only a memory. America could provide one such untainted environment; so could Israel.

In recent years, there have been several gatherings of Holocaust survivors—in Israel, in Washington, D.C., in Philadelphia, and in Ottawa. According to journalist Daniel Henninger, who covered the gathering in the United States capital, "one sensed a powerful current running between the Holocaust, America and Israel. For them, and one suspects for many other Jews, the three elements are joined in memory, purpose, gratitude and allegiance." In describing the speech of Benjamin Meed, a leader of the survivors organization, Henninger wrote that he welcomed everyone "to the capital of the free world." Applause. Meed praised "the Americans who liberated us." More applause. "Thank you, America." Every mention of America brought bursts of applause. The writer observed that he might well have been attending an American Legion convention. The most sustained applause greeted President Reagan when he said: "As a man whose heart is with you—and as president of a people you are now so much a part of—I promise you that the security of your safe havens, here and in Israel, will never be compromised."[3] Undoubtedly, the words spoken at this gathering, along with the feelings evoked, strengthen what for the present is a triangular relationship that forms the foundation of American Jewish identification: America at the top with Israel and the Holocaust at the base—the three are inseparable. And not only Jews perpetuate the memory of the Holocaust; it is becoming part of the American tradition as well.

The Holocaust has left its mark on America in various ways. Approximately 80,000 survivors of the Holocaust, including several members of Congress, live in the United States. Although the number is small, the Justice Department nonetheless has a staff whose job is to ferret out Nazis safely melted into American society and bring them to trial. Many non-Jewish members of Congress have concerned themselves with Holocaust issues. A bill was passed by the Congress bestowing honorary citizenship on Swedish hero Raoul Wallenberg. As journalist Wolf Blitzer points out:

> It is undeniable that the extermination of six million Jews during World War II . . . has left a lasting imprint on Presidents, Cabinet Secretaries, other government officials and members of Congress.

The tragedy of the Holocaust has generated sympathy and support for Israel and other issues of Jewish concern.[4]

Most impressive is the appointment by President Carter of a commission for the purpose of establishing a museum and a memorial to the Holocaust in Washington, D.C. Perhaps, as Jacob Neusner asserts, this commission was set up as a bid for the support of Jewish voters.[5] The mere fact of its existence, however, continues to strengthen the place of the Holocaust in American consciousness: Holocaust Remembrance Day is now observed every year. James Oliver Robertson points out that "America has a calendar. . . . And it . . . marks an annual cycle of specifically American secular and religious ritual celebrations, which make the year American and which provide for the annual renewal of American ideals and national myths."[6] With the remembrance of the Holocaust fixed on this calendar, the event is strengthened as an Americanized memory within the American tradition.

Historian Yehuda Bauer observed that "Carter's appointment of the Commission and his public observance of the Holocaust Memorial Day . . . stand out as symbols of deep American feelings of identification with the Jewish contents of the Holocaust." At the same time, however, Bauer also expressed concern that Americanization may de-Judaize the Holocaust.[7] Americanization is often perceived in a pejorative sense, as a process that divests everything it touches of its uniqueness, stripping it of its individuality. However, Americanization can also connote the idea of integrating into the myth of liberty and equality. In considering the importance of film and television in creating images and myths, we see that the cumulative effect of a series of American films on the Holocaust is such that de-Judaization of the Holocaust need not be a worry. On the contrary. While the Holocaust has followed various routes on its path toward Americanization, it has, at the same time, evolved from a universal symbol in *The Diary of Anne Frank* to a specifically Jewish event in *Holocaust*. A key figure in sustaining the memory of the Holocaust is writer Elie Wiesel, the first head of the President's commission that helped assure that the event would retain much of its specific Jewishness. So far, it appears that the Jewishness of the Holocaust and the Americanizing of the event can coexist.

Recently, the Bitburg affair cast some doubt on America's role in sustaining the memory of the Holocaust. President Ronald

Reagan agreed to visit the German town of Bitburg in May 1985 and to lay a wreath at the military cemetery there, a cemetery in which are buried members of the Nazi SS.[8] Undoubtedly, the visit turned out to have been a grievous mistake. Beforehand, Reagan was pressured not only by Jewish groups but also by a majority of Congress and American war veterans to alter his plans. The press was unanimous in its condemnation of the visit. We recall the extraordinary moment of Elie Wiesel's impassioned plea to the President not to go to Bitburg, to reaffirm his place with the victims of the Nazis. We also recall that his plea was covered live on television because he was being presented with the Congressional Gold Medal of Achievement, the highest honor bestowed upon a civilian by the United States government, by the President of the United States.

No, it was too hasty a judgment to accuse Reagan, or his staff, of obscuring the importance of the Holocaust. Rather, in Charles Silberman's view:

> In short, the Reagan administration discovered that even an inadvertent display of insensitivity to Jewish sensibilities carried a heavy price. And it *was* inadvertent. Reagan's intention was not to slight the Jews but to pay off a political debt to Chancellor Helmut Kohl by helping him with conservative elements in his own party.[9]

The issue is not one of the veiling of memory but the inability to comprehend just how important memory of the Holocaust is to American Jewry. Certainly, Bitburg opened wounds. But it also clarified matters, as columnist William Safire explains:

> Ronald Reagan, a month ago, had no real grasp of the moral priorities of the Holocaust or the fear of forgetting that prevents forgiveness. His journey to understanding—his own "painful walk into the past"—opened the minds of millions. . . . [H]is incredible series of blunders turned out to be a blessing.[10]

Much of this drama (except for the actual visit to the Bitburg cemetery) was played out before the television cameras. Bitburg turned into a rekindling of memory.

I stress the presence of the television camera, for it seems that today, no event "exists" without its intrusion. From war and starvation to award ceremonies, the camera captures it all for public consumption (and for posterity). It followed Elie Wiesel to Oslo,

Norway, where he was awarded the 1986 Nobel Prize for Peace (a further means of assuring the Holocaust its importance in history) and to Jerusalem, where he was honored in a ceremony at the Holocaust memorial, Yad Vashem. While the *kaddish*, the memorial prayer for the dead, was recited for the six million Jews in the Hall of Remembrance, the cameras clicked and rolled. Possibly this might be construed by some as commercialism or as a symbol of the "cult of celebrity." But more important, the ubiquitous camera—a fact of contemporary existence—helped, at that moment, to strengthen the memory of the Holocaust in the public mind.

Certainly, individual Americans have been influenced by media penetration of the Holocaust but often in their own particular fashion. One issue of the national news daily *USA Today* devoted a special page to anti-Semitism in America. In "Views from Across the USA," the question was asked: "Do you think it's important to remember the Holocaust?" A Catholic priest in Chicago worries that if we forget it, we can repeat it, that in the nuclear age man is capable of exhibiting, once again, the total disregard for human life. The Holocaust is thus a paradigm of tragedy. A black expresses the concern that the type of people who killed the Jews still exist today in groups like the Ku Klux Klan. For him, the Holocaust is a metaphor and a lesson to be remembered in order to ensure that it not happen again.[11] The courtrooms of America are teaching the Holocaust too. For example, it happened that swastikas were painted on cars during a teachers' meeting in New Jersey. The guilty parties were apprehended, and the presiding judge—Judge Callahan—seeing that they knew nothing of Nuremberg or *Kristallnacht,* ordered them to read Max Dimont's *Jews, God and History,* Lucy Dawidowicz's *The War Against the Jews,* and Anne Frank's *The Diary of a Young Girl.* The three men had to return a month later to answer questions about the Holocaust.[12]

Needless to say, distortions are bound to occur as a result of the Americanization of the Holocaust and its inevitable popularization. This is not peculiar to the Holocaust but simply part of the fabric of American society—a society that places special emphasis on freedom of speech; and a society that is steeped in commercial traditions. Such distortions include comparing Vietnam to Auschwitz and even certain memorials to the Holocaust as well. The Martyrs Memorial and Museum of the Holocaust in Los Angeles (affiliated with the Los Angeles Jewish Federation) has a simulated boxcar that serves as an exit from the museum. Combining a mistrust of the visitor's capability to comprehend with an American penchant for utilizing the latest technology and special effects, the exit has been described as follows:

> The most dramatic features of the room are a small sanctuary area and a simulated transport boxcar that serves as an exit. The passage is dark, except for a yellow light behind the slats on the walls which display the names of once-flourishing Jewish communities in Europe. Under foot one hears the metallic clanking of the train and envisions the horror of Jews crammed into cattle cars.[13]

Alvin Rosenfeld, in his article on popular culture and the Holocaust, speaks of the entrance of the Holocaust idiom into romantic novels, humor, and anti-Semitic remarks. "All of its [sic] draws upon the easy circulation of Holocaust language and Holocaust related images, the ready availability of the words and pictures of Jewish victimization."[14] Although this is most surely an outcome of media projection of the Holocaust, especially film and television, at the same time it is a misreading of the images. Crude as it may seem, this is the price of perpetuating the memory of the Holocaust in a free society. We cannot lose sight of the fact that the mission of memorializing the Holocaust—be it via Holocaust centers or the television film *Holocaust*—bears a resemblance to a commercial endeavor. And there are always people who will exploit new images in a perverse manner, even without the mass media. One simply cannot monitor all potential receivers of information. As it is, American society, and society in general, has seen a resurgence in the fascination with fascism and its symbols—[15] this too, an outcome of the dissemination of Holocaust images. The perpetrator of the crimes is transformed into an anti-hero, a nihilistic figure. Elie Wiesel pointed out some time ago that "everyone takes up the subject without the slightest embarrassment. Accessible to every mind, to every intellect in search of stimulation, this has become the topic of fashionable conversation. Why not?"[16] Of course, there is an understandable sarcasm to Wiesel's tone; yet the question he asks—"Why not?"—derives from the very essence of the democratic structure.

Lawrence Langer speaks a truth when he refers to the Holocaust as a drama of doom: Men died for nothing. Though I would disagree with Langer's interpretation of the upbeat ending in America's vision of the Holocaust, he is probably correct in observing that works like the play (and film) of *The Diary of Anne Frank*, the film *Judgment at Nuremberg*, or the TV series *Holocaust* try "to parlay hope, sacrifice, justice, and the future into a victory that will mitigate despair. Perhaps it is characteristically American, perhaps merely human . . ."[17] In dealing with the idea of "human" we confront the paradox of the Holocaust: It was hardly human—yet it was. Susan Sontag has written: "We live in a time in which tragedy is not an art form but a form of history."[18]

If the films under discussion can confront this most tragic history, and perhaps even reflect hope through this history, then they serve a function. The bleak vision of the Holocaust belongs only to the period itself. After Auschwitz either there is hope or there is nothing. American films on the Holocaust seek an answer in a typically American idiom—in hope—that attempts to give some meaning to the Final Solution. There are those who would argue, among them Alvin Rosenfeld, that films are not a replacement for historical knowledge of the Holocaust.[19] Perhaps. Certainly, the Americanization of the Holocaust through film does not necessarily imply knowledge, that is, that the American public has a scientifically historical perspective of the event. Indeed, historian of education Diane Ravitch has voiced a concern about America's sense of history in general. She bemoans the decreasing time devoted to the study of history in American public schools. Naomi Miller, chairman of the history department of Hunter College in New York City, told Ravitch that "we are in danger of bringing up a generation without historical memory."[20] Therefore, we might turn to film and television as a stimulus to further knowledge, for in speaking of German students, *New York Times* correspondent Judith Miller observes: "Film, in particular, is enormously effective in stirring interest in the past and in helping young people to comprehend the horror of the genocide during World War II."[21]

These American films have successfully disseminated images of the Nazi genocide against the Jews to a broad international audience. And with the Holocaust often serving as a metaphor for current events, these films confront contemporary history as well. At the same time, the manner in which the Holocaust evolves in film also reflects the society's more general trends and patterns. The event both shapes and is shaped by society.

As early as 1929, a two-year study on the influence of film on attitudes was undertaken. It was learned that "the cumulative effect of two or more motion pictures on a given social issue is greater than that produced by a single film." Follow-up some years later showed that "there is a demonstrable persistence of effect of the films on attitudes."[22] With regard to the films we are analyzing in this study, images of and attitudes toward the Jew evolve in the direction of a more positive portrait. Therefore we see in these films, if not the cause, at least an aid in helping to create a better environment for the Jew. Of course, many of these improved changes come as a result of knowledge of the Holocaust.

We have seen intermingled with the Nazi persecution of the Jews a host of external influences that affected the content of American films dealing with the Holocaust. In the earliest films on the subject, paralleling the rise and fall of Nazism, the image of the Jew evolves from the European type in *The House of Rothschild* (both in the physical image and in the Jew's overriding concern with money) to the acceptable American type in *Gentleman's Agreement*. At the same time, these films warn the public of the dangers confronting European Jewry, most movingly in *The Great Dictator*. Despite its ambiguous portrait of the Jew, *The House of Rothschild*, which appeared in the middle of the Depression, means to free the Jew from the negative characteristics commonly attributed to him. *The Great Dictator*, dating from the period of the war itself, turns to the Jew as the symbol of good in the battle being waged with the forces of evil. *Gentleman's Agreement*, appearing in the shadow of the Holocaust after the war, addresses the dangers of anti-Semitism.

It is during this immediate postwar period that Jews themselves became institutionalized as part of American society, in great part because of "horror at the Holocaust and sympathy with the emergence of Israel . . ."[23] This coincided with a period of conformity, out of which emerged the play and film *The Diary of Anne Frank*, one of the first international symbols of the Holocaust, molded in the American idiom to reflect the concerns of Americans during the 1950s. It began the process of the universalization of the Holocaust. The times extolled the values of social and political conformity, which the adaptation of Anne's diary parallels in its attempt to see the Holocaust as just another part of the entire arena of human suffering: Sometimes one race suffers, sometimes another.

By the time *Judgment at Nuremberg* appeared in 1961, attitudes were clearly changing in America. The film reflects this. At the same time, the Eichmann trial helped influence the dissemination of information on the Final Solution. *Judgment* deals with principles of justice, a theme that would predominate in the 1960s, especially with regard to the black struggle for civil rights and the war in Vietnam. *Judgment* also universalizes the Holocaust through compared, or shared, history: The Jews were victims among the many victims. Films appearing after *Judgment* use the Holocaust as a metaphor and paradigm to reflect contemporary concerns. *The Pawnbroker* is a metaphor for trouble in Harlem; *Ship of Fools* reflects contemporary chaos, as does *Cabaret*; and *Voyage of the Damned* and *Julia* mirror a period of introspection ruled by guilt, both collective and individual. Finally, television, influenced in part by a resurgence of ethnicity in the United States, turned to the subject with the major series *Holocaust*. *Holocaust* returns the Final Solution to its proper role in history by depicting its specific Jewishness and by attempting to recount the history of the destruction of Europe's Jews. *Holocaust* has proved invaluable in disseminating as a coherent whole what had been a series of discrete images and pieces of information, and to an unprecedentedly large audience. This has allowed the event to find its proper place in the history of America, not to be forgotten.

In fact, since *Holocaust*, many more American films have appeared that continue to explore the Final Solution. Among these are *Sophie's Choice* (1982), criticized in some circles for its focus on a Polish Catholic survivor of Auschwitz despite the fact that both William Styron's novel and the film emphasize the Jewish specificity of the Holocaust, and *Wallenberg: A Hero's Story* (1985), shown on NBC/TV and scripted by Gerald Green, in which the Hanukkah song is in this instance sung in its original Hebrew.

The road having been paved, young Jewish filmmakers are entering the Holocaust discourse, as for example, Laurence Jarvik's *Who Shall Live and Who Shall Die?* (1981), focusing on America's foreign policy, which prevented Jewish refugees from entering the United States during the Nazi period; and most recently, Josh Waletsky's *Partisans of Vilna* (1986), a nonfictional depiction of the resistance movement that sprang from the Vilna ghetto. Incidentally, Aviva Kempner, the producer of *Partisans of Vilna*, claims that it was *Holocaust* that sparked what she calls "her awakening."[24]

Several recent European films were conceived, according to their filmmakers, because of *Holocaust*: Markus Imhoof's *The Boat is Full* (1981), about the Swiss authorities who sent Jews from Switzerland back to occupied Europe and destruction; and Edgar Reitz's *Heimat* (1984), a fifteen-hour West German television series distributed internationally. According to Reitz, he made *Heimat* "partly in reaction against the American soap opera *Holocaust*."[25] It follows the lives of German villagers in the mythic town of Shabbach before, during and after the war. Neither Jews nor Nazis have much to do with Shabbach. *Heimat*, as pointed out by Judith Miller, fits perhaps into what is called revisionist history. Angry over the absence of Nazis in the film, German historian Hans Mommsen sees as its message that "this terrible thing, National Socialism, was done to us by a few brutes called Nazis, a tiny minority who seized power and distorted the peaceful life of ordinary German people."[26]

The latest and perhaps most important European film is Claude Lanzmann's highly acclaimed 9-hour and 23-minute work, *Shoah* (1985), which was begun years before it appeared— and before *Holocaust* was broadcast. Nonetheless, we might recall Pierre Sorlin's notion of "readiness" and say that Lanzmann's film appeared at the right moment. Opening on the heels of Reagan's visit to Bitburg, it provided intellectuals with a sorely needed counterpoint to *Holocaust*. At last, here is a film that honors its subject, they felt. No melodrama; not even archival photographs or film. *Shoah* is art that is memory—of survivors, of the perpetrators, and of the bystanders. Indeed, Lanzmann has created a film at whose very foundation is history. Undoubtedly, the antecedents that had helped to establish the Final Solution in the popular imagination, especially *Holocaust*, provided a receptive atmosphere for *Shoah*.

It becomes more evident that today's images, ideas, and myths are generally shaped by film and, especially, television. They are part of the phenomenon of popular, or mass, culture—not necessarily "lowbrow," but having a broad-based appeal. Because of this, aesthetic criteria, or even the depth of seriousness attached to a subject like the Holocaust, are relatively unimportant in our discussion. James Oliver Robertson writes that "the social process of explaining and understanding is often very different from the realities of the actual phenomenon being examined, the difference is vividly true of wars."[27] He might easily be describing the process of the Americanization of the Holocaust in film: It is inevitable that the Holocaust as interpreted in American film is different from the realities of Auschwitz. Attempts to confront the Holocaust are attempts to know the unknowable. Yet we should not dismiss films, be they products of Hollywood or of commercial television, for they have indeed served a function outside of their role as documents for analysis; they have helped through their images and portrayal of history to imprint the Holocaust on the American memory.

American films on the Holocaust have perhaps succeeded in this where other attempts have failed; they have contributed to the Americanization of the event. If the Holocaust cannot be understood, perhaps it can give meaning to a general public. It may be that the memory of the Holocaust can save the lives of those who suffer, now and in the future. When a Holocaust memorial was dedicated in New Haven, Connecticut, Mayor Frank Logue said at the ceremony: "People are still being persecuted for their religion and color and as long as that happens this monument will remind us to be vigilant in defense of freedom."[28] One hopes, too, that films and television programs will do the same. In reminding us of the past, they may serve to deter future tragedy and suffering.

Notes

Notes to Introduction

1. Jacob Sloan, ed. and trans., *Notes from the Warsaw Ghetto: The Journal of Emmanuel Ringelblum* (1958; reprint, New York: Schocken Paperbacks, 1974), 296.

2. George Steiner, *Language and Silence* (New York: Atheneum, 1970), 166.

3. Hannah Arendt, *The Origins of Totalitarianism* (1951; reprint, New York: Harcourt Brace Jovanovich, Inc., 1973), xiv.

4. Paul Lazarsfeld, Introduction, in *The Apathetic Majority*, by Charles Y. Glock, Gertrude Selznick, and Joe C. Spaeth (New York: Harper and Row, 1970), xiii.

5. Arthur M. Schlesinger, Jr., "Forward," in *American History/American Film*, ed. John E. O'Connor and Martin A. Jackson (New York: Frederick Ungar Publishing Co., 1979), x.

6. Deborah Lipstadt, *Beyond Belief: The American Press and the Coming of the Holocaust, 1933–1945* (New York: The Free Press, 1986).

7. Seymour Martin Lipset and Earl Raab, *The Politics of Unreason* (New York: Harper and Row, 1973), 492.

8. Letter from Rabbi Marc Tannenbaum to Robert D. Kasmire, Vice-President, Corporate Affairs, NBC, 25 July 1977, Titus Files. re a study of the American Jewish Committee on teaching of the Holocaust, and Lucy S. Dawidowicz, *The Holocaust and the Historians* (Cambridge: Harvard University Press, 1981), 23.

9. Alfred Kazin, "Can Today's Movies Tell the Truth About Fascism?" *New York Times*, 2 Jan. 1975.

10. Leo C. Rosten, *Hollywood: The Movie Colony, The Movie Makers* (New York: Harcourt, Brace and Co., 1941), 10, 161.

11. Michael J. Arlen, *The Camera Age* (England: Penguin Books, 1982), 13.

12. For example, Annette Insdorf, in her study *Indelible Shadows: Film and the Holocaust* (New York: Vintage Books, 1983), does include the so-called popular films in her study; but she is more concerned with the aesthetic and moral issues in Holocaust film rather than their historical context.

13. Raul Hilberg, *The Destruction of the European Jews* (Chicago: Quadrangle Books, 1961).

14. The French have seen their history discussed in such films as Michel Drach's *Les Violons du Bal* (1973), Louis Malle's *Lacombe, Lucien* (1974) and Michel Mitrani's *Black Thursday* (1974). In these and other films the themes of collaboration and the deportation of French Jews are portrayed. These films began a period in France referred to as "retro cinema." See such articles, for example, as an interview with Michel Foucault on "Anti-Retro" in *Cahiers du Cinema* 251/252 (July–Aug. 1974); or R. M. Friedman, "Exorcising the Past: Jewish Figures in Contemporary Films," *Journal of Contemporary History* 19, no. 3, July 1984.

15. Glock, Selznick, and Spaeth, 172.

16. The study of film by historians is a continually expanding field. Journals are published on the subject as well as a growing number of scholarly works. Of special importance for my study, especially for its

information on methodology, is Pierre Sorlin's *The Film in History: Restaging the Past* (Totowa, N.J.: Barnes and Noble Books, 1980).

17. George L. Mosse, *Germans & Jews* (New York: Universal Library, Grosset and Dunlap, 1971), 62.

Notes to Chapter One

1. Leo C. Rosten, *Hollywood: The Movie Colony, The Movie Makers* (New York: Harcourt, Brace and Co., 1941), 360.

2. Peter Grose, *Israel in the Mind of America* (New York: Alfred A. Knopf, 1983), 108.

3. See K. R. M. Short, "The Experience of Eastern Jewry in America as Portrayed in the Cinema of the 1920's and 30's," in *History and Film: Methodology, Research, Education,* ed. K. R. M. Short and Karsten Fledelius (Copenhagen: Eventus, 1980), 113–150; or, for a more general view of Jewish films and themes in Hollywood, see Lester D. Friedman, *Hollywood's Image of the Jew* (New York: Frederick Ungar Publishing Co., 1982) and Patricia Evens, *The Jew in American Cinema* (Bloomington: Indiana University Press, 1984).

4. Pierre Sorlin, *The Film in History: Restaging the Past* (Totowa, N.J.: Barnes and Noble Books, 1980), 32.

5. Morton Keller, "Jews and the Character of American Life Since 1930," in *Jews in the Mind of America,* by Charles Stember et al. (New York: Basic Books, 1966), 261–263. See also Alan Brinkley, *Voices of Protest: Huey Long, Father Coughlin, and the Great Depression* (New York: Vintage Books, 1983).

6. John Higham, "American Anti-Semitism Historically Reconsidered," in Stember et al., 250.

7. Sorlin, 71.

8. Leonard Mosley, *Zanuck* (London: Granada Publishing Ltd., 1984), 195.

9. Nunnally Johnson, Oral History, Oct. 1968, from project "An Oral History of the Motion Picture in America," directed by Professor Howard Suber, UCLA, 23–24.

10. This scene, as well as others in the film, was negative enough to be "borrowed" by the Nazis for their viciously anti-Semitic Nazi propaganda film *The Eternal Jew* (1940).

11. See Norman Cohn, *Warrant for Genocide* (England: Penguin Books, 1970), 172–180 (and for other references in this work to the *Protocols of the Elders of Zion*).

12. H. Richard Watts, Review from the *New York Herald Tribune,* 18 Mar. 1934, quoted in K. R. M. Short, "Hollywood Fights Anti-Semitism, 1940–1945," in *Film and Radio Propaganda in World War II,* ed. K. R. M. Short (Knoxville: University of Tennessee Press, 1983), 147.

13. See Gordon W. Allport, *The Nature of Prejudice* (1954; reprint, New York: Anchor Books, 1959), 188–189; and Charles Herbert Stember, "The Recent History of Public Attitudes," in Stember et al., 55–57.

14. Stember, 59.

15. John J. Appel, "Jews in American Caricature: 1820–1914," *American Jewish History,* Sept. 1981, 103–133. See also, for the image

of the Jew in American popular literature, Michael Dobkowski, *The Tarnished Dream* (Westport, Conn.: Greenwood Press, 1979).

16. Appel, 113.

17. Benjamin De Casseres, *Motion Picture Herald*, 24 Mar. 1934, 44.

18. Elias Canetti, *Crowds and Power* (New York: Viking Press, 1962), 183–188.

19. Oscar Handlin, "American Views of the Jew at the Opening of the Twentieth Century," *Publication of the American Jewish Historical Society* 40, June 1951, 329.

20. Rudolf Glanz, quoted in Higham, 250.

21. Higham, 251.

22. Stember, 137.

23. Rosten, 153–154.

24. Rosten, 326–327.

25. Charles Chaplin, "I Made the Great Dictator Because," n.d.

26. See George K. Anderson, *The Legend of the Wandering Jew* (Providence: Brown University Press, 1965) for all references to the legend.

27. Carl Combs, *Hollywood Citizen*, 12 Nov. 1940.

28. Richard Grunberger, *The Twelve-Year Reich: A Social History of Nazi Germany, 1933–1945* (New York: Holt, Rinehart and Winston, 1971), 331.

29. "Cartoon Cache," *International Herald Tribune*, 5 July 1984.

30. Nachman Blumental quoted in Lucy Dawidowicz, *The Holocaust and the Historians* (Cambridge: Harvard University Press, 1981), 133–134.

31. Bosley Crowther, "Still Supreme," *New York Times*, 20 Oct. 1940.

32. Charles Chaplin, *My Autobiography* (England: Penguin Books, 1974), 387–388.

33. Robert Payne, "Charlie Chaplin: Portrait of the Moralist," in *Film: An Anthology*, ed. Daniel Talbot (Berkeley: University of California Press, 1970), 362.

34. Hannah Arendt, *The Jew as Pariah: Jewish Identity and Politics in the Modern Age*, ed. Ron H. Feldman (New York: Grove Press, 1978), 81.

35. Gerald P. Nye, Appendix, Congressional Record, 4 Aug. 1941, A3975–A3977.

36. Gerald P. Nye, testimony, "Moving Picture Screen and Radio Propaganda," transcript, 9 Sept. 1941, pp. 27–44, Wisconsin Center for Film and Theater Research, UA Collection, O'Brien Legal File, Box 187.

37. Nye testimony, 122.

38. Letter from W. H. Mitchell of Mitchell, Poellnitz, in Florence, Alabama, to Ed Raftery of O'Brien, Driscoll, Raftery, 10 Sept. 1941, Wisconsin Center for Film and Theater Research, UA Collection, O'Brien Legal File.

39. Darryl F. Zanuck, testimony, "Moving Picture Screen and Radio Propaganda," transcript, 26 Sept. 1941, p. 990, Wisconsin Center for Film and Theater Research, UA Collection, O'Brien Legal File, Box 187.

40. The Germans tried to hide their activities related to the Final Solution. By late fall of 1941, however, according to Deborah Lipstadt in *Beyond Belief: The American Press and the Coming of the Holocaust, 1933–1945* (New York: The Free Press, 1986) the press had indeed accepted the fact of Nazi persecution of the Jews. In summer 1941, as the *Einsatzgruppen*, the mobile killing units, began their brutal mass murders of Jews in Soviet territory, scattered reports appeared in the press. Deportations of Jews from Germany to the East were being reported, along with stories on the ghettoization of the Jews. The systematic process of destruction in the gas chambers of death camps had not yet begun.

41. This information and excerpts from the *Government Information Manual for the Motion Picture Industry* comes from K. R. M. Short, "Documents," *Historical Journal of Film, Radio and Television*, Oct. 1983, 171–180.

42. Short, "Hollywood Fights Anti-Semitism, 1940–1945," 146–172.

43. Gertrude J. Selznick and Stephen Steinberg, *The Tenacity of Prejudice* (New York: Harper and Row, 1969), 63.

44. Letter from Herman Shumlin to Albert Hackett and Frances Goodrich, 1 Dec. 1943, Wisconsin Center for Film and Theater Research, Goodrich/Hackett File, Box 12.

45. Allport, 63, 74.

46. Robert Sklar, *Movie-Made America* (New York: Vintage Books, 1976), 249.

47. Stember, 84.

48. Stember, 142.

49. Stember, 142.

50. Mark Wischnitzer, *To Dwell in Safety* (Philadelphia: Jewish Publication Society of America, 1949), 260–285.

51. Short, "Hollywood Fights Anti-Semitism, 1940–1945," 169.

52. Pauline Kael, "Movies, the Desperate Art," in Daniel Talbot, 62–63.

53. Ibid., 62.

54. K. R. M. Short, "Hollywood Fights Anti-Semitism, 1945–1947," in *Feature Films as History*, ed. K. R. M. Short (Knoxville: University of Tennessee Press, 1981), 175.

55. It is of interest to note that director Elia Kazan apparently believed that those involved with the film had opted out in selecting Gregory Peck, 'a quintessential Wasp,' to play the role of the Jew in *Gentleman's Agreement*. See Mosley, p. 327.

56. Kathy's statement finds a parallel in the words of Harry Austryn Wolfson in 1922. Wolfson, who held the first chair in Judaic Studies at Harvard University, wrote: "All men are not born equal. Some are born blind, some deaf, some lame, and some are born Jews." Therefore, as the physically handicapped are deprived of certain advantages, ". . . to be isolated, to be deprived of many social goods and advantages, is our common lot as Jews." Quoted in Charles Silberman, *A Certain People* (New York: Summit Books, 1985), pp. 30–31. Wolfson was resigned; Kathy fearful. But, as *Gentleman's Agreement* explains, neither attitude was viable in America of 1947.

57. Quoted in Allport, 313.

58. Kael, "Movies," 63.

Notes to Chapter Two

1. David Bernstein, "Europe's Jews: Summer, 1947," *Commentary*, Aug. 1947, 101.

2. Seymour Martin Lipset and Earl Raab, *The Politics of Unreason* (New York: Harper and Row, 1973), 209–214.

3. Robin M. Williams, Jr., "Changes in Value Orientation," in *Jews in the Mind of America*, by Charles Stember et al. (New York: Basic Books, 1966), 348.

4. There seem to have been differing opinions as to the influence of the Holocaust on America's attitudes toward its Jews. Charles Stember in "The Recent History of Public Attitudes," in Stember et al., 215–216, feels that polls showed that the Holocaust had little influence re attitudes toward Jews. However, it is according to Ben Halpern in "Anti-Semitism in the Perspective of Jewish History," in Stember et al., especially p. 290, that I am basing my assumption on the lasting impact of the Holocaust.

5. Since the 1950s, the authenticity of Anne's diary has been questioned by neo-Nazis. The Netherlands Institute for War Documentation published, in 1986, a 714-page, three-volume edition of the diary, which includes Anne's first diary, her own corrected version, and the version selected by her father, Otto Frank, which is the one under discussion. Otto Frank did not alter Anne's words but rather deleted segments he felt to be private. It is Mr. Frank's selections of Anne's writings that have been read throughout the world and adapted by the Hacketts as a play and film (and TV film in 1980). The only changes in Mr. Frank's version, as proved by laboratory tests, were corrections in spelling and grammar. See Harry Mulisch, "Death and the Maiden," *The New York Review*, 17 July 1986 or "The Diary of Anne Frank," in *Patterns of Prejudice*, vol. 20, no. 3, July 1986.

6. Report of the Jewish Film Advisory Committee, May 1971, from the Community Relations Committee files of the Jewish Federation Council of Greater Los Angeles, Los Angeles, Calif.

7. Victor S. Navasky, *Naming Names* (New York: The Viking Press, 1980), 78–79. See also Larry Ceplair and Steven Englund, *The Inquisition in Hollywood* (Berkeley: University of California Press, 1983) for its history of politics in the film community between the years 1930 and 1960.

8. Howard Suber, "Politics and Popular Culture: Hollywood at Bay, 1933–1953," *American Jewish History*, June 1979, 532.

9. Suber, 530.

10. Navasky, 406.

11. Lipset and Raab, 222–223.

12. Ibid., 240.

13. Navasky, 112–113.

14. Ibid., 118–121.

15. Ibid., 338–339.

16. Ibid., 109–112.

17. Stember, 161.

18. Ibid., 192–193.

19. Benjamin B. Ringer, "Jews and the Desegregation Crisis," in Stember et al., 197–201.

20. Stember, 208–213; and see Leonard Dinnerstein. "Anti-Semi-

tism Exposed and Attacked, 1945–1950," *American Jewish History* 1, Sept. 1981, 134–149.

21. Thomas F. O'Dea, "The Changing Image of the Jews and the Contemporary Religious Situation: An Exploration of Ambiguities," in Stember et al., 308.

22. Henry Popkin, "The Vanishing Jew of Our Popular Culture," *Commentary*, July 1952, 46–55.

23. Report of the Jewish Film Advisory Committee, May 1971.

24. Letter from Otto Frank to Meyer Levin, 28 June 1952, received from Meyer Levin.

25. *The Diary of Anne Frank* was first published in the United States by Doubleday in 1952.

26. Meyer Levin has written two books on the subject, one nonfiction, *The Obsession*, and the other, a fictionalized account of the Anne Frank litigation, *The Fanatic*.

27. Portions of this diary appeared in *The New York Times*, and the rest was taken from the Wisconsin Center for Film and Theater Research, Goodrich-Hackett File.

28. One can see how careful the Hacketts were in approaching the subject of Anne's diary as well as their sensitivity in dealing with Otto Frank, with whom they corresponded during the writing of the play and the film. The Hacketts also gave scholarships to Brandeis and the Hebrew University. Wisconsin Center for Film and Theater Research, Goodrich-Hackett File.

29. English, we must remember, was not Mr. Frank's native language. Letter from Otto Frank to the Hacketts, 14 June 1954, Wisconsin Center for Film and Theater Research, Goodrich-Hackett File.

30. *Anne Frank: The Diary of a Young Girl* (1952: New York: Pocket Books Edition, 1959), 184.

31. Acting version of the play, Wisconsin Center for Film and Theater Research, Goodrich-Hackett File.

32. Several people have pointed out that in Lillian Hellman's memoir, "Julia" (in *Pentimento*), when Lilly asks Julia who the money she has smuggled into Germany is for, Julia includes Catholics and Communists along with Jews (see, for example, Sidra Ezrahi, *Not By Words Alone* (Chicago: University of Chicago Press, 1980). "Julia" was written much later than the *Diary*, and there is a question as to the authenticity of "Julia." Nonetheless, it is interesting to contemplate.

33. Wisconsin Center for Film and Theater Research, Goodrich-Hackett File.

34. Letter from the Hacketts to Otto Frank, 3 July 1956, Wisconsin Center for Film and Theater Research, Goodrich-Hackett File.

35. Letter from Otto Frank to the Hacketts, 9 Nov. 1955, Wisconsin Center for Film and Theater Research, Goodrich-Hackett File.

36. Letter from Margaret Scaltiel to Leah Salisbury, 25 Sept. 1957, Wisconsin Center for Film and Theater Research, Goodrich-Hackett File.

37. Letter from Leah Salisbury to the Hacketts, 10 Jan. 1957, Wisconsin Center for Film and Theater Research, Goodrich-Hackett File.

38. The Goodrich-Hackett File includes the record of the litigation proceedings as well as letters from Levin requesting consideration of his daughter, Dominique, to star as Anne in the film version of the *Diary*.

Levin intimated he would be willing to stop his litigation if Dominique were to get the role. George Stevens refused his "offer." Levin, incidentally, was involved in another court case because he was unhappy with the results of the dramatization and filming of his novel *Compulsion.*

39. Letter from John Stone to George Stevens, 23 Dec. 1957, Wisconsin Center for Film and Theater Research, Goodrich-Hackett File.

40. Quoted in a San Francisco newspaper, 10 Feb. 1959.

41. Letter from Frances Goodrich to Otto Frank, 22 Feb. 1959, Wisconsin Center for Film and Theater Research, Goodrich-Hackett File.

42. Letter from the Hacketts to Rabbi Max Nussbaum, 8 Aug. 1959, Wisconsin Center for Film and Theater Research, Goodrich-Hackett File.

43. See also Lawrence Langer, "The Americanization of the Holocaust on Stage and Screen," in *From Hester Street to Hollywood,* ed. Sarah Blacher Cohen (Bloomington: Indiana University Press, 1983). Langer bases his notion of Americanization on the upbeat ending common in American popular culture.

44. *Variety,* "How 'Cheerful' is Anne Frank?" 1 Apr. 1959.

45. Bruno Bettelheim, "The Ignored Lesson of Anne Frank," *Harper's Magazine,* Nov. 1960, 45–46. See also Bettelheim, *The Informed Heart* (Great Britain: Paladin, 1970).

46. See Judith E. Doneson, "The Jew as a Female Figure in Holocaust Film," *Shoah: A Review of Holocaust Studies and Commemorations* 1, no. 1, 1978, 12. This theme is a common one in many films on the Holocaust, American and otherwise, and in light of Jewish history, a logical one.

47. Stember, 171–195.

48. French agent Margaret Scaltiel, in a letter to the Hacketts of 3 Sept. 1957 concerning corrections for the French version of the play, pointed out that Albert Camus, who had read and liked the play, found this particular scene unsympathetic to the Jewish characters. Wisconsin Center for Film and Theater Research, Goodrich-Hackett File.

49. Bettelheim, "The Ignored Lesson of Anne Frank."

50. Pierre Sorlin, *The Film in History: Restaging the Past* (Totowa, N.J.: Barnes and Noble Books, 1980), 21.

51. Kermit Bloomgarden notes to the Hacketts, 9 Sept. 1954, Wisconsin Center for Film and Theater Research, Bloomgarden File, Box 5, Folder 2.

52. Letter from Otto Frank to a Mr. Ecker, 27 Feb. 1956, Wisconsin Center for Film and Theater Research, Goodrich-Hackett File.

53. Letter from Otto Frank to the Hacketts, 10 Oct. 1959, Wisconsin Center for Film and Theater Research, Goodrich-Hackett File.

54. Letter from Mrs. Charlotte Pfeffer to the Hacketts, 8 Apr. 1957, Wisconsin Center for Film and Theater Research, Goodrich-Hackett File.

55. Letter from the Hacketts to Mrs. Charlotte Pfeffer, 25 Apr. 1957, Wisconsin Center for Film and Theater Research, Goodrich-Hackett File.

56. André Maurois, *L'Avant Scène,* n.d.

57. Letter from Louis de Jong to George Stevens, 20 Apr. 1959,

Wisconsin Center for Film and Theater Research, Goodrich-Hackett File.

58. Sorlin, 64.

Notes to Chapter Three

1. Morris Dickstein, "Cold War Blues: Notes on the Culture of the Fifties," in *Writers and Politics*, ed. Edith Kurzweil and William Phillips (Boston: Routledge and Kegan Paul, 1983), 288–289.

2. Christopher Lasch, *The Culture of Narcissism* (New York: W. W. Norton and Co., Inc., 1978), 148.

3. Elie Wiesel, *One Generation After* (New York: Random House, 1970), 172.

4. Lawrence Langer, "The Americanization of the Holocaust on Stage and Screen," in *From Hester Street to Hollywood*, ed. Sarah Blacher Cohen (Bloomington: Indiana University Press, 1983), 224.

5. Letter from Dalton Trumbo to Gov. Edmund Brown of California, 27 Apr. 1960, Wisconsin Center for Film and Theater Research, Trumbo File.

6. Bruno Bettelheim, "Freedom from Ghetto Thinking," *Midstream*, Spring 1962.

7. Ibid., 24–25.

8. Martha Ackelsberg et al., "Pride, Prejudice and Politics: Jewish Jews on the American Left," *Response*, Autumn 1982, 10.

9. Ibid., 12.

10. Jacob Neusner, *Stranger at Home: "The Holocaust," Zionism, and American Judaism* (Chicago: University of Chicago Press, 1981), 79.

11. Gertrude J. Selznick and Stephen Steinberg, *The Tenacity of Prejudice* (New York: Harper Torchbook, Harper and Row, 1971), 104, 34–35.

12. Alan Spiegel, "A Typology of the Jew in the Contemporary American Film," in Sarah Blacher Cohen.

13. Ben Halpern, "Anti-Semitism in the Perspective of Jewish History," in *Jews in the Minds of America*, by Charles Herbert Stember et al. (New York: Basic Books, 1966), 297.

14. Charles Herbert Stember, "The Recent History of Public Attitudes," in Stember et al., 64, 66–67. According to Lipset and Raab in *The Politics of Unreason* (New York: Harper and Row, 1973), the potential for adhering to stereotypes is very strong, and Americans did not undergo any great ideological changes because of Hitler. Aided, however, by the process of Americanization and an improved popular image of the Jew in film and TV, Stember's assessment seems valid.

15. Stember, 194.

16. Susan Sontag, "Reflections on the Deputy," in *Against Interpretation* (New York: Delta Books, Dell Publishing Co., 1966).

17. Most of my information on the Eichmann trial comes from Charles Y. Glock, Gertrude Selznick, and Joe C. Spaeth, *The Apathetic Majority* (New York: Harper and Row, 1970), and Stember, 193–195.

18. Glock, Selznick, and Spaeth, 167–168.

19. Murray Schumach, "Hollywood Trial," *New York Times*, 30 Apr. 1961.

20. *Variety*, 8 Mar. 1961.

21. Abby Mann, foreword to published screenplay of *Judgment at Nuremberg*, Aug. 1961.

22. Pierre Sorlin, *The Film in History: Restaging the Past* (Totowa, N.J.: Barnes and Noble Books, 1980), 44.

23. Quoted in Pauline Kael, *Kiss Kiss Bang Bang* (New York: Bantam Books, 1969), 255.

24. Hollis Alpert, *Saturday Review*, 2 Dec. 1961, 43.

25. Stanley Kramer, *The American Film Institute: Dialogue on Film*, 2, no. 9, July 1973, from Stanley Kramer Collection, Department of Special Collections, University Research Library, UCLA, Box 255.

26. Lasch, 21.

27. Glock, Selznick, and Spaeth, 28.

28. Quotes are taken from the film and the final revised script, 7 July 1961, Stanley Kramer Collection, Department of Special Collections, University Research Library, UCLA.

29. Telford Taylor, "Large Questions in the Eichmann Case," *New York Times Magazine*, 22 Jan. 1961, 111.

30. Harry Golden, *Carolina Israelite* (n.d., 1961).

31. Stanley Kramer interviewed by Alberto Shatowsky in *Nanchete*, Stanley Kramer Collection, Department of Special Collections, University Research Library, UCLA, Box 38, publicity folder.

32. Raul Hilberg, *The Destruction of the European Jews* (Chicago: Quadrangle Books, 1961), 110–111.

33. Memo from Gunther Schiff on his conversation with Judge James Brand, 22 Feb. 1961, Stanley Kramer Collection, Department of Special Collections, University Research Library, UCLA.

34. Letter from Gershom Scholem to Hannah Arendt, 23 June 1963, in Hannah Arendt, *The Jew as Pariah*, ed. Ron H. Feldman (New York: Grove Press, 1978), 241.

35. Lucy S. Dawidowicz, "Visualizing the Warsaw Ghetto: Nazi Images of the Jews Refiltered by the BBC," *Shoah: A Review of Holocaust Studies and Commemorations*, 1, no. 1, 1978, 5–6, 17–18. Also, the death camps in the East (Poland) were liberated by Russian troops. Recently, two West German film makers, Bengt and Irmgard von Zur Muehlen, discovered footage in Russian archives and compiled two documentary films: *The Liberation of Auschwitz* (1986) and *Majdanek 1944—Victims and Criminals* (1986). The narration in *The Liberation of Auschwitz* tends to universalize the victims throughout: Jews, Poles, Yugoslavs, and other nationalities were destroyed in Auschwitz.

36. Letter from Gunther Schiff to Telford Taylor, 28 Feb. 1961, Kramer Collection, Box 39. Judge Brand, incidentally, concurs with Taylor's view in Brand's letter to Gunther Schiff of 7 Mar. 1961. Stanley Kramer Collection, Department of Special Collections, University Research Library, UCLA.

37. Sorlin, 21.

38. Publicity memo to Fred Goldberg from Myer P. Beck, 14 Aug. 1961, Stanley Kramer Collection, Department of Special Collections, University Research Library, UCLA.

39. From Myer P. Beck, notes of meeting held in United Artists boardroom, 5 June 1961, Stanley Kramer Collection, Department of Special Collections, University Research Library, UCLA, Box 39.

40. From the speech of Mayor Willy Brandt in Kongress Halle, 14 Dec. 1961, Stanley Kramer Collection, Department of Special Collections, University Research Library, UCLA.

41. Nathan Broch, *Los Angeles Mirror*, 25 Dec. 1961.

42. Harold Myers, "Emotional 'Nuremberg' Premier," *Variety*, 20 Dec. 1961.

43. Letter from Michael Musmanno to Stanley Kramer, n.d., Stanley Kramer Collection, Department of Special Collections, University Research Library, UCLA.

44. Lee Belser, *Los Angeles Mirror*, 15 Dec. 1961.

45. UA Publicity Release, n.d., Stanley Kramer Collection, Department of Special Collections, University Research Library, UCLA, Box 38.

46. Eleanor Roosevelt, "Nuremberg Revisited," *New York Post*, 2 Nov. 1961.

47. Letter to Stanley Kramer from Senator Jacob Javits, 25 Apr. 1962, Stanley Kramer Collection, Department of Special Collections, University Research Library, UCLA, Box 36.

48. Kael, *Kiss Kiss Bang Bang*, 256.

49. Andrew Sarris, "Notes on the Fascination of Fascism," *Village Voice*, 30 Jan. 1978, 33.

50. Morris Dickstein, "Black Humor and History," in Gerald Howard, ed., *The Sixties* (New York: Washington Square Press publication of Pocket Books, 1982), 272–292.

51. Susan Sontag, *Against Interpretation*, 265–267. Gerald Howard writes in *The Sixties*: "Despite the fact that Happenings were often elaborate put-ons or near-physical assaults on the audience, they were quite the rage in the early Sixties with the well-heeled art crowds . . ." 267.

52. Richard Walton, "Kennedy Remembered," *Newsweek*, 28 Nov. 1983.

53. Susan Sontag, "Going to the Theatre, etc.," in *Against Interpretation.*

54. Selznick and Steinberg, 117, 131.

55. For a general picture of events and culture of the 1960s, I referred to William L. O'Neill, *Coming Apart* (New York: Quadrangle Books, The New York Times Book Co., 1978).

56. Abby Mann, Speech at Temple Israel of Hollywood, 22 Feb. 1965, University of Southern California, Archives of Performing Arts, Mann Collection.

57. *Boxoffice*, 26 Apr. 1965.

58. Bosley Crowther, *New York Times*, 2 May 1965.

59. Penelope Gilliat, *The Observer Weekend*, 16 Oct. 1966.

60. Bosley Crowther, *New York Times*, 2 May 1965.

61. Judith E. Doneson, "The Jew as a Female Figure in Holocaust Film," *Shoah: A Review of Holocaust Studies and Commemorations*, 1, no. 1, 1978, 12. Bruno Bettelheim would see this image as a reflection of the Jews' ghetto thinking.

62. Pauline Kael, in her scathing article on Stanley Kramer, Abby Mann, and *Ship of Fools*, writes on the film's message and lumps it together with a wave of works in fiction, theater, and movies that deal in platitudes about the responsibility people must share for evil. As Miss

Kael views it: ". . . this inane, lofty it-tolls-for-thee-ism is taking its toll on our good sense." *Kiss Kiss Bang Bang*, 259.

63. Abby Mann, Oral History, interviewed by Stephen Farber, from project "An Oral History of the Motion Picture in America," directed by Professor Howard Suber, UCLA, 1968–1969, 5.

64. Letter from Katherine Anne Porter to Stanley Kramer, 28 July 1964, Stanley Kramer Collection, Department of Special Collections, University Research Library, UCLA, Box 75.

65. Letter from Abby Mann to Allen Rivkin, 23 Dec. 1964, University of Southern California Theater Arts Library, Archives of Performing Arts, Mann Collection.

66. Bettelheim, "Freedom from Ghetto Thinking," 19.

67. Kael, *Kiss Kiss Bang Bang*, 260.

68. *Variety*, 11 May 1965.

69. Seth Cagin and Philip Dray, *Hollywood Films of the Seventies* (New York: Harper and Row, 1984), 22.

70. James A. Sleeper, "The Case for Religious Radicalism," in *The New Jews*, ed. James A. Sleeper and Alan Mintz (New York: Vintage Books, 1970), 50.

71. Robert Brustein, *Revolution As Theater* (New York: Liveright, 1971), 78–79.

72. Sarris, 36.

73. Barbara Rose, "Protest in Art," in Kurzweil and Phillips, 240.

74. *Time*, 24 Dec. 1973.

75. Morton Keller, "Jews and the Character of American Life Since 1930," in Stember et al., 270–271.

76. Patricia Erens has done a good deal of work on the image of the Jew in American films. See, for example, "Gangsters, Vampires, and J.A.P.'s: The Jew Surfaces in American Movies," *The Journal of Popular Film* 4, no. 3, 1975, and, more recently, *The Jew in American Cinema* (Bloomington: Indiana University Press, 1984).

77. Tom Tugend, "Hollywood, The Gilded Ghetto," *Jewish Chronicle*, 22 Nov. 1974.

78. Letter dictated by Dore Schary, 15 Aug. 1972, Jewish Film Advisory Committee Files.

79. From minutes, Special Committee Meeting, 20 May 1971, Jewish Film Advisory Committee Files.

80. Quoted from letter to Martin Gang from Charles Posner, 4 Feb. 1971, Jewish Film Advisory Committee Files.

81. Lasch, 68.

82. Cagin and Dray, 161.

83. Interview with Bob Fosse by Lil Picard in *Inter/view*, Mar. 1972.

84. Barbara Rose, 246 and 238.

85. Picard.

86. Stephen Farber, *New York Times*, 20 Feb. 1972.

87. Lasch, 4, 14.

88. Neusner, 78 and Leon Jick, "The Holocaust: Its Use and Abuse Within the American Public," *Yad Vashem Studies*, vol. 14 (Jerusalem: Yad Vashem 1981).

89. Letter from Allen Rivkin to Joel Ollander, 4 Nov. 1974, Jewish Film Advisory Committee Files.

90. Richard Reeves, "If the Jews Will Not Be for Themselves, Who Will Be for Them?" *New York Magazine*, 23 Dec. 1974, 45–51.

91. Letter from Allen Rivkin to Charles Posner, 11 Mar. 1975, Jewish Film Advisory Committee Files.

92. Letter from Rivkin to Joel Ollander, 21 Apr. 1975, Jewish Film Advisory Committee Files.

93. Letter from Rivkin to Sherril Corwin, 1 May 1975, Jewish Film Advisory Committee Files.

94. *Newsweek*, 27 Dec. 1976.

95. Doneson, 11–13, 18.

96. Sarris, 33.

97. Synopsis of *Watch On the Rhine*, Wisconsin Center for Film and Theater Research, Shumlin Collection.

98. Final draft of *Watch On the Rhine*, Wisconsin Center for Film and Theater Research, Shumlin Collection.

99. Michael Billington, *The Illustrated London News*, Mar. 1974; Clive James in *At the Pillars of Hercules* from "What Becomes A Legend Most?" in *Village Voice*, 3 Mar. 1980; Sidney Hook, "Lillian Hellman's Scoundrel Time," *Encounter*, Feb. 1977; Mary McCarthy in Wolcott, *Village Voice*. In fact, Hellman sued McCarthy and the case was still pending at the time of Miss Hellman's death in July 1984. We might add to this journalist Martha Gellhorn's accusations about Lillian Hellman's inability to write the truth. Gellhorn, once the wife of Ernest Hemingway, claims Miss Hellman's writings about her experiences during the Spanish Civil War and her meetings with Hemingway tend to be apocryphal. See Martha Gellhorn, "On Apocryphism," "Guerre de Plume," in *The Paris Review* "79": *25th Anniversary Double Issue* 23, no. 79, Spring 1981.

100. Muriel Gardiner, *Code Name "Mary"* (New Haven: Yale University Press, 1983).

101. Bonnie Lyons, "Lillian Hellman: The First Jewish Nun on Prytani Street," in Sarah Blacher Cohen, 112.

102. *Variety*, 8 Feb. 1978. Interestingly, two years later, "legitimate" Jewish organizations called for a nationwide "tune-off" of *Playing for Time*, in which Redgrave plays Fania Fenelon, a "half-Jewish" prisoner in Auschwitz.

103. Paul Rosenfield, "Film Clips," *Los Angeles Times*, 4 Feb. 1978.

104. John J. O'Connor, "TV: Oscar Awards Back in Old Form," *New York Times*, 15 Apr. 1978, C28.

Notes to Chapter Four

1. Alvin H. Rosenfeld, "The Holocaust in American Popular Culture," *Midstream*, June/July 1983.

2. Michael J. Arlen, *The Camera Age* (England: Penguin Books, 1982), 6.

3. David Dortort, "The Jewish Image in Television—A Disaster Area," 1973, Jewish Film Advisory Committee Files.

4. Gustave Le Bon, *The Crowd* (1895; reprint, New York: Ballantine Books, 1969).

5. Martin Esslin, *The Age of Television* (San Francisco: W.H. Freeman and Co., 1982), 53–54.

6. Esslin, Personal Preface.

7. Robin M. Williams, Jr., "Changes in Value Orientation," in *Jews in the Mind of America*, by Charles Stember et al. (New York: Basic Books, 1966), 347.

8. See Nathan Glazer, *Ethnic Dilemmas, 1964–1982* (Cambridge: Harvard University Press, 1983).

9. Jacob Neusner, *Stranger at Home: "The Holocaust," Zionism, and American Judaism* (Chicago: University of Chicago Press, 1981), 89–90.

10. Quoted in Robert Alter, "Deformations of the Holocaust," *Commentary*, Feb. 1981.

11. Ibid., 50.

12. Leon Hadar, "A Chill in the Air," *Jerusalem Post*, 4 Dec. 1981, 10–11, quoting from Professors Harold Quinley and Charles Y. Glock in *Anti-Semitism in America* (New York: Free Press, 1979). Attitudes remain divided as to the future of American Jewry. Charles Silberman in *A Certain People* (New York: Summit Books, 1985) believes that American Jewry has reached a "golden period"; while Arthur Hertzberg, in his review of Silberman's book ("The Triumph of the Jews," *The New York Review*, 21 Nov. 1985) fears for the future of American Jewry because of intermarriage and assimilation, and the ability to sustain a Jewish life based primarily on activism. Both would agree that Jewish life in America has never been more comfortable.

13. Wolf Blitzer, "Dateline Washington," *Hadassah Magazine*, Apr. 1984, 42.

14. Drew Middleton, "Why TV Is Fascinated with the Hitler Era," *New York Times*, 16 Nov. 1980.

15. " 'Baby Boom' Attitudes Tend to Be Traditional," *International Herald Tribune*, 12 Dec. 1983, 3.

16. Andrew Sarris, *Village Voice*, 3 Sept. 1979.

17. Quoted in Howard Chapnick's book review of *Delcorso's Gallery* by Philip Caputo, *International Herald Tribune*, 10 Nov. 1983, 14.

18. Milton Shulman, *BBC Radio Times*, quoted in *Encounter*, Dec. 1978.

19. James Oliver Robertson, *American Myth, American Reality* (New York: Hill and Wang, 1981), 208.

20. Frank Rich, *Time*, 17 Apr. 1978. We might add that Claude Lanzmann's 9-hour, 23-minute film *Shoah* has been showing in movie houses internationally though not to the enormous number of viewers *Holocaust* reached. It also might be argued that in several areas, *Holocaust* helped lay the groundwork for the appearance of *Shoah*.

21. See, e.g., Neusner (above), Alter (above), and Paula Hyman, "New Debate on the Holocaust," *New York Times Magazine*, 14 Sept. 1980.

22. Israel Shenker, *New York Times*, 4, 5, 6 Mar. 1975.

23. Draft of publicity synopsis for *Holocaust*, n.d., from Titus Files.

24. Letter from Rabbi Jordan Pearlson to Alan Morris re script changes and suggestions, 15 June 1977, Titus Files.

25. Esslin, 53–54.

26. Letter from Rabbi Marc Tannenbaum to Robert D. Kasmire, Vice-President for Corporate Affairs, NBC, 25 July 1977, Titus Files.

27. Frank Rich, *Time*, 17 Apr. 1978.

225

Notes

28. See Seth Cagin and Philip Dray, *Hollywood Films of the Seventies* (New York: Harper and Row, 1984).

29. See Henry Feingold, *The Politics of Rescue* (New Brunswick, N.J.: Rutgers University Press, 1970) and Arthur Morse, *While Six Million Died* (New York: Random House, 1967).

30. Ben Halpern, "Anti-Semitism in the Perspective of Jewish History," in Stember et al., 297.

31. Christopher Lasch, *The Culture of Narcissism* (New York: W. W. Norton and Co., Inc., 1978), 68.

32. Wolfgang Ernst, "DIStory: Cinema and Historical Discourse," *Journal of Contemporary History*, July 1983, 399.

33. Michiko Kakutani, "Forty Years After, Artists Still Struggle with the Holocaust," *New York Times*, 5 Dec. 1982.

34. Susan Sontag, *Against Interpretation* (New York: Delta Books, Dell Publishing Co., 1966), 125–126.

35. Isaac Deutscher, *The Non-Jewish Jew and Other Essays* (London: Oxford University Press, 1968), 163–164.

36. Elie Wiesel, "Trivializing the Holocaust: Semi-Fact and Semi-Fiction," *New York Times*, 16 Apr. 1978.

37. Letter to Herbert Brodkin from Harvey Scheter, Regional Director of ADL in Los Angeles, 21 Apr. 1978, Titus Files.

38. Letter from Rabbi Jordan Pearlson to Robert E. Mulholland, Pres., NBC Network, 16 Mar. 1978, Titus Files.

39. Letter from Herbert Brodkin to Herbert Schlosser of NBC, 13 May 1977, Titus Files.

40. Letter from Rabbi Jordan Pearlson to Alan Morris, 15 June 1977, Titus Files.

41. Tom Shales, "NBC's Powerful 'Holocaust,' " *Washington Post*, Apr. 1978.

42. Rich.

43. Proposal of Gerald Green, Titus Files.

44. Lucy Dawidowicz, *A Holocaust Reader* (New York: Behrman House, 1976), 26–27.

45. Shooting script of *Holocaust*, Titus Files.

46. Green Proposal, Titus Files.

47. Green Proposal, Titus Files.

48. Letter from Robert Berger to Marvin Chomsky, director of *Holocaust*, 17 Mar. 1977, Titus Files.

49. Gerald Green, "A Wreath on the Graves of the Six Million," *TV Guide*, 15 Apr. 1978.

50. Lance Morrow, "Television and the Holocaust," *Time*, 1 May 1978.

51. Rich.

52. Lawrence Langer, "The Americanization of the Holocaust on Stage and Screen," in *From Hester Street to Hollywood*, ed. Sarah Blacher Cohen (Bloomington: Indiana University Press, 1983), 229. It is interesting to note that even in the so-called artistic films dealing with the theme of the Holocaust, the end is generally not a vision of darkness but one of hope. One can see this in Polish, French, Italian, and Czech films on the Holocaust, as well as those from America. For example, Wanda Jakubowska's *The Last Stop* (1948) filmed on location in Auschwitz, Alexander Ford's *Border Street* (1948), both Polish films; or *Distant*

Journey (1949) a film from Czechoslovakia. These and many other serious films end with a hopeful vision of the future.

53. Neusner, 82–83.

54. Green Proposal, Titus Files.

55. All quotes from *Holocaust* used here are taken from the shooting script, Titus Files.

56. In his comments to Alan Morris, Rabbi Pearlson indicated the improbability of this act, but thought it would be lost on most. Pearlson to Morris, 15 June 1977, Titus Files.

57. Judith E. Doneson, "The Jew as a Female Figure in Holocaust Film," *Shoah: A Review of Holocaust Studies and Commemorations* 1, no. 1, 1978.

58. Doneson, 12. Quote from Alan T. Davies, *Anti-Semitism and the Christian Mind* (New York: Herder and Herder, 1969), 37.

59. Bruno Bettelheim, "The Holocaust," *Encounter*, Dec. 1978, 7.

60. The complicated role of the various Jewish councils functioning during the period of the Final Solution has been put into its proper perspective in Isaiah Trunk's now standard work *Judenrat* (New York: The Macmillan Co., 1972).

61. Letter from Rabbi Jordan Pearlson to Alan Morris, 17 June 1977, Titus Files.

62. Green.

63. Irving Greenberg. Letters, *New York Times*, 30 Apr. 1978.

64. Elie Wiesel, "Trivializing the Holocaust."

65. Letter from Gerald Green to Herbert Brodkin, 5 Aug. 1977, Titus Files.

66. Jerry Kuehl, "Truth Claims," *Sight and Sound*, Autumn 1981, 272.

67. Robertson, 206–208.

68. Arlen, 277.

69. Robert Sklar, "Politics in Film: How Moviemakers Handle Hot Issues," *New York Times*, 18 July 1982.

70. Susan Sontag, *On Photography* (New York: Delta Books, 1977), 20.

71. Claude Lanzmann's highly praised 9-hour, 23-minute documentary film *Shoah* (France, 1985) contains no archival film or photographs of the period. One wonders if such a choice would have been possible without the antecedents that had already established a visual representation of the Holocaust. This also hints at the problem connected with the use of archival visual material.

72. Langer, 227.

73. Wiesel, "Trivializing the Holocaust."

74. See articles by Daniel J. Landes and Sybil Milton in *Genocide: Critical Issues of the Holocaust*, eds. Alex Grobman and Daniel J. Landes (Los Angeles: Simon Wiesenthal Center and Chappaqua, N.Y.: Rossel Books, 1983).

75. Sybil Milton, "The Camera as a Weapon: Documentary Photography and the Holocaust," *Simon Wiesenthal Center Annual* (Chappaqua, N.Y.: Rossel Books, 1984) 45–68, and Sybil Milton, "Images of the Holocaust—Part I," in *Holocaust* and *Genocide Studies*, 1, no. 1, 1986, 27–61.

76. See Mendel Grossman, *With a Camera in the Ghetto* (Israel: Ghetto Fighters House, 1972) and *Notes from the Warsaw Ghetto: The Journal of Emmanuel Ringelblum* (1958: reprint New York: Schocken Paperbacks, 1974).

77. Susan Sontag, *On Photography* (Delta Books), 14–15.

78. A similar occurrence happened with the TV broadcast of *Judgment at Nuremberg*. Without Herbert Brodkin's permission, the station blanked out four or five references to Nazi gas chambers and gas ovens because the show's sponsor was the American Gas Association. *Time*, 27 Apr. 1959, called this a "source of some of the most naïve censorship ever to be inflicted on a show."

79. Letter from the Reverend Frederic A. Brussat, 17 Mar. 1978, Titus Files.

80. Sontag, *On Photography*, 6–7.

81. T. Fabre, "Media Notebook: NBC's Holocaust—Pro and Con," in the National Catholic News Service, Division of the U.S. Catholic Conference, Report of 27 Apr. 1978. Titus Files.

82. Henry Feingold, "Four Days in April: A Review of NBC's Dramatization of the Holocaust," *Shoah: A Review of Holocaust Studies and Commemorations*, 1, no. 4, 1978.

83. Charles Y. Glock, Gertrude J. Selznick, Joe L. Spaeth, *The Apathetic Majority* (New York: Harper and Row, 1970), 171.

84. Quoted from *The German Tribune* (A Weekly Review of the German Press), 4 Feb. 1979, from Bernd Nellessen, *Hannoversche Allgemeine*, 27 Jan. 1979.

85. Correspondence from the Boston Chapter of the Lithuanian-American Community of the USA, 30 Apr. 1978, Titus Files.

86. Letter from Gerald Green to Herbert Brodkin, 18 July 1977, Titus Files.

87. Lasch, 187.

88. Because of the limited framework of our analysis, a discussion on the mass media and popular culture is not relevant; whereas the accusation of trivialization is part of the response to *Holocaust*. However, for an interesting study on popular culture see Norman Jacobs, ed., *Culture for the Millions? Mass Media in Modern Society* (Boston: Beacon Press, 1964).

89. Donal Henahan, "For Conductors, A Downbeat," *International Herald Tribune*, 23 Dec. 1983, 7.

90. Langer, 228.

91. Esslin, 51.

92. Advertising and Promotion Bulletin, n.d., Titus Files.

93. Dore Schary, Letters in response to *Holocaust*, *New York Times*, 30 Apr. 1978.

94. T. Fabre, The National Catholic News Service, 27 Apr. 1978, Titus Files.

95. Esslin, 88.

96. T. Fabre, The National Catholic News Service, 27 Apr. 1978, Titus Files.

97. Siegfried Zielinski, "History as Entertainment and Provocation: The TV Series 'Holocaust' in West Germany," in Anson Rabinbach and Jack Zipes, eds., *Germans and Jews Since the Holocaust* (New York: Holmes and Meier, 1986), 279–280.

98. Clive James, from *The Observer* in *Encounter*, Dec. 1978, 16.

99. Sander A. Diamond, " 'Holocaust' Film's Impact on Americans," *Patterns of Prejudice*, July–Aug. 1978.

100. Letter from Olga Kovacs to Herbert Brodkin, n.d., Titus Files.

101. Letter from 1939 Club, Inc., to Herbert Brodkin, n.d., Titus Files.

102. Elie Wiesel, "Trivializing the Holocaust."

103. Joseph Papp, Letters in response to *Holocaust, New York Times*, 30 Apr. 1978.

104. Letter from Richard Maass of the American Jewish Committee to Herbert Brodkin and Robert Berger, 8 Feb. 1978, Titus Files.

105. Middleton, *New York Times*.

106. Molly Haskell, "A Failure to Connect," *New York Magazine*, 15 May 1978, 79–80.

107. The articles are, respectively: "U.S. Says Hanoi Acts Like Nazis," *International Herald Tribune*, 23–24 June 1979; "Cambodia: No Exit," *Newsweek*, 25 June 1979; Kathleen Teltsch, "U.S. Urged to Aid Boat People," *International Herald Tribune*, 27 June 1979; and "Diplomats Sought Relief for Boat People," *International Herald Tribune*, 23 July 1979.

108. Roy Walters, "Paperback Talk," *New York Times Book Review*, 16 Apr. 1978.

109. Alter, 49.

110. Herbert G. Luft, *Variety*, 3 Jan. 1979.

111. Harriet van Horne, *New York Post* quoted in Diamond.

112. Quoted in Elisabeth Pond, "Germany: Turmoil of 'Holocaust,' " *Christian Science Monitor*, 30 Jan. 1979.

113. Quoted in *Jerusalem Post*, 1 Feb. 1979.

114. Ernie Meyer, " 'Holocaust': Lesson for the Heart," *Jerusalem Post*, 2 Feb. 1979, 5.

115. John Dornberg, "Dachau," *International Herald Tribune*, 9 July 1979, 12.

116. In fact, France has already received a "lesson" from its own film industry in Marcel Ophuls' *The Sorrow and the Pity* (1970), Louis Malle's *Lacombe, Lucien* (1974), André Hilami's *Singing Under the Occupation* (1976), and other films. Information on the French reaction to *Holocaust* comes from: Edwin Eytan, " 'Holocaust' To Be Aired in France Despite Strike of Technicians," *JTA Daily News Bulletin*, 13 Feb. 1979; *Variety*, 14 Feb. 1979; Jack Maurice, " 'Holocaust' Proves To Be Hot Potato in France," *Jerusalem Post*, 22 Feb. 1979; and *Variety*, 28 Feb. 1979.

117. Jean Ziegler, " 'Holocaust' and Swiss Myths," *International Herald Tribune*, 7–8 July 1979, 4.

118. NBC News Release, 4 Sept. 1979, Titus Files.

119. Letter from Herbert Brodkin to Herb Schlosser of NBC, 28 Feb. 1979, Titus Files.

120. Rabbi Marc Tannenbaum, NBC News Release, 4 Sept. 1979, Titus Files.

121. Charles Fenyvesi, "On Surviving After the Holocaust," *International Herald Tribune*, 19 Apr. 1983, 4.

Notes to Conclusion

1. James Oliver Robertson, *American Myth, American Reality* (New York: Hill and Wang, 1981), 29.

2. Robert Warshow, *The Immediate Experience* (New York: Atheneum, 1972), 244.

3. Daniel Henninger, "Human Dignity and the Holocaust," *Wall Street Journal*, 27 Apr. 1983, 6.

4. Wolf Blitzer, "Dateline Washington," *Hadassah Magazine*, Apr. 1984.

5. Jacob Neusner, *Strangers at Home: "The Holocaust," Zionism, and American Judaism* (Chicago: University of Chicago Press, 1981), 90.

6. Robertson, 9.

7. Yehuda Bauer, "Whose Holocaust?" *Midstream*, Nov. 1980, 42.

8. For an overview of the Bitburg affair, see Geoffrey Hartman, ed., *Bitburg in Moral and Political Perspective* (Bloomington: Indiana University Press, 1986).

9. Charles Silberman, *A Certain People* (New York: Summit Books, 1985), 363–364.

10. William Safire, "I Am a Jew . . . ," in Hartman, 212–214.

11. "Views from Across the USA/Do You Think It's Important to Remember the Holocaust?" *USA Today*, 15 Apr. 1983.

12. *Jerusalem Post*, 1 July 1980, 10.

13. Gary Rosenblatt, "The Simon Wiesenthal Center: State-of-the-Art Activism or Hollywood Hype?" *Baltimore Jewish Times*, 14 Sept. 1984, 67.

14. Alvin H. Rosenfeld, "The Holocaust in American Popular Culture," *Midstream*, June/July 1983, 53–59.

15. This too has been represented in such films as *The Damned* (1969) and *Night Porter* (1974). More serious discussions on the phenomenon can be found in Susan Sontag, "Fascinating Fascism," in *Movies and Methods*, ed. Bill Nichols (Berkeley: University of California Press, 1976), 31–43; and Saul Friedländer, *Reflections of Nazism* (New York: Harper and Row, 1984).

16. Elie Wiesel, *Legends of Our Time* (New York: Holt, Rinehart and Winston, 1968), 178.

17. Lawrence Langer, "The Americanization of the Holocaust on Stage and Screen," in *From Hester Street to Hollywood*, ed. Sarah Blacher Cohen (Bloomington: Indiana University Press, 1983), 213.

18. Susan Sontag, *Against Interpretation* (New York: Delta Books, Dell Publishing Co., 1966), 125.

19. Rosenfeld, 58.

20. Diane Ravitch, "Decline and Fall of Teaching History," *New York Times Magazine*, 19 Nov. 1985, 52.

21. Judith Miller, "Erasing the Past: Europe's Amnesia About the Holocaust," *New York Times Magazine*, 16 Nov. 1986, 110.

22. From a study carried out by R. C. Peterson and L. L. Thurston, as mentioned in Irwin C. Rosen, "The Effect of the Motion Picture 'Gentleman's Agreement' On Attitudes Toward Jews," *The Journal of Psychology*, 26, 1946, 525–536.

23. Dennis H. Wrong, "The Psychology of Prejudice and the Future of Anti-Semitism in America," in *Jews in the Mind of America*, by Charles Stember et al. (New York: Basic Books, 1966), 331.

24. Annette Insdorf, "Saga of Jews Who Fought Back Against Nazi Oppression," *New York Times*, 14 Sept. 1986.

25. Timothy Garton Ash, "The Life of Death," *The New York Review*, 19 Dec. 1985, 26.

26. Miller, 33.

27. Robertson, 4.

28. Peter Black, "New Haven Dedicates Holocaust Memorial," *New Haven Ledger*, 3 Nov. 1977.

Bibliography

Archives

American Film Institute, Beverly Hills, Calif.
Israel Film Archive, Jerusalem, Israel
Jewish Film Advisory Committee Files, the Community Relations Council of the Jewish Federation of Los Angeles, Los Angeles, Calif.
Jewish Film Archive, The Hebrew University and World Zionist Organization, Jerusalem, Israel
Margaret Herrick Library of the Academy of Motion Picture Arts and Sciences, Beverly Hills, Calif.
Stanley Kramer Collection, Department of Special Collections, University Research Library, UCLA
Titus Productions, Inc., Files, New York, N.Y.
UCLA Film Collection, Westwood, Calif.
UCLA Department of Collections, University Research Library, Westwood, Calif.
UCLA Theater Arts Library, Westwood, Calif.
University of Southern California Archives of Performing Arts, Theater Arts Library, Los Angeles, Calif.
Wisconsin Center for Film and Theater Research, The State Historical Society of Wisconsin, Madison, Wis.

Works Consulted: Books, Articles, and Newspapers

Aaron, Daniel, ed. *America in Crisis.* New York: Knopf, 1952.
Ackelsberg, Martha, Paul Cowen, Jack Neufield, and Ellen Willis. "Pride, Prejudice and Politics: Jewish Jews on the American Left." *Response,* Autumn 1982, 3–39.
Agee, James. *Agee on Film.* Boston: Beacon Press, 1964.
Alexander, William. *Film on the Left: American Documentary Film from 1931 to 1942.* Princeton: Princeton University Press, 1981.
Allport, Gordon W. *The Nature of Prejudice.* 1954. Reprint. New York: Anchor Books, 1959.
Alpert, Hollis. Review of *Judgment at Nuremberg. Saturday Review,* 2 Dec. 1961.
Alter, Robert. "Deformations of the Holocaust." *Commentary,* Feb. 1981, 48–54.
―――. "Sentimentalizing the Jews." *Commentary,* Sept. 1965, 71–75.
American Jewish History Special Issue: The Jewish Impact on American Mass Culture, Sept. 1982.
Anderson, George K. *The Legend of the Wandering Jew.* Providence: Brown University Press, 1965.
Anne Frank: The Diary of a Young Girl. 1952. New York: Pocket Books Edition, 1959.
Appel, John J. "Jews in American Caricature: 1820–1914." *American Jewish History,* Sept. 1981, 103–133.
Arendt, Hannah. *Eichmann in Jerusalem.* New York: The Viking Press, 1968.
―――. *The Jew as Pariah: Jewish Identity and Politics in the Modern Age.* Edited by Ron H. Feldman. New York: Grove Press, 1978.
―――. *The Origins of Totalitarianism.* 1951. Reprint. New York: Harcourt Brace Jovanovich, Inc., 1973.

Arlen, Michael J. *The Camera Age.* England: Penguin Books, 1982.

Ash, Timothy Garton. "The Life of Death," The *New York Review of Books,* 19 Dec. 1985.

" 'Baby Boom' Attitudes Tend to Be Traditional." *International Herald Tribune,* 12 Dec. 1983.

Bauer, Yehuda. "Whose Holocaust?" *Midstream,* Nov. 1980, 42–46.

Bazin, André. *What is Cinema?* Vol. 1. Translated by Hugh Gray. Berkeley: University of California Press, 1967.

Belser, Lee. *Los Angeles Mirror,* 15 Dec. 1961.

Bernstein, David. "Europe's Jews: Summer, 1947: A Firsthand Report by an American Observer." *Commentary,* Aug. 1947, 101–109.

Bettelheim, Bruno. "Freedom from Ghetto Thinking." *Midstream,* Spring 1962, 16–25.

———. "The Holocaust." *Encounter,* Dec. 1978, 7–19.

———. "The Ignored Lesson of Anne Frank." *Harper's Magazine,* Nov. 1960, 45–50.

———. *The Informed Heart.* Great Britain: Paladin, 1970.

Billington, Michael. *The Illustrated London News,* Mar. 1978.

Black, Peter. "New Haven Dedicates Holocaust Memorial." *New Haven Ledger,* 3 Nov. 1977.

Blitzer, Wolf. "Dateline Washington." *Hadassah Magazine,* Apr. 1984.

Boorstin, Daniel J. *The Image: A Guide to Pseudo-Events in America.* 1961. Reprint. New York: Atheneum, 1982.

Boxoffice, 16 Apr. 1965.

Brinkley, Alan. *Voices of Protest: Huey Long, Father Coughlin, and the Great Depression.* New York: Vintage Books, 1983.

Broch, Nathan. *Los Angeles Mirror,* 25 Dec. 1961.

Brown, Les, and Savannah Waring Walkers, eds. *Fast Forward: The New Television and American Society.* Kansas City: Andrews and McMeel, Inc., 1983.

Brustein, Robert. *Revolution as Theater.* New York: Liveright, 1971.

Cagin, Seth, and Philip Dray. *Hollywood Films of the Seventies.* New York: Harper and Row, 1984.

"Cambodia: No Exit." *Newsweek,* 25 June 1979.

Campbell, Russell. "The Ideology of the Social Consciousness Movie: Three Films of Darryl F. Zanuck." *Quarterly Review of Film,* Winter 1978, 49–71.

Canetti, Elias. *Crowds and Power.* New York: Viking Press, 1962.

Carroll, Peter N. *It Seemed Like Nothing Happened: The Tragedy and Promise of America in the 1970s.* New York: Holt, Rinehart and Winston, 1982.

"Cartoon Cache." *International Herald Tribune,* 5 July 1984.

Ceplair, Larry, and Steven Englund. *The Inquisition in Hollywood: Politics in the Film Community 1930–1960.* Berkeley: University of California Press, 1983.

Chaplin, Charles. "I Made 'The Great Dictator' Because." N.d.

———. "Mr. Chaplin Answers His Critics." *The New York Times,* 27 Oct. 1940.

———. *My Autobiography.* England: Penguin Books, 1974.

Chapnick, Howard. "Book Review of *Delcorso's Gallery* by Philip Caputo." *International Herald Tribune,* 10 Nov. 1983.

Clark, M.J., ed. *Politics and the Media.* Oxford: Pergamon Press, 1979.

Cohen, Eliot. "Mr. Zanuck's 'Gentleman's Agreement.' " *Commentary*, Jan. 1948, 51–56.

Cohen, Sarah Blacher, ed. *From Hester Street to Hollywood.* Bloomington: Indiana University Press, 1983.

Cohn, Norman. *Warrant for Genocide.* England: Penguin Books, 1970.

Combs, Carl. *Hollywood Citizen,* 12 Nov. 1940.

Crowther, Bosley. "Hollywood's Producer of Controversy." *The New York Times Magazine,* 10 Dec. 1961.

———. "Lost Opportunity or Where Was Hollywood When the Lights Went Out?" *The New York Times,* 23 June 1940.

———. *The New York Times,* 2 May 1965.

———. "Still Supreme." *The New York Times,* 20 Oct. 1940.

Dawidowicz, Lucy S. *A Holocaust Reader.* New York: Behrman House, 1976.

———. "American Jews and the Holocaust." *The New York Times Magazine,* 18 April 1982.

———. *The Holocaust and the Historians.* Cambridge: Harvard University Press, 1981.

———. *On Equal Terms.* New York: Holt, Rinehart and Winston, 1984.

———. "Visualizing the Warsaw Ghetto: Nazi Images of the Jews Refiltered by the BBC." *Shoah: A Review of Holocaust Studies and Commemorations,* 1, no. 1, 1978, 5–6, 17–18.

———. *The War Against the Jews.* New York: Holt, Rinehart and Winston, 1975.

De Casseres, Benjamin. "De Casseres Calls 'Rothschild' First Full-Sized World Picture." *Motion Picture Herald,* 24 Mar. 1934, 40, 44.

Deutscher, Isaac. *The Non-Jewish Jew and Other Essays.* London: Oxford University Press, 1968.

Diamond, Sander A. " 'Holocaust' Film's Impact on Americans." *Patterns of Prejudice,* July-Aug. 1978, 1–9, 17.

"The Diary of Anne Frank." *Patterns of Prejudice,* 20, no. 3, July 1986, 36–38.

Dickstein, Morris. "Cold War Blues: Notes on the Culture of the Fifties." In *Writers and Politics,* edited by Edith Kurzweil and William Phillips, 269–292. Boston: Routledge and Kegan Paul, 1983.

———. "Black Humor and History," in Gerald Howard, ed. *The Sixties.* New York: Washington Square Press publication of Pocket Books, 1982, 272–292.

Dinnerstein, Leonard. "Anti-Semitism Exposed and Attacked, 1945–1950." *American Jewish History,* Sept. 1981, 134–149.

"Diplomats Sought Relief for Boat People." *International Herald Tribune,* 23 July 1979.

Dobkowski, Michael. *The Tarnished Dream.* Westport, Conn.: Greenwood Press, 1979.

Doneson, Judith E. "The Jew as a Female Figure in Holocaust Film." *Shoah: A Review of Holocaust Studies and Commemorations* 1, no. 1, 1978, 11–13, 18.

Dornberg, John. "Dachau." *International Herald Tribune,* 9 July 1979.

Dresner, Samuel. "The Vanishing Hero: Christian Drama, Jewish Tragedy." *Midstream,* June–July 1982, 44–46.

Edinburgh '77 Magazine: History/Production/Memory, 2.

Eisenstein, Sergei. *Notes of a Film Director.* New York: Dover Publications, 1970.

Erens, Patricia. "Gangsters, Vampires, and J.A.P.'s: The Jew Surfaces in American Movies." *The Journal of Popular Film* 4, no. 3, 1975, 208–222.

———. *The Jew in American Cinema.* Bloomington: Indiana University Press, 1984.

Ernst, Wolfgang. "DIStory: Cinema and Historical Discourse." *Journal of Contemporary History,* July 1983, 397–409.

Esslin, Martin. *The Age of Television.* San Francisco: W. H. Freeman and Co., 1982.

Eytan, Edwin. " 'Holocaust' to Be Aired in France Despite Strike of Technicians." *JTA Daily News Bulletin,* 13 Feb. 1979.

Ezrahi, Sidra. *Not By Words Alone.* Chicago: University of Chicago Press, 1980.

Fabre, T. "Media Notebook: NBC's Holocaust—Pro and Con." The National Catholic News Service, 27 Apr. 1978.

Farber, Steven. *The New York Times,* 20 Feb. 1972.

Feingold, Henry. "Four Days in April: A Review of NBC's Dramatization of the Holocaust." *Shoah: A Review of Holocaust Studies and Commemorations* 1, no. 1, 1978, 15–17.

———. *The Politics of Rescue.* New Brunswick, N.J.: Rutgers University Press, 1970.

Fenyvesi, Charles. "On Surviving After the Holocaust." *International Herald Tribune,* 19 Apr. 1983.

Ferro, Marc. *Cinéma et Histoire.* Paris: Denoël/Gonthier, 1977.

Foucalt, Michel. "Interview on 'Anti-Retro.' " Translated by Martin Jardin. *Edinburgh '77 Magazine: History/Production/Memory,* no. 2, 20–25.

Freedman, Samuel G., "Bearing Witness: The Life and Works of Elie Wiesel." *The New York Times Magazine,* 23 Oct. 1983.

Friedländer, Saul. *Reflections of Nazism: An Essay on Kitsch and Death.* Translated by Thomas Weyr. New York: Harper and Row, 1984.

Friedman, Lester D. *Hollywood's Image of the Jew.* New York: Frederick Ungar Publishing Co., 1982.

Friedman, R. M. "Exorcising the Past: Jewish Figures in Contemporary Films." *Journal of Contemporary History,* July 1984.

Frye, Northrop. "The Great Charlie." *The Canadian Forum,* Aug. 1941, 148–150.

Gardiner, Muriel. *Code Name "Mary."* New Haven: Yale University Press, 1983.

Gellhorn, Martha. "On Apocryphism," "Guerre de Plume." *The Paris Review "79": 25th Anniversary Double Issue* 23, no. 79, Spring 1981, 281–301.

Gilliat, Penelope. *The Observer Weekend,* 16 Oct. 1966.

Glazer, Nathan. *Ethnic Dilemmas, 1964–1982.* Cambridge: Harvard University Press, 1983.

Glock, Charles Y., Gertrude J. Selznick, and Joe C. Spaeth. *The Apathetic Majority.* New York: Harper and Row, 1970.

Golden, Harry. *Carolina Israelite,* n.d., 1961.

Green, Gerald. "A Wreath on the Graves of the Six Million." *TV Guide,* 15 Apr. 1978, 4–8.

———. *The Artists of Terezin.* New York: Hawthorn Books, Inc., 1969.

Greenberg, Irving. "Letters." *The New York Times,* 30 Apr. 1978, p. D-30.

Grobman, Alex. "Hollywood on the Holocaust." *Shoah,* Fall/Winter, 1983–1984, 6–10.

Grose, Peter. *Israel in the Mind of America.* New York: Alfred A. Knopf, 1983.

Grossman, Mendel. *With a Camera in the Ghetto.* Israel: Ghetto Fighters House, 1972.

Grunberger, Richard. *The Twelve-Year Reich: A Social History of Nazi Germany, 1933–1945.* New York: Holt, Rinehart and Winston, 1971.

Hadar, Leon. "A Chill in the Air." *The Jerusalem Post,* 4 Dec. 1981.

Halpern, Ben. "Anti-Semitism in the Perspective of Jewish History." In *Jews in the Mind of America,* by Charles Herbert Stember et al., 273–301. New York: Basic Books, 1966.

Handlin, Oscar. "American Views of the Jew at the Opening of the Twentieth Century." *Publication of the American Jewish Historical Society,* 40, June 1951.

Hartmann, Geoffrey, ed. *Bitburg in Moral and Political Perspective.* Bloomington: Indiana University Press, 1986.

Harvey, Stephen. "Why Today's Films Turn to History." *The New York Times,* 28 Aug. 1983.

Haskell, Molly. "A Failure to Connect." *New York Magazine,* 15 May 1978, 79–80.

Hellman, Lillian. *Pentimento.* New York: New American Library, 1974.

———. *Scoundrel Time.* New York: Bantam Edition, 1982.

Henahan, Donal. "For Conductors, a Downbeat." *International Herald Tribune,* 23 Dec. 1983.

Henninger, Daniel. "Human Dignity and the Holocaust." *Wall Street Journal,* 27 Apr. 1983.

Hertzberg, Arthur. "The Triumph of the Jews," *The New York Review of Books,* 21 Nov. 1985.

Higham, John. "American Anti-Semitism Historically Reconsidered." In *Jews in the Mind of America,* by Charles Herbert Stember et al., 237–258. New York: Basic Books, 1966.

Hilberg, Raul. *The Destruction of the European Jews.* Chicago: Quadrangle Books, 1961.

Hook, Sidney. "Lillian Hellman's *Scoundrel Time.*" *Encounter,* Feb. 1978.

"How 'Cheerful' is Anne Frank?" *Variety,* 1 Apr. 1959.

Howard, Gerald, ed. *The Sixties.* New York: Washington Square Press publication of Pocket Books, 1982.

Howe, Irving. *World of Our Fathers.* New York: Bantam Edition, 1980.

Huff, Theodore. *Charlie Chaplin.* New York: Arno Press and The New York Times, 1972.

Hyman, Paula. "New Debate on the Holocaust." *The New York Times Magazine,* 14 Sept. 1980.

Insdorf, Annette. *Indelible Shadows: Film and the Holocaust.* New York: Vintage Books, 1983.

———. "Saga of Jews Who Fought Back Against Nazi Oppression." *The New York Times,* 14 Sept. 1986.

Jacobs, Norman, ed. *Culture for the Millions? Mass Media in Modern Society.* Boston: Beacon Press, 1964.

James, Clive. From *The Observer.* In *Encounter*, Dec. 1978.

The Jerusalem Post, 1 Feb. 1979.

The Jerusalem Post, 1 July 1980, 10.

Jick, Leon A. "The Holocaust: Its Use and Abuse Within the American Public." In *Yad Vashem Studies*, Vol. 14. Jerusalem: Yad Vashem, 1981.

Johnson, Nunnally. Interview. "An Oral History of the Motion Picture in America." UCLA, 1968–1969.

Kael, Pauline. *Kiss Kiss Bang Bang.* New York: Bantam Books, 1969.

———. "Movies, the Desperate Art." In *Film: An Anthology*, edited by Daniel Talbot, 51–71. Berkeley: University of California Press, 1970.

Kakutani, Michiko. "Forty Years After, Artists Still Struggle with the Holocaust." *The New York Times*, 5 Dec. 1982.

Kammen, Michael. *People of Paradox.* New York: Oxford University Press, 1980.

Katsch, Abraham I. Ed. and trans. *Scroll of Agony: The Warsaw Diary of Chaim A. Kaplan.* New York: The Macmillan Co., 1965.

Kazin, Alfred. "Can Today's Movies Tell the Truth About Fascism?" *The New York Times*, 2 Jan. 1975.

Keller, Morton. "Jews and the Character of American Life Since 1930." In *Jews in the Mind of America*, by Charles Stember et al., 259–272. New York: Basic Books, 1966.

"Kennedy Remembered." *Newsweek*, 28 Nov. 1983.

Knight, Arthur. "Review of *Judgment at Nuremberg*." *Saturday Review*, 2 Dec. 1961.

Kramer, Stanley. *The American Film Institute: Dialogue on Film* 2, no. 9, July 1973.

Kuehl, Jerry. "Truth Claims." *Sight and Sound*, Autumn 1981, 272–274.

Kurzweil, Edith, and William Phillips, eds. *Writers and Politics: A Partisan Review Reader.* Boston: Routledge and Kegan Paul, 1983.

Lampell, Millard. "The Jew in Celluloid." *Jewish Life*, Feb. 1949, 14–16.

Landes, Daniel J. "Modesty and Self-Dignity in Holocaust Films." In *Genocide: Critical Issues of the Holocaust*, edited by Alex Grobman and Daniel Landes, 11–13. Los Angeles: Simon Wiesenthal Center and Chappaqua, N.Y.: Rossel Books, 1983.

Langer, Lawrence. "The Americanization of the Holocaust on Stage and Screen." In *From Hester Street to Hollywood*, edited by Sarah Blacher Cohen, 213–230. Bloomington: Indiana University Press, 1983.

Lanzmann, Claude. *Shoah: An Oral History of the Holocaust.* New York: Pantheon Books, 1985.

Laquer, Walter, and George L. Mosse, eds. *Journal of Contemporary History: Historians and Movies: The State of the Art.* July 1983.

Lasch, Christopher. *The Culture of Narcissism.* New York: W. W. Norton and Co., Inc., 1978.

———. *The Minimal Self.* New York: W. W. Norton and Co., Inc., 1984.

Lazarsfeld, Paul. Introduction to *The Apathetic Majority*, by Charles Y.

Glock, Gertrude Selznick, and Joe C. Spaeth, xii–xvi. New York: Harper Torchbook, Harper and Row, 1970.

Le Bon, Gustave. *The Crowd.* 1895. Reprint New York: Ballantine Books, 1969.

Leuchtenberg, William E. *A Troubled Feast: American Society Since 1945.* Boston: Little, Brown & Co., 1973.

Levin, Meyer, "Bitch Time." *The Jerusalem Post,* 16 Apr. 1977, 14.

Lipset, Seymour Martin, and Earl Raab. *The Politics of Unreason: Rightwing Extremism in America, 1790–1970.* New York: Harper Torchbook, Harper and Row, 1973.

Lipstadt, Deborah. *Beyond Belief: The American Press and the Coming of the Holocaust, 1933–1945.* New York: The Free Press, 1986.

Luft, Herbert G. *Variety,* 3 Jan. 1979.

Lyons, Bonnie. "Lillian Hellman: The First Jewish Nun on Prytani Street." In *From Hester Street to Hollywood,* edited by Sarah Blacher Cohen, 106–122. Bloomington: Indiana University Press, 1983.

Mann, Abby. Foreword to published screenplay of *Judgment at Nuremberg,* Aug. 1961.

———. Interview in "An Oral History of the Motion Picture in America." UCLA, 1968–1969.

Manvell, Roger. *Films and the Second World War.* New York: Delta Books, 1976.

Maurice, Jack. " 'Holocaust' Proves to be Hot Potato in France." *The Jerusalem Post,* 22 Feb. 1979.

Maurois, André. *L'Avant Scène,* n.d.

May, Larry L., and Elaine Tyler May. "Why Jewish Movie Moguls: An Exploration in American Culture." *American Jewish History,* Sept. 1982, 6–25.

Maynard, Richard A. *Propaganda on Film: A Nation at War.* Rochelle Park, N.J.: Hayden Book Co., Inc., 1975.

Meyer, Ernie. " 'Holocaust': Lesson for the Heart." *The Jerusalem Post,* 2 Feb. 1979.

Middleton, Drew. "Why TV Is Fascinated with the Hitler Era." *The New York Times,* 16 Nov. 1980, 31.

Miller, Judith. "Erasing the Past: Europe's Amnesia About the Holocaust." *The New York Times Magazine,* 16 Nov. 1986.

Milton, Sybil. "The Camera as Weapon: Documentary Photography and the Holocaust." *Simon Wiesenthal Center Annual.* Chappaqua, N.Y.: Rossel Books, 1984, 45–68.

———. "Images of the Holocaust—Part I." *Holocaust and Genocide Studies.* 1, no. 1, 1986, 27–61.

———. "Sensitive Issues About Holocaust Films." In *Genocide: Critical Issues of the Holocaust,* edited by Alex Grobman and Daniel Landes, 8–11. Los Angeles: Simon Wiesenthal Center and Chappaqua, N.Y.: Rossel Books, 1983.

Morris, Charles R. *A Time of Passion: America 1960–1980.* New York: Penguin Books, 1986.

Morrow, Lance. "Television and the Holocaust." *Time,* 1 May 1978, 50–51.

Morse, Arthur. *While Six Million Died.* New York: Random House, 1967.

Mosley, Leonard. *Zanuck.* London: Granada Publishing, Ltd., 1984.

Mosse, George L. *Germans and Jews.* New York: Universal Library, Grosset and Dunlap, 1971.

Mulisch, Harry. "Death and the Maiden." *The New York Review of Books,* 17 July 1986.

Myers, Harold, "Emotional 'Nuremberg' Premiere." *Variety,* 20 Dec. 1961.

Navasky, Victor S. *Naming Names.* New York: The Viking Press, 1980.

Nellessen, Bernd. From *The German Tribune,* 4 Feb. 1979.

Neusner, Jacob. *Strangers At Home: "The Holocaust," Zionism, and American Judaism.* Chicago: University of Chicago Press, 1981.

Newcomb, Horace, and Robert S. Alley. *The Producer's Medium: Conversations with Creators of American TV.* New York: Oxford University Press, 1983.

Newsweek, 27 Dec. 1976.

O'Connor, John E., and Martin A. Jackson, eds. *American History/American Film, Interpreting the Hollywood Image.* New York: Frederick Ungar Publishing Co., 1979.

O'Connor, John J. "Diverse Views of Nazi Germany." *The New York Times,* 9 Sept. 1979.

———. "TV: Oscar Awards Back in Old Form." *The New York Times,* 15 Apr. 1978.

O'Dea, Thomas F. "The Changing Image of the Jew and the Contemporary Religious Situation: An Exploration of Ambiguities." In *Jews in the Mind of America,* by Charles Herbert Stember et al., 302–322. New York: Basic Books, 1966.

O'Neill, William L. *Coming Apart.* New York: Quadrangle Books, The New York Times Book Co., 1978.

Papp, Joseph. "Letters." *The New York Times,* 30 Apr. 1978, D29.

Payne, Robert. "Charlie Chaplin: Portrait of the Moralist." In *Film: An Anthology,* edited by Daniel Talbot, 361–374. Berkeley: University of California Press, 1970.

Picard, Lil. "Interview with Bob Fosse." *Inter/View,* Mar. 1972.

Pickard, Roy. *The Oscar Movies From A–Z.* England: Hamlyn Paperbacks, 1982.

Poe, Elizabeth. "Blacklisting and Censorship in Motion Pictures." *Mass Media,* July 1959, 14–18.

Pond, Elisabeth. "Germany: Turmoil of 'Holocaust.' " *Christian Science Monitor,* 30 Jan. 1979.

Popkin, Henry. "The Vanishing Jew of Our Popular Culture." *Commentary,* July 1952, 46–55.

Rabinbach, Anson, and Jack Zipes, eds. *Germans and Jews Since the Holocaust: The Changing Situation in West Germany.* New York: Holmes and Meier, 1986.

Rabinowitz, Dorothy. "A Powerful Accurate Drama of Dark History." *Wall Street Journal,* 14 Apr. 1978.

Ravitch, Diane. "Decline and Fall of Teaching History." *The New York Times Magazine,* 17 Nov. 1985.

Reeves, Richard. "If Jews Will Not Be for Themselves, Who Will Be for Them?" *New York Magazine,* 23 Dec. 1974, 45–51.

Rich, Frank. *Time,* 17 Apr. 1978.

Ringer, Benjamin B. "Jews and the Desegregation Crisis." In *Jews in the Mind of America,* by Charles Herbert Stember et al., 197–207. New York: Basic Books, 1966.

Robertson, James Oliver. *American Myth, American Reality.* New York: Hill and Wang, 1981.

Roosevelt, Eleanor. "Nuremberg Revisited." *The New York Post,* 2 Nov. 1961.

Rose, Barbara. "Protest in Art." In *Writers and Politics: A Partisan Review Reader,* edited by Edith Kurzweil and William Phillips, 235–246. Boston: Routledge and Kegan Paul, 1983.

Rose, Peter I. *The Ghetto and Beyond: Essays on Jewish Life in America.* New York: Random House, 1969.

Rosen, Irwin C. "The Effect of the Motion Picture 'Gentleman's Agreement' On Attitudes Toward Jews." *The Journal of Psychology,* 26, 1946, 525–536.

Rosenblatt, Gary. "The Simon Wiesenthal Center: State-of-the-Art Activism or Hollywood Hype?" *Baltimore Jewish Times,* 14 Sept. 1984.

Rosenblum, Ralph, and Robert Karen. *When the Shooting Stops . . . The Cutting Begins: A Film Editor's Story.* Middlesex, England: Penguin Books, 1980.

Rosenfeld, Alvin H. "The Holocaust in American Popular Culture." *Midstream,* June/July 1983, 53–59.

———. "On Holocaust and History." *Shoah: A Review of Holocaust Studies and Commemorations* 1, no. 1, 1978, 19.

———. *Imagining Hitler.* Bloomington: Indiana University Press, 1985.

Rosenfield, Paul. "Film Clips." *The Los Angeles Times,* 4 Feb. 1978.

Rosten, Leo C. *Hollywood: The Movie Colony, The Movie Makers.* New York: Harcourt, Brace and Co., 1941.

Safire, William. "I Am a Jew." In Geoffrey Hartman, ed. *Bitburg in Moral and Political Perspective.* Bloomington: Indiana University Press, 1986, 212–214.

Sarris, Andrew. "Notes on the Fascination of Fascism." *Village Voice,* 30 Jan. 1978, 33.

———. *Village Voice,* 3 Sept. 1979.

Sayre, Nora. *Running Time: Films of the Cold War.* New York: Dial Press, 1978.

Schary, Dore. "Letters." *The New York Times,* 30 Apr. 1978, D30.

Schiff, Ellen. *From Stereotype to Metaphor: The Jew in Contemporary Drama.* Albany: State University of New York Press, 1982.

Schlesinger, Arthur, Jr. "Review of *Judgment at Nuremberg.*" *Show,* Dec. 1961.

Schumach, Murray. "Hollywood Trial." *The New York Times,* 30 Apr. 1961.

Selznick, Gertrude J., and Stephen Steinberg. *The Tenacity of Prejudice.* New York: Harper Torchbook, Harper and Row, 1971.

Shales, Tom. "NBC's Powerful 'Holocaust.' " *The Washington Post,* Apr. 1978.

Sheldon, James H. " 'America First' and the Nazi-like Film Probe." *Variety,* 7 Jan. 1942.

Shenker, Israel. *The New York Times,* 4, 5, and 6 Mar. 1975.

Short, K. R. M. "Documents." *Historical Journal of Film, Radio and Television,* Oct. 1983, 171–180.

——. "The Experience of Eastern Jewry in America as Portrayed in the Cinema of the 1920's and 30's." In *History and Film: Methodology, Research, Education,* edited by K. R. M. Short and Karsten Fledelius, 113–150. Copenhagen: Eventus, 1980.

——. "Hollywood Fights Anti-Semitism, 1940–1945." In *Film and Radio Propaganda in World War II,* edited by K. R. M. Short, 146–172. Knoxville: University of Tennessee Press, 1983.

——. "Hollywood Fights Anti-Semitism, 1945–1947." In *Feature Films as History,* edited by K. R. M. Short, 157–189. Knoxville: University of Tennessee Press, 1981.

Shulman, Milton. *BBC Radio Times* from *Encounter,* Dec. 1978.

Silberman, Charles. *A Certain People.* New York: Summit Books, 1985.

Simovic, Drogos. "How Hitler Saw 'The Great Dictator.'" *Review Yugoslav Monthly Magazine,* Oct. 1963, 30–31.

Singerman, Robert. "The American Career of the *Protocols of the Elders of Zion.*" *American Jewish History,* Sept. 1981, 48–78.

Sklar, Robert. *Movie-Made America.* New York: Vintage Books, 1976.

——. "Politics in Film: How Moviemakers Handle Hot Issues." *The New York Times,* 18 July 1982.

Sleeper, James A., and Alan L. Mintz. *The New Jews.* New York: Vintage Books, 1971.

Sloan, Jacob, ed. and trans. *Notes from the Warsaw Ghetto: The Journal of Emmanuel Ringelblum.* 1958. Reprint. New York: Schocken Paperbacks, 1974.

Sontag, Susan. *Against Interpretation.* New York: Delta Books, Dell Publishing Co., 1966.

——. "Fascinating Fascism." In *Movies and Methods,* edited by Bill Nichols, 31–43. Berkeley: University of California Press, 1976.

——. *On Photography.* New York: Delta Books, Dell Publishing Co., 1979.

Sorlin, Pierre. *The Film in History: Restaging the Past.* Totowa, N.J.: Barnes and Noble Books, 1980.

Sowell, Thomas. *Ethnic America.* New York: Basic Books, Inc., 1981.

Speigel, Alan. "A Typology of the Jew in the Contemporary American Film." In *From Hester Street to Hollywood,* edited by Sarah Blacher Cohen, 257–275. Bloomington: Indiana University Press, 1983.

Steiner, George. *Language and Silence.* New York: Atheneum, 1970.

Stember, Charles Herbert, et al. *Jews in the Mind of America.* New York: Basic Books, 1966.

——. "The Recent History of Public Attitudes." In *Jews in the Mind of America,* by Charles Herbert Stember et al., 31–234. New York: Basic Books, 1966.

Suber, Howard. "Politics and Popular Culture: Hollywood at Bay, 1933–1953." *American Jewish History,* June 1979, 517–533.

Talbot, Daniel, ed. *Film: An Anthology.* Berkeley: University of California Press, 1970.

Talbot, David, and Barbara Zheutlin. *Creative Differences: Profiles of Hollywood Dissidents.* Boston: South End Press, 1978.

Taylor, Telford. "Large Questions in the Eichmann Case." *The New York Times Magazine,* 22 Jan. 1961.

Teltsch, Kathleen, "U.S. Urged to Aid Boat People." *International Herald Tribune,* 27 June 1979.

Time, 24 Dec. 1973.

Trunk, Isaiah. *Judenrat*. New York: The Macmillan Co., 1972.

Tugend, Tom. "Hollywood: The Gilded Ghetto." *Jewish Chronicle*, 22 Nov. 1974, 36–42, 94.

"U.S. Says Hanoi Acts Like Nazis." *International Herald Tribune*, 23–24 June, 1979.

Variety, 8 Mar. 1961.

Variety, 11 May 1965.

Variety, 8 Feb. 1978.

Variety, 14 Feb. 1979.

Variety, 28 Feb. 1979.

Varon, Benno Weiser. "The Haunting of Meyer Levin." *Midstream*, Aug./Sept. 1976, 7–23.

"Views From Across the USA/Do You Think It's Important to Remember the Holocaust?" *USA Today*, 15 Apr. 1983.

Walters, Ray. "Paperback Talk." *The New York Times Book Review*, 16 Apr. 1978.

Warshow, Robert. *The Immediate Experience*. New York: Atheneum, 1972.

Weinberg, David. "The 'Socially Acceptable' Immigrant Minority Group: The Image of the Jew in American Popular Films." *North Dakota Quarterly*, Autumn 1972, 60–68.

Werner, M. R. "The Screen." *The New York Times*, 22 June 1941.

Wiesel, Elie. *Legends of Our Time*. New York: Holt, Rinehart and Winston, 1968.

———. *One Generation After*. New York: Random House, 1970.

———. "Trivializing the Holocaust: Semi-Fact and Semi-Fiction." *The New York Times*, 16 Apr. 1978.

Wieseltier, Leon. "Auschwitz and Peace." *The New York Times*, 10 Mar. 1978.

Williams, Robin M., Jr. "Changes in Value Orientation." In *Jews in the Mind of America*, by Charles Herbert Stember et al., 341–353. New York: Basic Books, 1966.

Wischnitzer, Mark. *To Dwell in Safety*. Philadelphia: Jewish Publication Society of America, 1949.

Wolcott, James. "What Becomes a Legend Most?" *Village Voice*, 3 Mar. 1980, 51.

Wrong, Dennis W. "The Psychology of Prejudice and the Future of Anti-Semitism in America." In *Jews in the Mind of America*, by Charles Herbert Stember et al., 323–340. New York: Basic Books, 1966.

Yarnell, Allen. *The Postwar Epoch: Perspectives on American History Since 1945*. New York: Harper and Row, 1972.

Ziegler, Jean. " 'Holocaust' and Swiss Myths." *International Herald Tribune*, 7–8 July 1979.

Zielinski, Siegfried, "History as Entertainment and Provocation: The TV Series 'Holocaust' in West Germany." In Anson Rabinbach and Jack Zipes, eds. *Germans and Jews Since the Holocaust: The Changing Situation in West Germany*, 258–283. New York: Holmes and Meier, 1986.

Filmography

List of Films Cited in the Text

Annie Hall. U.S., 1977. Director: Woody Allen; Script: Woody Allen and Marshall Brickman.

Black Thursday. France, 1974. Director: Michel Mitrani; Script: Albert Cossery and Michel Mitrani.

Blazing Saddles. U.S., 1974. Director: Mel Brooks; Script: Mel Brooks et al.

The Boat Is Full. Switzerland/West Germany/Austria, 1981. Director and Script: Markus Imhoof.

Bonnie and Clyde. U.S., 1967. Director: Arthur Penn; Script: David Newman and Robert Benton.

Border Street. Poland, 1948. Director Alexander Ford; Script: Ludwig Starski, Jan Fethke, and Alexander Ford.

Cabaret. U.S., 1972. Director: Bob Fosse; Script: Jay Presson Allen.

A Clockwork Orange. Great Britain, 1971. Director and Script: Stanley Kubrick.

Confessions of a Nazi Spy. U.S., 1939. Director: Anatole Litvak; Script: Milton Krims and John Wexley.

Crossfire. U.S., 1947. Director: Edward Dmytryk; Script: John Paxton.

The Damned. Italy, 1964. Director: Luigi Visconti; Script: N. Badulucco, E. Medioli, and L. Visconti.

The Diary of Anne Frank. U.S., 1959. Director: George Stevens; Script: Frances Goodrich and Albert Hackett.

The Distant Journey. Czech., 1949. Director and Script: Alfred Radok.

The Eternal Jew. Germany, 1940. Director: Fritz Hippler.

Exodus. U.S., 1960. Director: Otto Preminger; Script: Dalton Trumbo.

Genocide. U.S., 1981. Director: Arnold Schwartzman; Script: Martin Gilbert and Rabbi Marvin Hier.

Gentleman's Agreement. U.S., 1947. Director: Elia Kazan; Script: Moss Hart.

The Grapes of Wrath. U.S., 1940. Director: John Ford; Script: Nunnally Johnson.

The Great Dictator. U.S., 1940. Director and Script: Charles Chaplin.

Harold and Maude. U.S., 1971. Director: Hal Ashby; Script: Colin Higgins.

Heimat. West Germany, 1984. Director: Edgar Reitz; Script: Edgar Reitz and Peter Steinbach.

Hitler's Children. U.S., 1943. Director: Edward Dmytryk; Script: Emmet Lavery.

Holocaust. U.S., 1978. NBC/TV, Director: Marvin Chomsky; Script: Gerald Green.

The House of Rothschild. U.S., 1934. Director: Alfred Werker; Script: Nunnally Johnson.

The Illegals. U.S., 1948. Director: Meyer Levin.

Juarez. U.S., 1939. Director: William Dieterle.

Jud Seuss. Germany, 1940. Director: Veit Harlan.

Judgment at Nuremberg. U.S., 1961. Director: Stanley Kramer; Script: Abby Mann.

Julia. U.S., 1977. Director: Fred Zinnemann; Script: Alvin Sargent.

Lacombe, Lucien. France, 1974. Director: Louis Malle; Script: Patrick Modiano and Louis Malle.

The Last Stop. Poland, 1948. Director: Wanda Jakubowska; Script: Gerda Schneider and Wanda Jakubowska.

The Liberation of Auschwitz. West Germany, 1986. Producer and Director: Bengt and Irmgard von Zur Muehlen.

Little Big Man. U.S., 1970. Director: Arthur Penn; Script: Calder Willingham.

Majdenek. West Germany, 1986. Producer and Director: Bengt and Irmgard von Zur Muehlen.

The Mortal Storm. U.S., 1940. Director: Frank Borzage; Script: Claudine West, Anderson Ellis, and George Froeschel.

Mr. Smith Goes to Washington. U.S., 1939. Director: Frank Capra; Script: Sidney Buchman.

Night Porter. Italy, 1974. Director: Liliana Cavani; Script: Italo Moscati and Liliana Cavani.

Partisans of Vilna. U.S., 1986. Director: Josh Waletsky.

The Pawnbroker. U.S., 1965. Director: Sidney Lumet; Script: Morton Find and David Friedkin.

Playing for Time. U.S., 1980. CBS/TV, Director: Daniel Mann; Script: Arthur Miller.

Ragtime. U.S., 1981. Director: Milos Forman; Script: Michael Weller.

Roots. U.S., 1977. ABC/TV, Director: David Green; Script: William Blinn and Ernest Kinoy.

The Seventh Cross. U.S., 1944. Director: Fred Zinnemann.

Ship of Fools. U.S., 1965. Director: Stanley Kramer; Script: Abby Mann.

Shoah. France, 1985. Director: Claude Lanzmann.

The Shop on Main Street. Czech., 1965. Directors: Jan Kadar and Elmar Klos; Script: Ladislav Grosman.

Skokie. U.S., 1981. CBS/TV, Director: Herbert Wise; Script: Ernest Kinoy.

Sophie's Choice. U.S., 1982. Director and Script: Alan Pakula.

The Sorrow and the Pity. France, 1970. Director: Marcel Ophuls.

The Sound of Music. U.S., 1965. Director: Robert Wise; Script: Ernest Lehman.

Straw Dogs. Great Britain, 1971. Director: Sam Peckinpah; Script: David Z. Goodman.

To Be Or Not To Be. U.S., 1942. Director: Ernst Lubitsch; Script: Edwin Justus Mayer, Melchior Lengyel, and Ernst Lubitsch.

Torn Curtain. U.S., 1966. Director: Alfred Hitchcock; Script: Brian Moore.

Les Violons du Bal. France, 1973. Director and Script: Michel Drach.

Voyage of the Damned. U.S. and Great Britain, 1976. Director: Stuart Rosenberg; Script: Steve Shagan and David Butler.

Wallenberg: A Hero's Story. U.S., 1985. NBC/TV, Director: Lamont Johnson; Script: Gerald Green.

Watch on the Rhine. U.S., 1943. Director: Herman Shumlin; Script: Dashiell Hammett.

Who Shall Live and Who Shall Die? U.S., 1981. Director: Laurence Jarvik.

The Winds of War. U.S., 1983. Director: Dan Curtis; Script: Herman Wouk.

Zelig. U.S., 1983. Director and Script: Woody Allen.

Selected Filmography

And the Fifth Horseman is Fear. Czechoslovakia, 1968. Director: Zbynek Brynych.

Angry Harvest. West Germany, 1985. Director: Agnieszka Holland.

Ashes and Diamonds. Poland, 1958. Director: Andrzej Wajda; Script: Jerzy Andrzejewski and Andrzej Wajda.

Black Thursday. France, 1974. Director: Michel Mitrani. Script: Albert Cossery and Michel Mitrani.

Charlotte. Holland/West Germany, 1981. Director: Franz Weisz; Script: Judith Herzberg.

Diamonds of the Night. Czechoslovakia, 1964. Director: Jan Nemec; Script: Arnost Lustig and Jan Nemec.

Distant Journey. Czechoslovakia, 1949. Director: Alfred Radok; Story by: K. Kolar and M. Drvota.

Elysium. Hungary, 1986. Director: Erika Szanto. Script: Eva Schultze and Erika Szanto.

The Garden of the Finzi-Continis. Italy, 1970. Director: Vittorio De Sica. Script: Cesare Zavattini, Vittorio Bonicelli and Ugo Pirro.

Generation. Poland, 1955. Director: Andrzej Wajda. Script: Bohdan Czeszko.

Genocide. Great Britain, 1975. For *World at War,* Thames/TV. Director: Michael Darlow. Script: Charles Bloomberg.

The Gold of Rome. Italy, 1961. Director: Carlo Lizzani; Script: Lucio Baltistrada, Giuliani de Negri, Alberto Lecco and Carlo Lizzani.

Image Before My Eyes. U.S., 1980. Director: Josh Waletsky; Script: Jerome Badanes.

Kapo. Italy, 1960. Director: Gillo Pontecorvo. Script: Franco Solinas and Gillo Pontecorvo.

Landscape After Battle. Poland, 1970. Director: Andrzej Wajda. Script: Andrzej Brozozowski and Andrzej Wajda.

The Last Metro. France, 1980. Director: Francois Truffaut; Script: Suzanne Schiffman, Jean-Claude Grumberg and Francois Truffaut.

Kanal. Poland, 1956. Director: Andrzej Wajda. Script: Jerszy S. Stawinski.

Mr. Klein. France, 1976. Director: Joseph Losey. Script: Franco Solinas.

Madame Rosa. France, 1977. Director and Script: Moshe Mizrahi.

Me and the Colonel. U.S., 1958. Director: Peter Glenville; Script: S. N. Behrman.

Mein Kampf. Sweden, 1960. Director: Erwin Leiser.

The Memory of Justice. France, 1976. Director and Script: Marcel Ophuls.

Night and Fog. France, 1955. Director: Alain Resnais; Script: Jean Cayrol.

The Passenger. Poland, 1962. Director: Andrej Munk (completed Witold Lesiewicz). Script: Zofia Posmysz and Andrej Munk.

Professor Mamlock. USSR, 1938. Directors: Adolf Minkin and Herbert Rappaport; Script: Friedrich Wolff, Adolf Minkin and Herbert Rappaport.

The Revolt of Job. Hungary, 1981. Directors: Imre Gyöngössy and Barna Kabay. Script: Katalin Petenyi.

Samson. Poland, 1961. Director: Andrzej Wajda; Script: Kasimierz Brandys and Andrzej Wajda.

The Search. Switzerland/U.S., 1948. Director: Fred Zinnemann; Script: Richard Schweizer and David Wechsler.

Seven Beauties. Italy, 1975. Director and Script: Lina Wertmüller.

Stars. Bulgaria/East Germany, 1959. Director: Konrad Wolf; Script: Anzhel Vagenstein and Christa Wernicke.

Sweet Light in a Dark Room. Czechoslovakia, 1960. Director: Jiri Weiss; Script: Jan Otcenasek.

The Tin Drum. West Germany, 1979. Director: Volker Schlöndorff; Script: Jean-Claude Carriere, Franz Seitz and Volker Schlöndorff.

The Two of Us. France, 1966. Director and Script: Claude Berri.

Warsaw Ghetto. Great Britain, 1968. For BBC/TV.

The Young Lions. U.S., 1958. Director: Edward Dmytryk; Script: Edward Anhalt.

Index

Note: Page numbers in *italics* indicate illustrations.